Diabetes Comfort Food

Johanna Burkhard

Barbara Selley, BA, RD
Nutrition Editor

Robert
ROSE

For complete cataloguing information, see page 275.

Disclaimer

The recipes in this book have been carefully tested by our kitchen and our tasters. To the best of our knowledge, they are safe and nutritious for ordinary use and users. For those people with food or other allergies, or who have special food requirements or health issues, please read the suggested contents of each recipe carefully and determine whether or not they may create a problem for you. All recipes are used at the risk of the consumer.

We cannot be responsible for any hazards, loss or damage that may occur as a result of any recipe use.

For those with special needs, allergies, requirements or health problems, in the event of any doubt, please contact your medical adviser prior to the use of any recipe.

Design & Production: PageWave Graphics Inc.

Editor: Sue Sumeraj

Cover photography: Colin Erricson

Inside photography: Mark T. Shapiro

Food Stylist: Kate Bush

Props Stylist: Charlene Erricson

Cover image: Chicken Curry with Red Peppers (see recipe, page 87)

We acknowledge the financial support of the Government of Canada through the Book Publishing Industry Development Program (BPIDP) for our publishing activities.

Published by: Robert Rose Inc.
120 Eglinton Ave. E., Suite 800, Toronto, Ontario, Canada M4P 1E2
Tel: (416) 322-6552   Fax: (416) 322-6936

Printed in Canada

1 2 3 4 5 6 7 8 9 10   CPL   13 12 11 10 09 08 07 06

Contents

Acknowledgments

A cookbook is never a solo effort, and I would like to sincerely thank my family, friends and colleagues who lent a generous hand in crafting this book.

Thanks to my former Montreal colleagues Julian Armstrong of the *Gazette* and Linda Kay of Concordia University for their continued support and inspiration in my writing career.

Thanks also to the creative team at Robert Rose: publisher Bob Dees; Marian Jarkovich for her expert marketing skills; dietitian Barbara Selley for her meticulous attention to the nutritional information; Sue Sumeraj for her creative editing; Andrew Smith, Joseph Gisini and Kevin Cockburn of PageWave Graphics for the superb book design and layout; and food stylist Kate Bush, props stylist Charlene Ericson and food photographer Mark Shapiro for the wonderful photography.

Warmest thanks to my family for sharing my passion for food.

This book is dedicated to my children, Nicole and Patrick, who are now adults and have set up their own homes and kitchens — a heartfelt thanks for the many happy, loving memories and meals we shared around the table, with many more to come.

Introduction

Each of us has our own favorite comfort foods — whether they be special-occasion meals that bring back memories of time spent with family and friends, or cherished recipes that evoke raves when you serve them. People with diabetes (and those planning and cooking meals for them) sometimes assume they will no longer be able to enjoy their favorite comfort foods. Not true. This book will help you prepare healthy, soul-satisfying meals using familiar recipes that every member of the family, including those with diabetes, will enjoy — meals with a variety of breads and other grain products; vegetables and fruit; lean meat, poultry and fish; and lower-fat dairy products.

For people with diabetes, one of the primary goals is maintaining or achieving a healthy weight. This means controlling calorie intake and limiting total fat to no more than 30% of calories and saturated fat to no more than 10% of calories.[1] For a person eating 2,000 calories a day, for example, the total fat consumed should be about 65 grams, including no more than 22 grams of saturated fat.

Controlling sodium is also important. Sodium in the diet comes primarily from salt, whether it be used in cooking, added at the table or hidden in manufactured and prepared foods. Consider that one teaspoon (5 mL) of salt contains about 2,400 mg of sodium. The American Diabetes Association limits sodium to 2,400–6,000 mg per day, while the Canadian Diabetes Association suggests 2,000–4,000 mg. In both cases, the lower end of the range is recommended.[2]

There is a common misconception that those with diabetes should avoid carbohydrates, especially sugar. This is not true, but you should control the total amount of carbohydrate eaten and spread it evenly throughout the day's meals and snacks. Glycemic index — the degree to which a particular type of carbohydrate raises blood sugar — is also important. Foods such as legumes, vegetables and whole-grain foods have the lowest glycemic indexes and should be consumed often. To learn more about glycemic index, consult your diabetes educator or visit **www.diabetes.org** or **www.diabetes.ca**.

The recipes in *Diabetes Comfort Food* call for ingredients that are readily available in supermarkets, and the cooking directions are easy to follow. Time-saving shortcuts, practical information and nutrition tips are also provided. In addition, each recipe includes a nutritional analysis that breaks down calories, total carbohydrate (and fiber), protein, total fat (plus saturated fat and cholesterol) and sodium per serving, and America's Exchanges and Canada's Choices are listed. When you're planning meals, use this information to compensate for recipes that are higher in fat, sodium or carbohydrate with those that are lower.

The calculations for America's Exchanges were based on the following values:

GROUPS/LISTS	NUTRIENTS PER EXCHANGE		
	CARBOHYDRATE (g)	PROTEIN (g)	FAT (g)
Carbohydrate Group			
Starch	15	3	0–1
Fruit	15	–	–
Milk			
Fat-free, low-fat	12	8	0–3
Reduced-fat	12	8	5
Whole	12	8	8
Other Carbohydrates	15	v	v*
Vegetables	5	2	–
Meat and Meat Substitutes Group			
Very lean	–	7	0–1
Lean	–	7	3
Medium-fat	–	7	5
High-fat	–	7	8
Fat Group	–	–	5

* v = variable

Source: Adapted from *Exchange Lists for Meal Planning,* American Diabetes Association and American Dietetic Association, 2003.

The calculations for Canada's Choices were based on the values in the table below. Carbohydrate (less dietary fiber) from all ingredients was totaled and reported as Carbohydrate Choices; one Choice contains 15 grams of available carbohydrate.

CANADA'S CHOICES	NUTRIENTS PER CHOICE		
	CARBOHYDRATE (g)	PROTEIN (g)	FAT (g)
Carbohydrate	15	0	0
Grains & Starches	15	3	0
Fruits	15	1	0
Milk (1%) & Alternatives	15	8	2.5
Other Choices	15	v	v*
Vegetables	<5 (most)	2	0
Meat and Alternatives	0	7	3
Fats	0	0	5
Extras	<5	0	0

* v = variable

Source: Adapted from *Beyond the Basics: Meal Planning, Healthy Eating and Diabetes Prevention and Management*, Version 2, Canadian Diabetes Association, December 20, 2005.

For more information on food exchanges, food choices and all aspects of managing diabetes, visit **www.diabetes.org** or **www.diabetes.ca**.

There's no greater pleasure than the time spent around the table with friends and family. I hope this book inspires you to create some special new memories based on healthful, great-tasting recipes that everyone can enjoy.

---

1 Canadian Diabetes Association, "2003 Clinical Practice Guidelines for the Prevention and Management of Diabetes in Canada," *Can J Diabetes* 27, Suppl. no. 2 (2003): S21–S23.

2 American Diabetes Association, "Standards of Medical Care in Diabetes — 2006," *Diabetes Care* 29 (2006): S4–S42; Canadian Diabetes Association, "2003 Clinical Practice Guidelines for the Prevention and Management of Diabetes in Canada," *Can J Diabetes* 27, Suppl. no. 2 (2003): S21–S23.

Appetizers

MAKES 40 PIECES
(2 per serving)

Want a great start to a meal? Begin here. I always have containers of this delicious mushroom spread in my freezer ready to defrost in the microwave when friends or family drop by. The same applies for the bread, which I slice, pack into plastic bags and freeze.

Tips

Butter, walnuts and Parmesan cheese are all high in fat, so it's best to set your limit at one serving of these tasty snacks.

Mushroom-walnut filling can be frozen for up to 1 month.

To wash or not to wash mushrooms? You can wipe them with a damp cloth, if you wish. However, I feel that it's important to wash all produce that comes into my kitchen. I quickly rinse mushrooms under cold water and immediately wrap in a clean, dry kitchen towel or paper towels to absorb excess moisture.

NUTRITIONAL ANALYSIS PER SERVING

Calories	71
Carbohydrate	7 g
Fiber	1 g
Protein	3 g
Fat, total	4 g
Fat, saturated	2 g
Sodium	135 mg
Cholesterol	8 mg

Creamy Mushroom Walnut Toasts

● *Preheat oven to 375°F (190°C)* ● *Baking sheet*

1 lb	mushrooms (an assortment of white, oyster and portobello), coarsely chopped	500 g
2 tsp	butter	10 mL
1/3 cup	finely chopped green onions	75 mL
2	cloves garlic, minced	2
1/2 tsp	dried thyme leaves	2 mL
4 oz	light cream cheese or goat cheese, cut into pieces	125 g
1/4 cup	freshly grated Parmesan cheese (plus extra for topping)	50 mL
1/4 cup	finely chopped walnuts	50 mL
2 tbsp	finely chopped fresh parsley	25 mL
	Freshly ground black pepper	
40	crostini (toasted baguette slices) (see box, page 12)	40

1. In a food processor, finely chop mushrooms in batches, using on-off turns.

2. In a large nonstick skillet, heat butter over medium-high heat. Add mushrooms, green onions, garlic and thyme; cook for 5 to 7 minutes or until mushrooms are softened. Cook 1 to 2 minutes more, if necessary, until all moisture has evaporated. (Mixture should be dry and almost crumbly.) Remove from heat.

3. Add cream cheese, stirring until smooth. Add Parmesan cheese, walnuts and parsley. Season with pepper to taste. Transfer to a bowl; cover and let cool.

4. Spread toasted baguette slices with a generous teaspoonful (5 to 7 mL) of mushroom mixture. Arrange on baking sheet. Sprinkle tops with additional Parmesan cheese. Bake in preheated oven for 8 to 10 minutes or until edges are toasted.

AMERICA'S EXCHANGES PER SERVING

1/2	Other Carbohydrate
1/2	Fat

CANADA'S CHOICES PER SERVING

1/2	Carbohydrate
1/2	Fat

MAKES 36 PIECES
(3 per serving)

Get a head start on your party preparations with these tasty appetizers designed to be stored in the freezer. When the festivities are about to begin, just pop them into a hot oven.

Tips

To freeze, spread bread slices with cheese mixture; arrange in a single layer on baking sheets and freeze. Transfer to a rigid container, separating layers with waxed paper; freeze for up to 1 month. No need to defrost before baking.

Wear rubber gloves when handling jalapeño peppers to avoid skin irritation.

Cheddar Jalapeño Toasts

● Preheat oven to 375°F (190°C) ● Baking sheets

8 oz	light Cheddar cheese, shredded	250 g
4 oz	light cream cheese, cubed	125 g
2 tbsp	finely diced red bell pepper	25 mL
2 tbsp	minced jalapeño peppers or 1 tbsp (15 mL) minced pickled jalapeño peppers	25 mL
2 tbsp	finely chopped fresh parsley	25 mL
36	baguette slices, cut 1/3-inch (8 mm) thick	36

1. In a food processor, purée Cheddar and cream cheese until very smooth. Transfer to a bowl; stir in red pepper, jalapeño peppers and parsley.
2. Spread bread slices with a generous teaspoonful (5 to 7 mL) of cheese mixture; arrange on baking sheets.
3. Bake in oven for 10 to 12 minutes (up to 15 minutes, if frozen) until tops are puffed and edges toasted. Serve warm.

NUTRITIONAL ANALYSIS PER SERVING	
Calories	123
Carbohydrate	9 g
Fiber	0 g
Protein	7 g
Fat, total	6 g
Fat, saturated	4 g
Sodium	320 mg
Cholesterol	20 mg

AMERICA'S EXCHANGES PER SERVING	
1/2	Starch
1	Medium-fat Meat

CANADA'S CHOICES PER SERVING	
1/2	Carbohydrate
1	Meat & Alternatives
1/2	Fat

Easy Artichoke Cheese Melts

● *Preheat oven to 375°F (190°C)* ● *Baking sheet*

Everyone likes to have a breezy appetizer in their repertoire. This is one of mine. It takes no time to prepare and tastes great.

Tips

You might think olives are the main source of sodium here, but sodium is found in many foods, including the marinated artichokes, cheese, mayonnaise and bread in these appetizers.

Make this spread up to 3 days ahead, cover and refrigerate. Assemble appetizers just before serving or toasts will soften.

1	jar (6 oz/170 mL) marinated artichokes, well drained and finely chopped	1
½ cup	shredded light Cheddar or light Gouda cheese	125 mL
2 tbsp	freshly grated Parmesan cheese	25 mL
¼ cup	light mayonnaise	50 mL
24	crostini (toasted baguette slices) (see box, below)	24
¼ cup	finely diced red bell pepper	50 mL
8	Kalamata olives, cut into thin slivers	8

1. In a bowl, combine artichokes, Cheddar, Parmesan and mayonnaise. Spread over toasts; top with red pepper and olive slivers.

2. Arrange on a baking sheet; bake for 10 to 12 minutes or until tops are bubbly and edges are golden. Serve warm.

Crostini (Toasted Baguette Slices)

Cut 1 thin baguette into ⅓-inch (8 mm) thick slices. Arrange on baking sheet. Bake in 375°F (190°C) oven for 5 minutes or until edges are lightly toasted. Spread toasts with artichoke mixture just before baking to prevent them from turning soggy.

NUTRITIONAL ANALYSIS PER SERVING	
Calories	118
Carbohydrate	11 g
Fiber	1 g
Protein	4 g
Fat, total	7 g
Fat, saturated	2 g
Sodium	375 mg
Cholesterol	9 mg

AMERICA'S EXCHANGES PER SERVING	
½	Starch
1	Fat

CANADA'S CHOICES PER SERVING	
½	Carbohydrate
1½	Fat

Creamy Spinach Dip

**MAKES 3 CUPS
(750 ML)
(2 tbsp/25 mL per
serving)**

*Here's a dip that's so much
tastier than the ones made
with salty soup mixes.
Serve with vegetable
dippers such as carrot,
pepper, cucumber, celery,
broccoli, fennel and
cauliflower. I use any
leftovers as a dressing for
pasta or potato salads, or
as a spread for sandwiches.*

Tip

To grate lemon zest, use a
zester to remove the zest in
thin shreds and finely chop
with a knife. When lemons
are bargain-priced, stock up
for the future. Grate the
zest and squeeze the juice;
place in separate containers
and freeze.

I	package (10 oz/300 g) fresh or frozen spinach	I
I cup	crumbed light feta cheese (about 4 oz/125 g)	250 mL
1/3 cup	chopped green onions	75 mL
1/4 cup	chopped fresh dill	50 mL
I	clove garlic, minced	I
I tsp	grated lemon zest (see tip, at left)	5 mL
1 1/2 cups	light sour cream	375 mL
1/2 cup	light mayonnaise	125 mL

1. Remove tough stem ends from fresh spinach; wash in cold water. Place spinach with moisture clinging to leaves in a large saucepan. Cook over high heat, stirring, until just wilted. (If using frozen spinach, see tip, page 16.) Place spinach in a colander to drain. Squeeze out moisture by hand; wrap in a clean, dry towel and squeeze out excess moisture.

2. In a food processor, combine spinach, feta, green onions, dill, garlic and lemon zest. Process until very finely chopped.

3. Add sour cream and mayonnaise; process, using on-off turns, just until combined. Transfer to a serving bowl, cover and refrigerate until ready to serve. Serve in a bread bowl (see box, below), if desired, and accompany with vegetable dippers.

Bread Bowl for Serving Dip

Using a serrated knife, slice 2 inches (5 cm) off top of small (1 lb/500 g) unsliced round whole wheat or sourdough bread. Hollow out loaf, reserving contents, leaving a shell about 1-inch (2.5 cm) thick. Spoon dip into bread bowl. Cut reserved bread into strips or cubes and serve along with vegetable dippers.

NUTRITIONAL ANALYSIS PER SERVING	
Calories	45
Carbohydrate	3 g
Fiber	0 g
Protein	2 g
Fat, total	3 g
Fat, saturated	I g
Sodium	105 mg
Cholesterol	3 mg

AMERICA'S EXCHANGES PER SERVING
I Fat

CANADA'S CHOICES PER SERVING
I Fat

Warm Salsa Dip

MAKES 3 CUPS (750 ML)
(¼ cup/50 mL per serving)

This dip will draw raves from a gang of starving teens or a crowd around the TV set when the ball game is in progress. In our house, we usually can't agree if we want the dip hot or mild. The solution? I use mild salsa as the base, and once the dip is made, divide it into two bowls. I leave one mild and add plenty of hot sauce or minced pickled jalapeños to spice up the other.

1	can (19 oz/540 mL) white kidney beans, drained and rinsed	1
1 cup	mild or hot salsa	250 mL
2	cloves garlic, minced	2
1 tsp	ground cumin	5 mL
1 tsp	dried oregano leaves	5 mL
4 oz	light cream cheese, cubed and softened	125 g
1 cup	shredded part-skim mozzarella or light Cheddar cheese	250 mL
	Tortilla chips or pita crisps (see box, below)	

1. In a bowl, mash beans with a fork until quite smooth.
2. In a medium saucepan, combine beans, salsa, garlic, cumin and oregano. Place over medium heat, stirring often, until piping hot.
3. Stir in cream cheese; stir until dip is smooth. Add mozzarella; stir until melted. Serve warm with tortilla or pita crisps.

Microwave Method

1. Combine all the ingredients in microwave-safe bowl. Microwave at Medium-High (70%), stirring twice, for 5 to 7 minutes, or until heated through and cheese is melted. Serve warm with tortilla chips or pita crisps.

Pita Crisps

A lower-fat alternative to tortilla chips is pita crisps. To make them, separate three 7-inch (18 cm) pitas into rounds and cut each into 8 wedges. Place in a single layer on baking sheets; bake at 350°F (180°C) for 8 to 10 minutes or until crisp and lightly toasted. Let cool. Store in a covered container. Pita crisps can be made 1 day ahead.

NUTRITIONAL ANALYSIS PER SERVING

Calories	101
Carbohydrate	10 g
Fiber	4 g
Protein	7 g
Fat, total	4 g
Fat, saturated	2 g
Sodium	315 mg
Cholesterol	13 mg

AMERICA'S EXCHANGES PER SERVING

½	Vegetable
½	Other Carbohydrate
½	High-fat Meat

CANADA'S CHOICES PER SERVING

½	Carbohydrate
1	Meat & Alternatives

**MAKES 2 CUPS
(500 ML)
(¼ cup/50 mL per
serving)**

*With a can of crab meat
in the pantry and cream
cheese in the fridge, you're
all set to make a quick dip
in 5 minutes flat. You can
make it in the microwave
or just as easily on the
stovetop over medium heat.*

Tip

Serve with Melba toast
rounds or crisp vegetable
dippers.

Variation

5-Minute Clam Dip
Substitute 1 can
(5 oz/142 g) drained
clams for the crab. Stir
in 1 minced garlic
clove, if desired.

5-Minute Crab Dip

8 oz	light cream cheese	250 g
1	can (6 oz/170 mL) crab meat, drained, liquid reserved	1
¼ cup	finely chopped green onions	50 mL
2 tsp	freshly squeezed lemon juice	10 mL
½ tsp	Worcestershire sauce	2 mL
¼ tsp	paprika	1 mL
	Hot pepper sauce	

1. Place cream cheese in a medium-size microwave-safe bowl; microwave at Medium (50%) for 2 minutes or until softened. Stir until smooth.
2. Stir in crab, green onions, 2 tbsp (25 mL) reserved crab liquid, lemon juice, Worcestershire sauce, paprika and hot pepper sauce to taste. Microwave at Medium-High (70%) for 2 minutes or until piping hot. Serve warm.

**NUTRITIONAL ANALYSIS
PER SERVING**

Calories	83
Carbohydrate	2 g
Fiber	0 g
Protein	5 g
Fat, total	6 g
Fat, saturated	3 g
Sodium	345 mg
Cholesterol	20 mg

AMERICA'S EXCHANGES PER SERVING	
½	Medium-fat Meat
1	Fat

CANADA'S CHOICES PER SERVING	
½	Meat & Alternatives
1	Fat

**MAKES 3 CUPS
(750 ML)
(2 tbsp/25 mL per
serving)**

*When you've got the gang
coming over, serve this
warm dip and watch
it disappear. I like to
accompany it with white
or blue corn tortilla chips.*

Tips

If you want a hot version,
use 2 fresh or pickled
jalapeño peppers. Or for
a mild version, use 1 can
(4 oz/113 g) green chilies,
drained and chopped.

To defrost spinach, remove
packaging and place in a
4-cup (1 L) casserole dish.
Cover and microwave at
High, stirring once, for
6 to 8 minutes or until
defrosted and hot. Place
in a sieve and press out
excess moisture.

Warm Spinach and Cheese Dip

1	package (10 oz/300 g) fresh or frozen chopped spinach	1
8 oz	light cream cheese, softened (see tip, page 24)	250 g
1 cup	mild or medium salsa	250 mL
2	green onions, finely chopped	2
1	clove garlic, minced	1
1/2 tsp	dried oregano leaves	2 mL
1/2 tsp	ground cumin	2 mL
1/2 cup	shredded light Cheddar cheese	125 mL
1/2 cup	low-fat milk (approx.)	125 mL
	Salt	
	Hot pepper sauce	

1. Remove tough stem ends from fresh spinach; wash in cold water. Place spinach with moisture clinging to leaves in a large saucepan. Cook over high heat, stirring, until just wilted. (If using frozen spinach, see tip, at left.) Place spinach in a colander to drain. Squeeze out moisture by hand; wrap in a clean, dry towel and squeeze out excess moisture.

2. In a medium saucepan, combine spinach, cream cheese, salsa, green onions, garlic, oregano and cumin. Cook over medium heat, stirring, for 2 to 3 minutes or until smooth and piping hot.

3. Stir in cheese and milk; cook for 2 minutes or until cheese melts. Add more milk to thin dip, if desired. Season with hot pepper sauce to taste. Spoon into serving dish.

Microwave Method

1. In an 8-cup (2 L) casserole dish, combine spinach, cream cheese, salsa, onions, garlic, oregano and cumin; cover and microwave at Medium (50%) for 4 minutes, stirring once. Add cheese and milk; cover and microwave at Medium-High (70%), stirring once, for 2 to 3 minutes, or until cheese is melted. Season with hot pepper sauce to taste.

**NUTRITIONAL ANALYSIS
PER SERVING**

Calories	39
Carbohydrate	2 g
Fiber	1 g
Protein	2 g
Fat, total	3 g
Fat, saturated	2 g
Sodium	150 mg
Cholesterol	8 mg

**AMERICA'S EXCHANGES
PER SERVING**

1/2	Fat

**CANADA'S CHOICES
PER SERVING**

1/2	Fat

Do-Ahead Herb Dip

**MAKES 2 CUPS
(500 ML)
(2 tbsp/25 mL per
serving)**

This creamy dip relies on lower-fat dairy products and zesty herbs, so it clocks in with a lot less fat and calories than you might imagine. Make it at least a day ahead to let flavors develop. Serve with fresh veggies.

Tips

Other fresh herbs, including basil, can be added according to what you have in the fridge or growing in your garden. If you're fond of fresh dill, increase the amount to 2 tbsp (25 mL).

This dip also makes a great dressing for pasta and potato salads. Store in a covered container in the fridge for up to 1 week.

1 cup	creamed 1% cottage cheese	250 mL
½ cup	plain low-fat yogurt or light sour cream	125 mL
½ cup	light mayonnaise	125 mL
⅓ cup	finely chopped fresh parsley	75 mL
2 tbsp	finely chopped fresh chives or minced green onions	25 mL
1 tbsp	chopped fresh dill	15 mL
1½ tsp	Dijon mustard	7 mL
1 tsp	red wine vinegar or lemon juice	5 mL
	Hot pepper sauce	

1. In a food processor, purée cottage cheese, yogurt and mayonnaise until very smooth and creamy.

2. Transfer to a bowl; stir in parsley, chives, dill, mustard, vinegar and hot pepper sauce to taste. Cover and refrigerate.

NUTRITIONAL ANALYSIS PER SERVING	
Calories	40
Carbohydrate	2 g
Fiber	0 g
Protein	2 g
Fat, total	3 g
Fat, saturated	1 g
Sodium	130 mg
Cholesterol	4 mg

AMERICA'S EXCHANGES PER SERVING	
½	Medium-fat Meat

CANADA'S CHOICES PER SERVING	
½	Fat

*Variations of the popular
bean dip always make the
party circuit. Here's my
updated version. It has
an oregano-bean base, a
creamy jalapeño cheese
layer and a vibrant fresh
topping of tomatoes, olives
and cilantro.*

Tip

Fresh cilantro, also called
coriander and Chinese
parsley, lasts only a few
days in the fridge before
it deteriorates and turns
tasteless. Wash cilantro
well, spin dry and wrap
in paper towels; store
in plastic bag in the fridge.
Leave the roots on — they
keep the leaves fresh.

Always Popular Layered Bean Dip

● *8-inch (20 cm) shallow round serving dish or pie plate*

1	can (19 oz/540 mL) red kidney beans or black beans, drained and rinsed	1
1	clove garlic, minced	1
1 tsp	dried oregano leaves	5 mL
½ tsp	ground cumin	2 mL
1 tbsp	water	15 mL
1 cup	shredded light Cheddar cheese	250 mL
¾ cup	light sour cream	175 mL
1 tbsp	minced pickled jalapeño peppers	15 mL
2	tomatoes, seeded and finely diced	2
2	green onions, finely chopped	2
⅓ cup	sliced black olives	75 mL
⅓ cup	chopped fresh cilantro or parsley	75 mL

1. In a food processor, combine beans, garlic, oregano, cumin and water; process until smooth. Spread in serving dish.

2. In a bowl, combine cheese, sour cream and jalapeño peppers. Spread over bean layer. (Can be assembled earlier in day; cover and refrigerate.)

3. Just before serving, sprinkle with tomatoes, green onions, olives and cilantro. Serve with baked tortilla chips or pita crisps (see box, page 14).

*I like to serve this tasty
easy-to-make spread with
warm squares of focaccia
or pita crisps.*

Tip

Dip can be made up to
3 days ahead.

Variation

Instead of fresh basil,
increase chopped parsley
to 2 tbsp (25 mL) and
add ½ tsp (2 mL) dried
basil leaves to the onions
when cooking.

Italian White Bean Spread

2 tbsp	olive oil	25 mL
I	small onion, finely chopped	I
2	large cloves garlic, finely chopped	2
I tbsp	red wine vinegar	15 mL
I	can (19 oz/540 mL) white kidney beans, drained and rinsed	I
2 tbsp	finely chopped oil-packed sun-dried tomatoes	25 mL
I tbsp	chopped fresh parsley	15 mL
I tbsp	chopped fresh basil leaves	15 mL
	Freshly ground black pepper	

1. In a small saucepan, combine oil, onion and garlic; cook over medium-low heat, stirring occasionally, for 5 minutes or until softened (do not brown). Add vinegar and remove from heat. In a food processor, purée kidney beans and onion mixture until smooth.

2. Transfer to a bowl. Stir in sun-dried tomatoes, parsley and basil; season with pepper to taste. Cover and refrigerate.

NUTRITIONAL ANALYSIS PER SERVING	
Calories	51
Carbohydrate	6 g
Fiber	2 g
Protein	2 g
Fat, total	2 g
Fat, saturated	0 g
Sodium	75 mg
Cholesterol	0 mg

AMERICA'S EXCHANGES PER SERVING	
½	Other Carbohydrate
½	Lean Meat

CANADA'S CHOICES PER SERVING	
I	Extra

MAKES 2¼ CUPS (550 ML)
(¼ cup/50 mL per serving)

You can buy hummus, the classic spread from the Middle East, in most supermarkets, but I find it so easy to make in my home kitchen. Serve it as a dip with pita wedges or use as a sandwich spread.

NUTRITIONAL ANALYSIS PER SERVING	
Calories	120
Carbohydrate	12 g
Fiber	3 g
Protein	4 g
Fat, total	7 g
Fat, saturated	1 g
Sodium	225 mg
Cholesterol	0 mg

Hummus

1	can (19 oz/540 mL) chickpeas, rinsed and drained	1
⅓ cup	Kalamata olives, pitted (about 12)	75 mL
¼ cup	water	50 mL
3 tbsp	freshly squeezed lemon juice	45 mL
2 tbsp	tahini	25 mL
2 tbsp	olive oil	25 mL
2	cloves garlic, chopped	2
¼ tsp	ground cumin (optional)	1 mL
2 tbsp	finely chopped fresh parsley	25 mL

1. In a food processor, purée chickpeas, olives, water, lemon juice, tahini, olive oil, garlic and cumin, if using, until smooth.
2. Transfer to a bowl; stir in parsley. Cover and refrigerate.

AMERICA'S EXCHANGES PER SERVING	
½	Other Carbohydrate
½	Lean Meat
1	Fat

CANADA'S CHOICES PER SERVING	
½	Carbohydrate
½	Meat & Alternatives
1	Fat

MAKES 24 PITA BITES
(2 per serving)

NUTRITIONAL ANALYSIS PER SERVING	
Calories	71
Carbohydrate	11 g
Fiber	2 g
Protein	2 g
Fat, total	3 g
Fat, saturated	0 g
Sodium	130 mg
Cholesterol	0 mg

Hummus Pita Bites

2	7-inch (18 cm) thin soft pitas, split	2
1 cup	hummus	250 mL
½	small seedless cucumber	½
½	small red bell pepper, cut into thin strips	½

1. Spread the rough sides of each pita generously with hummus, leaving a small border.
2. Cut cucumber into 5-inch (12 cm) long strips, each ¼-inch (5 mm) thick. Place a few cucumber and red pepper strips along edge of pita halves and roll into a tight bundle. Wrap each in plastic wrap and refrigerate up until serving time.
3. To serve, trim ends and slice into 1-inch (2.5 cm) pieces. Place cut side up on a serving plate.

AMERICA'S EXCHANGES PER SERVING	
½	Starch
½	Fat

CANADA'S CHOICES PER SERVING	
½	Carbohydrate
½	Fat

Here's a modern spin to an old standby, chicken liver spread. Even if you're not a big fan of liver, you'll be instantly won over when you try this lightly sweetened pâté with currants and Port. Serve with warm toasted baguette slices.

Tips

Make the pâté up to 3 days ahead. Cover surface with plastic wrap and refrigerate. Or pack into containers and freeze for up to 1 month.

The taste of freshly grated nutmeg is so much better than the pre-ground variety. Whole nutmeg can be found in the spice section of your supermarket or bulk food store. Look for inexpensive nutmeg graters in kitchenware shops.

NUTRITIONAL ANALYSIS PER SERVING	
Calories	76
Carbohydrate	3 g
Fiber	0 g
Protein	4 g
Fat, total	5 g
Fat, saturated	3 g
Sodium	140 mg
Cholesterol	117 mg

Party Pâté

3 tbsp	dried currants	45 mL
3 tbsp	ruby Port	45 mL
1 lb	chicken livers	500 g
½ cup	water	125 mL
2 tbsp	butter	25 mL
1	medium onion, finely chopped	1
1 cup	peeled, chopped apples	250 mL
¾ tsp	salt	4 mL
½ tsp	dried sage leaves	2 mL
½ tsp	freshly ground black pepper	2 mL
¼ tsp	freshly grated nutmeg (see tip, at left)	1 mL
⅓ cup	butter, cut into small cubes	75 mL

1. In a small glass dish, combine currants and Port; microwave at High for 1 minute until plump. Set aside.

2. Trim chicken livers and cut into quarters. Place in a large nonstick skillet with water; bring to a boil over medium heat, stirring often, for 5 minutes or until no longer pink. Drain in sieve; transfer liver to food processor.

3. Rinse and dry skillet; add 2 tbsp (25 mL) butter and melt over medium heat. Add onion, apples, salt, sage, pepper and nutmeg; cook, stirring often, for 5 minutes or until softened.

4. Add onion-apple mixture to liver in bowl of food processor; purée until very smooth. Let cool slightly. Add butter cubes to liver mixture and purée until creamy. Add reserved currants and Port; pulse, using on-off turns, until just combined.

5. Spoon into a serving bowl. Cover surface with plastic wrap and refrigerate until firm, about 4 hours or overnight. Serve with toasted baguette slices (see box, page 12).

AMERICA'S EXCHANGES PER SERVING	
1	Medium-fat Meat

CANADA'S CHOICES PER SERVING	
½	Meat & Alternatives
1	Fat

Antipasto Nibblers

Here's another last-minute idea for tasty bites to serve when friends drop over. These small nibblers are a throwback to the cocktail-lounge scene of the 1960s, when appetizers often meant cold cuts wrapped around a pickle. I like them because they can be assembled in a few minutes and are a colorful addition to a tray of warm appetizers.

Tip

Appetizers are often high in sodium, so save them for special occasions and be careful not to eat too many. In these nibblers, the olives and cheese each contribute about half of the sodium.

24	stuffed green olives or Kalamata olives	24
8 oz	light Havarti cheese, cut into ¾-inch (2 cm) cubes	250 g
1	small red bell pepper, cut into 1-inch (2.5 cm) squares	1
1	small green bell pepper, cut into 1-inch (2.5 cm) squares	1
1 tbsp	olive oil	15 mL
1 tbsp	balsamic vinegar	15 mL
	Freshly ground black pepper	
2 tbsp	chopped fresh basil leaves or parsley	25 mL

1. Thread 1 olive, 1 cheese cube, then 1 pepper square on cocktail toothpicks. Arrange in attractive shallow serving dish. Cover and refrigerate until serving time.

2. In a small bowl, whisk together oil and balsamic vinegar; pour over kabobs. Season generously with pepper; sprinkle with basil and serve.

NUTRITIONAL ANALYSIS PER SERVING	
Calories	79
Carbohydrate	2 g
Fiber	0 g
Protein	5 g
Fat, total	5 g
Fat, saturated	2 g
Sodium	330 mg
Cholesterol	10 mg

AMERICA'S EXCHANGES PER SERVING	
½	Vegetable
½	High-fat Meat

CANADA'S CHOICES PER SERVING	
½	Meat & Alternatives
½	Fat

MAKES 48 PIECES
(3 per serving)

Here's an updated version of the classic cheese ball, an appetizer that dominated the party scene in the 1950s and 1960s. This recipe may seem to call for a lot of peppercorns, but it's not all that peppery. It just has a lively zip.

Tips

To crack peppercorns, place in a heavy plastic bag and, on a wooden board, crush using a rolling pin or heavy skillet.

Cheese logs can be frozen for up to 1 month. Defrost in the refrigerator for several hours before slicing.

Cheddar Pepper Rounds

8 oz	light Cheddar cheese, shredded	250 g
4 oz	light cream cheese	125 g
2 tbsp	brandy or sherry	25 mL
1/4 cup	finely chopped fresh parsley	50 mL
1 tbsp	cracked black peppercorns (see tip, at left)	15 mL
	Melba toasts	

1. In a food processor, combine Cheddar cheese, cream cheese and brandy. Process until mixture is very smooth. Transfer to a bowl; refrigerate for 3 hours or until firm.

2. Divide mixture into two pieces; wrap each in plastic wrap. Roll on a flat surface and shape into a smooth log measuring about 6 by 1 1/2 inches (15 by 4 cm).

3. Place parsley and cracked peppercorns on a plate. Unwrap cheese logs and roll in parsley-peppercorn mixture until evenly coated. Wrap again in plastic wrap and refrigerate until firm.

4. To serve, cut each log into 1/4-inch (0.5 cm) slices and place on Melba toasts.

NUTRITIONAL ANALYSIS PER SERVING	
Calories	108
Carbohydrate	8 g
Fiber	1 g
Protein	6 g
Fat, total	5 g
Fat, saturated	3 g
Sodium	260 mg
Cholesterol	16 mg

AMERICA'S EXCHANGES PER SERVING	
1/2	Starch
1/2	Medium-fat Meat
1/2	Fat

CANADA'S CHOICES PER SERVING	
1/2	Carbohydrate
1/2	Meat & Alternatives
1/2	Fat

**MAKES 1 1/4 CUPS
(300 ML)
(2 tbsp/25 mL per
serving)**

*You can whip up this
reliable recipe in only
a few minutes using
ingredients you keep on
hand in the pantry and
in the fridge. It's equally
good with crackers or
vegetable dippers. You'll
turn to it, as I have, time
and time again.*

Tips

Microwave cold cream
cheese at Medium (50%)
for 1 minute to soften.

Spread can be prepared up
to 2 days ahead, covered
and refrigerated.

Rosy Shrimp Spread

4 oz	light cream cheese, softened	125 g
1/4 cup	plain low-fat yogurt or light sour cream	50 mL
2 tbsp	prepared chili sauce	25 mL
1 tsp	prepared horseradish	5 mL
	Hot pepper sauce	
1	can (4 oz/113 g) small shrimp, drained and rinsed	1
1 tbsp	minced green onion tops or chopped fresh chives	15 mL

1. In a bowl, beat cream cheese until smooth. Stir
in sour cream, chili sauce, horseradish and hot
pepper sauce to taste.

2. Fold in shrimp and green onions. Transfer to serving
dish; cover and refrigerate until serving time.

NUTRITIONAL ANALYSIS PER SERVING	
Calories	45
Carbohydrate	2 g
Fiber	0 g
Protein	3 g
Fat, total	3 g
Fat, saturated	1 g
Sodium	150 mg
Cholesterol	21 mg

AMERICA'S EXCHANGES PER SERVING	CANADA'S CHOICES PER SERVING
1/2 Medium-fat Meat	1/2 Meat & Alternatives

Smoked Salmon Mousse

MAKES 2⅔ CUPS (650 ML)
(¼ cup/50 mL per serving)

This is one of my most-requested recipes. It delivers a wonderful smoked salmon flavor, but uses relatively little of that costly ingredient. My secret? I work magic with canned salmon, which keeps the cost reasonable so I can serve this appetizer more often.

Tips

I prefer to use canned sockeye salmon (instead of the pink variety) for its superior color and flavor.

The mousse can be prepared up to 4 days ahead for easy entertaining.

To get more juice out of a lemon, roll on counter top or microwave at High for 20 seconds before squeezing.

1	can (7½ oz/213 g) sockeye salmon	1
1	package (¼ oz/7 g) unflavored gelatin	1
½ tsp	grated lemon zest	2 mL
1 tbsp	freshly squeezed lemon juice	15 mL
¼ tsp	salt	1 mL
1½ cup	light sour cream	375 mL
4 oz	smoked salmon, finely chopped	125 g
2 tbsp	minced green onions	25 mL
2 tbsp	finely chopped fresh dill	25 mL
	Hot pepper sauce	
	Dill sprigs and lemon zest for garnish	

1. Drain salmon and place juice in small measuring cup. Add enough water to make ¼ cup (50 mL). Sprinkle gelatin over. Let stand 1 to 2 minutes to soften. Microwave at Medium (50%) for 45 to 60 seconds or until dissolved.

2. Remove any skin from salmon and discard. Place in a food processor with gelatin mixture, lemon zest and juice, and salt. Process until smooth. Transfer mixture to a bowl. Stir in sour cream, smoked salmon, green onions and dill. Season with hot pepper sauce to taste.

3. Spoon mixture into a serving dish. Cover loosely with plastic wrap (it should not touch surface of the mousse), refrigerate for 4 hours or overnight. Garnish top with dill sprigs and lemon zest; serve with Melba toast or pumpernickel rounds.

NUTRITIONAL ANALYSIS PER SERVING	
Calories	85
Carbohydrate	3 g
Fiber	0 g
Protein	8 g
Fat, total	4 g
Fat, saturated	1 g
Sodium	225 mg
Cholesterol	7 mg

AMERICA'S EXCHANGES PER SERVING	
1½	Lean Meat

CANADA'S CHOICES PER SERVING	
1	Meat & Alternatives

MAKES 24 PIECES
(2 per serving)

Everyone loves smoked salmon and these popular appetizers are always the first to go at a party.

Tips

These appetizers can be made earlier in the day or even the day before — just cover and refrigerate. Garnish shortly before serving.

Use this cream cheese and mustard spread instead of mayonnaise when you're making finger sandwiches with sliced smoked ham or turkey.

Irresistible Smoked Salmon Bites

4 oz	light cream cheese	125 g
1 tbsp	finely chopped fresh dill	15 mL
2 tsp	honey mustard	10 mL
2 tsp	grainy mustard	10 mL
2 tsp	freshly squeezed lemon juice	10 mL
6	slices dark rye or pumpernickel bread, crusts trimmed	6
6 oz	sliced smoked salmon	175 g
	Capers and dill sprigs for garnish	

1. Place cream cheese in a bowl; microwave at Medium (50%) for 1 minute to soften. Stir well. Blend in dill, honey mustard, grainy mustard and lemon juice.

2. Generously spread mustard mixture on bread; layer with smoked salmon. Cut each slice into 4 pieces. Garnish with capers and dill. Cover with plastic wrap and refrigerate.

NUTRITIONAL ANALYSIS PER SERVING

Calories	80
Carbohydrate	8 g
Fiber	1 g
Protein	5 g
Fat, total	3 g
Fat, saturated	1 g
Sodium	295 mg
Cholesterol	10 mg

AMERICA'S EXCHANGES PER SERVING

1/2	Starch
1/2	Medium-fat Meat

CANADA'S CHOICES PER SERVING

1/2	Carbohydrate
1/2	Meat & Alternative

MAKES 2 1/2 CUPS (625 ML) (1/4 cup/50 mL per serving)

Supermarket shelves are lined with great-tasting salsas. Take your favorite salsa, throw in a few roasted vegetables and voila! — you've got yourself a snazzy spread. This versatile sauce makes a wonderful condiment for sandwiches with cold cuts or cheese, or as a pizza topping.

Tips

Prepare ratatouille salsa ahead. It keeps well in a covered container in the refrigerator for 3 days or 1 month in the freezer.

Dice the vegetables into uniform 1/4-inch (0.5 cm) pieces.

Medium salsa gives a nice burst of heat to the sauce. If using mild salsa, add hot pepper sauce to taste.

Ratatouille Salsa

- *Preheat oven to 425°F (220°C)*
- *Baking sheet, sprayed with vegetable cooking spray*

1 1/2 cups	diced eggplant	375 mL
1 1/2 cups	diced zucchini	375 mL
1	red bell pepper, diced	1
1 tsp	dried basil leaves	5 mL
1 tbsp	olive oil	15 mL
1 1/2 cups	medium salsa	375 mL
1/4 cup	chopped fresh parsley	50 mL
1	clove garlic, minced	1

1. Spread eggplant, zucchini and red pepper on prepared baking sheet. Sprinkle with basil; drizzle with oil. Roast in oven, stirring occasionally, for about 20 minutes or until vegetables are tender and lightly colored.

2. Transfer to a bowl; stir in salsa, parsley and garlic. Cover and refrigerate.

NUTRITIONAL ANALYSIS PER SERVING	
Calories	33
Carbohydrate	5 g
Fiber	1 g
Protein	1 g
Fat, total	2 g
Fat, saturated	0 g
Sodium	170 mg
Cholesterol	0 mg

AMERICA'S EXCHANGES PER SERVING	
1	Vegetable
1/2	Fat

CANADA'S CHOICES PER SERVING	
1	Extra

*Who doesn't love meatballs
as an appetizer? As fast as
I fill the serving bowls with
them, they disappear.*

Tip

Cooked meatballs can be
made up to 1 day ahead
and kept covered in the
refrigerator, or frozen for
up to 2 months. To freeze,
place meatballs in a single
layer on trays; when
frozen, transfer to covered
containers. To defrost
quickly, place meatballs
in a casserole dish and
microwave at High for 4 to
5 minutes until just warmed
through, stirring once.

Appetizer Meatballs

- *Preheat oven to 400°F (200°C)*
- *Baking sheet, sprayed with vegetable cooking spray*

1 tbsp	vegetable oil	15 mL
1	medium onion, finely chopped	1
2	cloves garlic, minced	2
¾ tsp	salt	4 mL
½ tsp	dried thyme leaves	2 mL
½ tsp	freshly ground black pepper	2 mL
½ cup	reduced-sodium beef broth	125 mL
2 tsp	Worcestershire sauce	10 mL
2 lbs	lean ground beef	1 kg
1 cup	soft fresh bread crumbs	250 mL
2 tbsp	finely chopped fresh parsley	25 mL
1	large egg, lightly beaten	1

1. In a medium nonstick skillet, heat oil over medium
   heat. Add onion, garlic, salt, thyme and pepper; cook,
   stirring often, for 5 minutes or until softened. Stir in
   beef broth and Worcestershire sauce; let cool slightly.

2. In a bowl, combine onion mixture, ground beef,
   bread crumbs, parsley and egg; mix thoroughly.

3. Form beef mixture into 1-inch (2.5 cm) balls; arrange
   on prepared baking sheet. Bake in preheated oven for
   18 to 20 minutes or until nicely browned. Transfer
   to a paper towel–lined plate to drain.

NUTRITIONAL ANALYSIS PER SERVING	
Calories	78
Carbohydrate	2 g
Fiber	0 g
Protein	7 g
Fat, total	4 g
Fat, saturated	2 g
Sodium	125 mg
Cholesterol	28 mg

AMERICA'S EXCHANGES PER SERVING	
1	Medium-fat Meat

CANADA'S CHOICES PER SERVING	
1	Meat & Alternatives

*This versatile dipping
sauce is also good with
chicken or pork kebabs,
or with chicken wings.
For a spicy version, add
hot pepper sauce to taste.*

Tip

Soy sauce is a popular
condiment and ingredient,
but it is also high in sodium.
Use reduced-sodium soy
sauce to enjoy the flavor
with about 50% less
sodium. Brands vary, but
there is typically about
1,000 mg of sodium in
1 tbsp (15 mL) regular
soy sauce and 500 mg in
the same amount of the
reduced-sodium product.

Party Meatballs with Sweet-and-Sour Sauce

1/2 cup	orange juice	125 mL
3 tbsp	reduced-sodium soy sauce	45 mL
1/4 cup	ketchup	50 mL
1/4 cup	packed brown sugar	50 mL
2 tbsp	balsamic vinegar	25 mL
1	clove garlic, minced	1
1 1/2 tsp	cornstarch	7 mL
36	Appetizer Meatballs (half the recipe, see page 28)	36

1. In a medium saucepan, stir together orange juice, soy sauce, ketchup, brown sugar, vinegar, garlic and cornstarch until smooth. Bring to a boil over medium heat, stirring constantly, until sauce is thick and smooth.

2. Stir in cooked meatballs; cover and simmer for 5 minutes or until heated through.

NUTRITIONAL ANALYSIS PER SERVING

Calories	110
Carbohydrate	10 g
Fiber	0 g
Protein	8 g
Fat, total	5 g
Fat, saturated	2 g
Sodium	310 mg
Cholesterol	28 mg

AMERICA'S EXCHANGES PER SERVING

1/2	Other Carbohydrate
1	Medium-fat Meat

CANADA'S CHOICES PER SERVING

1/2	Carbohydrate
1	Meat & Alternatives

**MAKES 12 PIECES
(1 per serving)**

*Spinach and feta pie, a
classic Greek comfort
food, can be served warm
or at room temperature
as an appetizer or part
of a buffet.*

Tips

It's best to stick to one
serving of this delicious but
relatively high-fat appetizer.
The fat is mainly from olive
oil, a source of desirable
monounsaturated fat, but
even "good" fats should be
consumed in moderation.
When appetizers are higher
in fat, keep an eye on your
intake and make lower-fat
choices for the remainder
of the meal.

While you're working with
one phyllo sheet at a time,
cover the remainder with
plastic wrap and place a
damp towel on top to
prevent drying out.

Spanakopita

- Preheat oven to 375°F (190°C)
- 13- by 9-inch (3 L) baking pan, sprayed with vegetable cooking spray

2	bags (10 oz/300 g) fresh spinach	2
5 tbsp	olive oil (approx.)	75 mL
1 cup	sliced green onions	250 mL
2	eggs	2
1 cup	finely crumbled light feta cheese (about 5 oz/150 g)	250 mL
1/4 cup	chopped fresh dill	50 mL
	Freshly ground black pepper	
9	sheets phyllo pastry	9

1. Rinse spinach in cold water; remove tough ends. Place in large saucepan with just the water clinging to leaves; cook over medium-high heat, stirring, until just wilted. Drain well and squeeze dry; finely chop.

2. In a large nonstick skillet, heat 1 tbsp (15 mL) of the oil over medium-high heat; cook spinach and green onions, stirring, for 4 minutes or until spinach is just tender. Let cool.

3. In a bowl, beat eggs; add spinach mixture, feta and dill and season with pepper.

4. Place one sheet of phyllo on work surface and brush lightly with oil. Fit into baking pan with ends hanging over sides. Layer four more phyllo sheets in pan, brushing each with oil before adding the next. Evenly spread with spinach filling and fold ends over filling. Layer remaining four phyllo sheets on top, brushing each lightly with oil before adding the next. Carefully fold pastry edges under bottom pastry.

5. Using a sharp knife, cut the top phyllo layers into squares or a diamond pattern. Brush top with oil. Bake in preheated oven for 35 to 40 minutes or until golden. Let cool for 10 minutes before cutting into 12 pieces.

**NUTRITIONAL ANALYSIS
PER SERVING**

Calories	157
Carbohydrate	13 g
Fiber	2 g
Protein	6 g
Fat, total	10 g
Fat, saturated	3 g
Sodium	285 mg
Cholesterol	35 mg

**AMERICA'S EXCHANGES
PER SERVING**

1/2	Starch
1/2	Vegetable
1/2	Lean Meat
1 1/2	Fat

**CANADA'S CHOICES
PER SERVING**

1/2	Carbohydrate
1/2	Meat & Alternatives
1 1/2	Fat

Soups

Chicken Noodle Soup

Often called "Jewish penicillin," chicken soup is the perfect antidote to an oncoming cold. But there's more to its restorative powers. Rich and delicious, it can banish the winter blues and make you feel just plain good any day of the year.

Tips

Soups, including this one, often contain surprising amounts of sodium. Start by adding only half the salt called for in a recipe and taste to see if you really need to add the rest.

You don't have to slave over the stove to make this soul-satisfying soup. Adding the chicken and the vegetables to the pot at the same time streamlines the process and does away with the chore of making stock first. The results are every bit as pleasing.

3 lbs	whole chicken or chicken pieces, such as legs and breasts	1.5 kg
10 cups	water (approx.)	2.5 L
1	large onion, finely chopped	1
3	carrots, peeled and chopped	3
2	stalks celery, including leaves, chopped	2
2 tbsp	chopped fresh parsley	25 mL
1/2 tsp	dried thyme leaves	2 mL
1 1/2 tsp	salt	7 mL
1/4 tsp	freshly ground black pepper	1 mL
1	bay leaf	1
1 1/2 cups	medium or broad egg noodles	375 mL
1 cup	finely diced zucchini or small cauliflower florets	250 mL
2 tbsp	chopped fresh dill or parsley	25 mL

1. Rinse chicken; remove as much skin and excess fat as possible. Place in a large stockpot; add water to cover. Bring to a boil over high heat; using a slotted spoon, skim off foam as it rises to the surface.

2. Add onion, carrots, celery, parsley, thyme, salt, pepper and bay leaf. Reduce heat to medium-low; cover and simmer for about 1 1/4 hours or until chicken is tender.

3. Remove chicken with slotted spoon and place in a large bowl; let cool slightly. Pull chicken meat off the bones, discarding skin and bones. Cut meat into bite-size pieces. Reserve 2 cups (500 mL) for soup. (Use remainder for casseroles and sandwiches.)

4. Skim fat from surface of soup; bring to a boil. Add cubed chicken, noodles, zucchini and dill; cook for 10 minutes or until noodles and vegetables are tender. Remove bay leaf. Add pepper to taste.

NUTRITIONAL ANALYSIS PER SERVING

Calories	139
Carbohydrate	12 g
Fiber	3 g
Protein	15 g
Fat, total	3 g
Fat, saturated	1 g
Sodium	525 mg
Cholesterol	39 mg

AMERICA'S EXCHANGES PER SERVING

1/2	Starch
1	Vegetable
2	Very Lean Meat

CANADA'S CHOICES PER SERVING

1/2	Carbohydrate
2	Meat & Alternatives

Cheese-Smothered Onion Soup

SERVES 6
(1½ cups/375 mL per serving)

This savory soup will warm you up on cold blustery days. The assertive flavor of onions mellows and sweetens when cooked until golden. This classic makes an easy transition from an everyday dish to an entertainment standout.

Tip

The onion soup base can be made ahead and refrigerated for up to 5 days or frozen for up to 3 months.

Hate shedding tears when chopping onions? To minimize the weeping problem, use a razor-sharp knife to prevent loss of juices and cover the cut onions with a paper towel as you chop them to prevent the vapors from rising to your eyes.

2 tbsp	soft margarine or butter	25 mL
8 cups	thinly sliced Spanish onions (about 2 to 3)	2 L
¼ tsp	dried thyme leaves	1 mL
¼ tsp	freshly ground black pepper	1 mL
2 tbsp	all-purpose flour	25 mL
3 cups	reduced-sodium beef broth	750 mL
3 cups	water	750 mL
6	slices French bread, about ¾-inch (2 cm) thick	6
1½ cups	shredded light Swiss cheese	500 mL

1. In a Dutch oven or large heavy saucepan, melt butter over medium heat. Add onions, thyme and pepper; cook, stirring often, for 15 minutes or until onions are tender and a rich golden color. Blend in flour; stir in broth and water. Bring to a boil, stirring until thickened. Reduce heat to medium-low, cover and simmer for 15 minutes.

2. Meanwhile, position oven rack 6 inches (15 cm) from broiler; preheat broiler.

3. Arrange bread slices on baking sheet; place under broiler and toast on both sides.

4. Place toasts in deep ovenproof soup bowls; sprinkle with half the cheese. Arrange bowls in large shallow baking pan. Ladle hot soup into bowls. Sprinkle with remaining cheese. Place under broiler for 3 minutes or until cheese melts and is lightly browned. Serve immediately.

NUTRITIONAL ANALYSIS PER SERVING	
Calories	256
Carbohydrate	30 g
Fiber	3 g
Protein	13 g
Fat, total	9 g
Fat, saturated	4 g
Sodium	595 mg
Cholesterol	17 mg

AMERICA'S EXCHANGES PER SERVING	
1	Starch
2½	Vegetable
1	Medium-fat Meat
½	Fat

CANADA'S CHOICES PER SERVING	
2	Carbohydrate
1	Meat & Alternatives
1	Fat

SERVES 8
(1 1/2 cups/375 mL per serving)

My family came from the Netherlands to Southern Ontario in the 1950s and we were raised on this warming Dutch soup. When I lived in Quebec for several years, I discovered pea soup was also a key staple in that province's food heritage and I felt right at home.

Tip

For a wonderful rich flavor, I like to add a meaty ham bone to the soup as it simmers. As most hams sold today in supermarkets are boneless, however, the addition of both chopped smoked ham and chicken stock make a good substitute. If you have a ham bone, add it (first removing any fat) and use water instead of stock. Smoked pork hock is another alternative if a ham bone is not available.

Old-Fashioned Pea Soup with Smoked Ham

1 tbsp	canola oil	15 mL
1	medium leek, white and light green part only, chopped (see tip, page 43)	1
1	large onion, chopped	1
2	large cloves garlic, finely chopped	2
3	carrots, peeled and chopped	3
1	large stalk celery, including leaves, chopped	1
1 1/2 tsp	dried marjoram leaves	7 mL
1	bay leaf	1
1/4 tsp	freshly ground black pepper	1 mL
6 cups	reduced-sodium chicken broth	1.5 L
2 cups	water	500 mL
2 cups	chopped lean smoked ham	500 mL
1 1/2 cups	dried yellow or green split peas, rinsed and picked over	375 mL
1/4 cup	chopped fresh parsley	50 mL

1. In a Dutch oven or stockpot, heat oil over medium heat. Add leek, onion, garlic, carrots, celery, marjoram, bay leaf and pepper; cook, stirring often, for 8 minutes or until softened.

2. Stir in broth, water, ham and split peas. Bring to a boil; reduce heat, cover and simmer, stirring occasionally, for about 1 1/2 hours or until split peas are tender.

3. Remove bay leaf. Stir in parsley. Soup thickens as it cools; thin with additional stock or water to desired consistency.

NUTRITIONAL ANALYSIS PER SERVING	
Calories	208
Carbohydrate	29 g
Fiber	5 g
Protein	16 g
Fat, total	4 g
Fat, saturated	1 g
Sodium	685 mg
Cholesterol	14 mg

AMERICA'S EXCHANGES PER SERVING	
1	Starch
1	Vegetable
2	Very Lean Meat

CANADA'S CHOICES PER SERVING	
1 1/2	Carbohydrate
2	Meat & Alternatives

Curried Split Pea Soup

Here's a homey satisfying soup that's perfect to serve as the main event on cold, blustery days.

Tips

Purchased broths and stocks are often high in sodium. Look for reduced-sodium or salt-free products; check labels for ingredients and sodium levels.

This recipe makes a large batch of soup; freeze extra for another meal.

1 tbsp	vegetable oil	15 mL
2	medium onions, chopped	2
4	cloves garlic, finely chopped	4
1 tbsp	mild curry paste or powder	15 mL
1 tsp	ground cumin	5 mL
1 tsp	paprika	5 mL
¼ tsp	cayenne pepper	1 mL
3	large carrots, peeled and chopped	3
2	large stalks celery, including leaves, chopped	2
2 cups	yellow or green split peas, rinsed and sorted	500 mL
¼ cup	tomato paste	50 mL
10 cups	vegetable broth or reduced-sodium chicken broth	2.5 L
⅓ cup	chopped fresh cilantro or parsley	75 mL
	Freshly ground black pepper	
	Plain low-fat yogurt (optional)	

1. In a large Dutch oven or stockpot, heat oil over medium heat. Add onions, garlic, curry paste, cumin, paprika and cayenne pepper; cook, stirring, for 3 minutes or until softened.

2. Add carrots, celery, split peas, tomato paste and stock. Bring to a boil; reduce heat, cover and simmer for about 1 to 1½ hours or until peas are tender.

3. Stir in cilantro; season with pepper to taste. Ladle into bowls; top with a dollop of yogurt, if desired. Soup thickens as it cools, so you may want to thin with additional stock before serving.

NUTRITIONAL ANALYSIS PER SERVING	
Calories	267
Carbohydrate	45 g
Fiber	7 g
Protein	14 g
Fat, total	4 g
Fat, saturated	0 g
Sodium	680 mg
Cholesterol	0 mg

AMERICA'S EXCHANGES PER SERVING	
2	Starch
1	Other Carbohydrate
2	Vegetable
1	Very Lean Meat

CANADA'S CHOICES PER SERVING	
2½	Carbohydrate
1½	Meat & Alternatives

Basil Tomato-Rice Soup

*My pantry can be sparse,
but I can always count
on having these few
ingredients on hand to
make this last-minute soup
to serve with crusty whole-
grain bread and cheese.*

Tips

Parboiled rice should not
be confused with "instant"
rice; parboiled requires
about the same cooking
time as regular rice. Before
milling, a pressurized steam
process forces some of the
B vitamins to move from
the bran and germ into the
starchy portion. Parboiling
also lowers the glycemic
index, making this type of
rice a better choice for
people with diabetes.

For fresher flavor and
less sodium, replace
canned tomatoes with
4 large ripe tomatoes,
peeled and chopped.

If you prefer, substitute
2 tbsp (25 mL) chopped
fresh basil for the dried and
add with parsley.

I tbsp	olive oil	15 mL
I	large onion, chopped	I
2	stalks celery, chopped	2
2	cloves garlic, finely chopped	2
I tsp	dried basil leaves	5 mL
I	can (28 oz/796 mL) plum tomatoes, including juice	I
4 cups	reduced-sodium chicken broth	I L
2 cups	water	500 mL
½ cup	parboiled (converted) rice	125 mL
I tsp	granulated sugar (approx.)	5 mL
	Freshly ground black pepper	
2 tbsp	chopped fresh parsley	25 mL

1. In a Dutch oven or stockpot, heat oil over medium heat. Add onion, celery, garlic and basil; cook, stirring, for 5 minutes or until softened.

2. In a food processor, purée tomatoes with juice. Add to pot with broth, water and rice; season with sugar, salt and pepper to taste. Bring to a boil; reduce heat, cover and simmer for 30 to 35 minutes or until rice is tender. Stir in parsley.

NUTRITIONAL ANALYSIS PER SERVING

Calories	131
Carbohydrate	22 g
Fiber	2 g
Protein	5 g
Fat, total	3 g
Fat, saturated	0 g
Sodium	560 mg
Cholesterol	0 mg

AMERICA'S EXCHANGES PER SERVING

I	Starch
2½	Vegetable
½	Fat

CANADA'S CHOICES PER SERVING

1½	Carbohydrate
½	Fat

Creamy Tomato Soup

**SERVES 6
(1 cup/250 mL
per serving)**

*I always look forward to
late summer — when
baskets of lush ripe
tomatoes are the showpiece
in outdoor markets — so
I can make this silky
smooth soup. In winter,
vine-ripened greenhouse
tomatoes make a good
stand-in, particularly if you
use a little tomato paste for
extra depth. Just add 1 to
2 tbsp (15 to 25 mL)
when puréeing soup.*

Tip

If tomatoes aren't fully
ripened when you buy
them, place in a paper bag
on your counter for a day a
two. The ethylene gas given
off by the tomatoes speeds
up the ripening process.
Never store tomatoes in
the fridge — the cold
temperature numbs their
sweet flavor. A sunny
windowsill may seem
like a good place to ripen
tomatoes, but a hot sun
often bakes rather than
ripens them.

- *Preheat oven to 400°F (200°C)*
- *Large roasting pan*

1 tbsp	olive oil	15 mL
6	ripe tomatoes cored and quartered, (about 2 lbs/1 kg)	6
1	medium leek, white and light green part only, chopped (see tip, page 43)	1
1	small onion, coarsely chopped	1
2	medium carrots, peeled and coarsely chopped	2
1	stalk celery, including leaves, chopped	1
2	large cloves garlic, sliced	2
½ tsp	salt	2 mL
¼ tsp	freshly ground black pepper	1 mL
Pinch	freshly grated nutmeg	Pinch
2 cups	reduced-sodium chicken broth	500 mL
1 cup	water	250 mL
1 cup	light (5%) cream	250 mL
2 tbsp	chopped fresh herbs such as parsley, basil or chives	25 mL

1. Drizzle oil over bottom of a large shallow roasting pan. Add tomatoes, leek, onion, carrots, celery and garlic; season with salt, pepper and nutmeg.

2. Roast, uncovered, in preheated oven, stirring often, for 1¼ hours or until vegetables are very tender, but not brown.

3. Combine broth with water and add 2 cups (500 mL) to pan; purée mixture in batches, preferably in a blender or a food processor, until very smooth. Strain soup through a sieve into large saucepan.

4. Add cream and enough of the remaining broth to thin soup to desired consistency. Add pepper to taste. Heat until piping hot; do not let the soup boil or it may curdle. Ladle into warm bowls; sprinkle with fresh herbs.

NUTRITIONAL ANALYSIS PER SERVING

Calories	112
Carbohydrate	14 g
Fiber	3 g
Protein	4 g
Fat, total	5 g
Fat, saturated	2 g
Sodium	410 mg
Cholesterol	8 mg

AMERICA'S EXCHANGES PER SERVING

2	Vegetable
1	Fat

CANADA'S CHOICES PER SERVING

½	Carbohydrate
1	Fat

SERVES 6
(1½ cups/375 mL per serving)

Here's an inviting soup that's fragrant with garlic and brimming with fresh seafood in a rich wine and tomato broth. When I invite friends over for a relaxed dinner, I like to accompany this soup with crusty bread, followed by a simple salad and a fresh fruit dessert.

Tips

For a less expensive version of this recipe, replace shrimp and scallops with an equal quantity of mild fish. If using frozen fish in block form, remove packaging, place on plate and microwave at Medium (50%) for 5 minutes or until partly thawed. Cut into cubes; let stand for 15 minutes until completely thawed.

This soup can be prepared through Step 2, covered and refrigerated for up to 1 day or frozen for up to 3 months. When reheating, bring back to a full boil.

NUTRITIONAL ANALYSIS PER SERVING	
Calories	215
Carbohydrate	11 g
Fiber	2 g
Protein	26 g
Fat, total	6 g
Fat, saturated	1 g
Sodium	435 mg
Cholesterol	74 mg

Mediterranean Seafood Soup

2 tbsp	olive oil	25 mL
1	Spanish onion, chopped (about 1 lb/500 g)	1
3	cloves garlic, finely chopped	3
1	red bell pepper, diced	1
1	green bell pepper, diced	1
1	large stalk celery, including leaves, chopped	1
1	bay leaf	1
1 tsp	paprika	5 mL
¼ tsp	hot pepper flakes	1 mL
¼ tsp	saffron threads, crushed	1 mL
1	can (19 oz/540 mL) tomatoes, including juice, chopped	1
4 cups	fish stock or reduced-sodium chicken broth (approx.)	1 L
1 cup	dry white wine or vermouth or additional broth	250 mL
1 lb	halibut or other mild white fish, cubed	500 g
8 oz	raw medium shrimp, peeled and deveined, tails left on	250 g
8 oz	scallops, halved if large	250 g
⅓ cup	finely chopped fresh parsley	75 mL

1. In a Dutch oven or large saucepan, heat oil over medium-high heat. Add onion, garlic, peppers, celery, bay leaf, paprika, hot pepper flakes and saffron; cook, stirring often, for 5 minutes or until vegetables are softened.

2. Add tomatoes with juice, broth and wine. Bring to a boil; reduce heat to medium-low and simmer, covered, for 30 minutes.

3. Stir in halibut, shrimp, scallops and parsley; cover and simmer for 3 to 5 minutes or until fish is opaque. Serve immediately in warm soup bowls.

AMERICA'S EXCHANGES PER SERVING	
2	Vegetable
3	Very Lean Meat
1	Fat

CANADA'S CHOICES PER SERVING	
½	Carbohydrate
3½	Meat & Alternatives

SERVES 4
(1⅓ cups/325 mL
per serving)

*Thick and creamy, laden
with chunks of potatoes
and featuring the smoky
flavor of bacon, this
restaurant favorite is
easy to recreate in your
home kitchen.*

Clam Chowder

4	slices bacon, chopped	4
1	can (5 oz/142 g) clams, drained, juice reserved	1
1	small onion, finely chopped	1
1	stalk celery, finely diced	1
1	clove garlic, minced	1
1	bay leaf	1
1½ cups	potatoes, peeled, cut into ½-inch (1 cm) cubes	375 mL
1 cup	fish broth or reduced-sodium chicken broth	250 mL
2 cups	low-fat milk	500 mL
3 tbsp	all-purpose flour	45 mL
2 tbsp	finely chopped fresh parsley	25 mL
	Freshly ground black pepper	

1. In a large saucepan, cook bacon over medium heat, stirring, for 4 minutes or until crisp. Remove; blot with paper towels and set aside. Drain fat from pan.

2. Add drained clams, onion, celery, garlic and bay leaf; cook, stirring often, for 3 minutes or until vegetables are softened.

3. Stir in reserved clam juice, potatoes and broth; bring to a boil. Reduce heat to medium-low, cover and simmer for 15 minutes or until vegetables are tender.

4. In a bowl, blend a small amount of the milk into the flour to make a smooth paste. Stir in remaining milk until smooth and lump-free. Add to saucepan; bring to a boil over medium-high heat, stirring often, until mixture thickens.

5. Stir in bacon bits, parsley and pepper to taste. Remove bay leaf before serving.

NUTRITIONAL ANALYSIS PER SERVING	
Calories	199
Carbohydrate	24 g
Fiber	1 g
Protein	14 g
Fat, total	5 g
Fat, saturated	2 g
Sodium	425 mg
Cholesterol	23 mg

AMERICA'S EXCHANGES PER SERVING	
1	Starch
½	Milk, Fat-free/Low-fat
½	Vegetable
1	Lean Meat

CANADA'S CHOICES PER SERVING	
1½	Carbohydrate
1½	Meat & Alternatives

Hearty Mussel Chowder

Cultivated mussels are the perfect fast food. They come debearded (meaning the thread that holds them to stationary objects has already been removed) and require only a quick rinse under cold water before cooking. Just throw them in a pot, steam for 4 to 5 minutes and they're ready to eat.

Tip

To store mussels, place in a bowl and cover with damp paper towels. Never keep in a closed plastic bag or the mussels will suffocate. Also never put in a sink full of water or they will drown. For maximum freshness, use within 2 days of purchase.

2 lbs	cultivated mussels	1 kg
1 cup	white wine or water	250 mL
4	slices bacon, chopped	4
1	large leek, white and light green part only, chopped (see tip, page 43)	1
2	stalks celery, chopped	2
1½ cups	diced peeled potatoes	375 mL
½ tsp	salt	2 mL
¼ tsp	freshly ground black pepper	1 mL
½ cup	diced red bell pepper	125 mL
2 tbsp	all-purpose flour	25 mL
1½ cups	low-fat milk	375 mL
2 tbsp	finely chopped fresh parsley	25 mL

1. Place mussels and wine in a large saucepan. Cover and place over high heat; bring to a boil. Steam for 4 minutes or just until shells open. Drain, reserving cooking liquid. Add enough water or reduced-sodium fish broth to make 2 cups (500 mL) liquid. Remove mussel meat from shells and place in a bowl; discard any that do not open.

2. In a large saucepan over medium heat, cook bacon, stirring often, for 4 minutes or until crisp. Remove with slotted spoon; drain on paper towels. Drain fat from pan. Add leek and celery; cook, stirring, for 3 minutes or until softened. Add potatoes, reserved mussel broth, salt and pepper. Bring to a boil; reduce heat, cover and simmer for 15 minutes or until potatoes are tender. Stir in red pepper.

3. In a bowl, blend flour with ¼ cup (50 mL) milk to make a smooth paste; add remaining milk. Stir into saucepan; bring to a boil and cook, stirring, until thickened. Add reserved mussels, bacon bits and parsley; cook 2 minutes or until piping hot.

NUTRITIONAL ANALYSIS PER SERVING

Calories	231
Carbohydrate	25 g
Fiber	2 g
Protein	16 g
Fat, total	6 g
Fat, saturated	2 g
Sodium	605 mg
Cholesterol	30 mg

AMERICA'S EXCHANGES PER SERVING	
1	Starch
½	Milk, Fat-free/Low-fat
1	Vegetable
1	Lean Meat

CANADA'S CHOICES PER SERVING	
1½	Carbohydrate
1½	Meat & Alternatives

*The trademark ingredients
of Creole cooking —
onions, green pepper
and celery — have been
combined in a tomato and
cream base to create this
luscious fish soup.*

Tip

Any kind of fish, such as
cod, sole, haddock or
bluefish, can be used. If
using frozen fish fillets,
remove packaging and
arrange fish on plate;
microwave at High for 3 to
4 minutes or until partially
defrosted. Cut fish into
small cubes; let stand
15 minutes to complete
defrosting.

Creole Fish Soup

1 tbsp	olive oil	15 mL
4	green onions, chopped	4
1	large clove garlic, minced	1
2	stalks celery, including leaves, chopped	2
1	green bell pepper, diced	1
1 tsp	paprika	5 mL
½ tsp	dried thyme leaves	2 mL
Pinch	cayenne pepper	Pinch
2 cups	diced peeled potatoes	500 mL
1	can (19 oz/540 mL) stewed tomatoes, including juice, chopped	1
2 cups	fish or vegetable broth (approx.)	500 mL
1 lb	fresh or frozen fish fillets	500 g
	Freshly ground black pepper	

1. In a large saucepan, heat oil over medium heat. Add
   green onions, garlic, celery, green pepper, paprika,
   thyme and cayenne pepper; cook, stirring, for
   3 minutes or until softened. Add potatoes, stewed
   tomatoes with juice and broth; bring to a boil.
   Reduce heat, cover and simmer for 15 minutes
   or until vegetables are tender.

2. Add fish; simmer for 2 minutes or until fish flakes
   when tested with a fork. (Add more broth if soup is
   too thick.) Add pepper to taste.

NUTRITIONAL ANALYSIS PER SERVING	
Calories	304
Carbohydrate	28 g
Fiber	4 g
Protein	32 g
Fat, total	8 g
Fat, saturated	1 g
Sodium	595 mg
Cholesterol	41 mg

AMERICA'S EXCHANGES PER SERVING	
1	Starch
3	Vegetable
3	Very Lean Meat
½	Fat

CANADA'S CHOICES PER SERVING	
1½	Carbohydrate
4	Meat & Alternatives

This nourishing soup is chockful of vegetables and excels at chasing away the winter chills. It's soothing both to the body and the soul.

Tip

For fresher flavor and less sodium, replace canned tomatoes with 4 large ripe tomatoes, peeled and chopped.

Chunky Minestrone

1 tbsp	olive oil	15 mL
2	medium onions, chopped	2
4	cloves garlic, finely chopped	4
3	medium carrots, peeled and diced	3
2	stalks celery, including leaves, chopped	2
1½ tsp	dried basil leaves	7 mL
1 tsp	dried oregano or marjoram leaves	5 mL
½ tsp	freshly ground black pepper	2 mL
8 cups	reduced-sodium chicken broth	2 L
2 cups	water	500 mL
1	can (19 oz/540 mL) tomatoes, including juice, chopped	1
2 cups	small cauliflower florets	500 mL
1½ cups	green beans, cut into 1-inch (2.5 cm) lengths	375 mL
¾ cup	small pasta shapes, such as tubetti or shells	175 mL
1	can (19 oz/540 mL) chickpeas or small white beans, drained and rinsed	1
⅓ cup	chopped fresh parsley	75 mL
	Freshly grated Parmesan cheese	

1. In a Dutch oven or large stockpot, heat oil over medium heat. Add onions, garlic, carrots, celery, basil, oregano and pepper; cook, stirring, for 5 minutes or until softened.

2. Stir in broth, water, tomatoes with juice, cauliflower and beans. Bring to a boil; reduce heat to medium-low and simmer, covered, for 20 minutes or until vegetables are tender.

3. Stir in pasta; cover and simmer for 10 minutes, stirring occasionally, until pasta is just tender.

4. Add chickpeas and parsley; cook 5 minutes more or until heated through. Ladle soup into heated bowls and sprinkle with Parmesan.

NUTRITIONAL ANALYSIS PER SERVING

Calories	132
Carbohydrate	21 g
Fiber	4 g
Protein	6 g
Fat, total	3 g
Fat, saturated	0 g
Sodium	505 mg
Cholesterol	0 mg

AMERICA'S EXCHANGES PER SERVING

1	Starch
1½	Vegetable
½	Fat

CANADA'S CHOICES PER SERVING

1	Carbohydrate
1	Meat & Alternatives

SERVES 8
(1 ½ cups/375 mL
per serving)

With all the glamorous foods out there now, cabbage is often neglected. That's a shame. Cabbage is an excellent partner to soothing potatoes and smoky sausage in this robust soup — which shows just how rich an addition this underrated vegetable can be. Taste it and you'll see.

Tips

To clean leeks, trim dark green tops. Cut down center almost to root end and chop. Rinse in a sink full of cold water to remove sand; scoop up leeks and place in colander to drain or use a salad spinner.

Store soup in covered container in refrigerator for up to 5 days.

Leek, Potato and Cabbage Soup

1 tbsp	olive oil	15 mL
2	medium leeks, white and light green part only, chopped (see tip, at left)	2
2	cloves garlic, finely chopped	2
¼ tsp	freshly ground black pepper	1 mL
¼ tsp	caraway seeds (optional)	1 mL
2 cups	peeled and cubed potatoes	500 mL
4 cups	finely shredded green cabbage	1 L
6 cups	reduced-sodium beef broth	1.5 L
4 oz	kielbasa, or other cooked smoked sausage, cut into small cubes	125 g
¼ cup	chopped fresh parsley	50 mL

1. In a large saucepan, heat oil over medium heat. Add leeks, garlic, pepper and caraway seeds, if using; cook, stirring, for 4 minutes or until softened.

2. Stir in potatoes, cabbage and broth. Bring to a boil; reduce heat to medium-low and simmer, covered, for 20 minutes or until vegetables are tender.

3. Add sausage and parsley; cook 5 minutes more or until sausage is heated through.

NUTRITIONAL ANALYSIS PER SERVING

Calories	113
Carbohydrate	13 g
Fiber	3 g
Protein	6 g
Fat, total	5 g
Fat, saturated	1 g
Sodium	520 mg
Cholesterol	10 mg

AMERICA'S EXCHANGES PER SERVING

½	Starch
1	Vegetable
½	High-fat Meat

CANADA'S CHOICES PER SERVING

½	Carbohydrate
½	Meat & Alternatives
½	Fat

**SERVES 6
(1 cup/250 mL per
serving)**

*Watercress adds a vibrant
color and nip to the classic
combo of creamed potato
and leek soup.*

Tip

You can make this soup
a day ahead and reheat
until piping hot. It's also
delicious served cold.

Perfect Potato
and Leek Soup

1 tbsp	soft margarine or butter	15 mL
2	medium leeks, white and light green part only, chopped (see tip, page 43)	2
2 cups	diced peeled potatoes	500 mL
1 tsp	dried tarragon or fines herbes	5 mL
2 tbsp	all-purpose flour	25 mL
4 cups	reduced-sodium chicken broth	1 L
1	bunch watercress, tough stems removed, chopped	1
1 cup	low-fat milk	250 mL
	Freshly ground black pepper	
	Watercress sprigs	

1. In a large saucepan, melt butter over medium heat. Add leeks, potatoes and tarragon; cook, stirring, for 5 minutes or until leeks are softened but not browned. Blend in flour; stir in broth. Bring to a boil; reduce heat, cover and simmer, stirring occasionally, for 20 minutes or until potatoes are very tender.

2. Add watercress; simmer 1 minute until watercress is limp and bright green in color.

3. In a food processor or blender, purée soup in batches until smooth. Return to saucepan. Stir in milk; season with pepper to taste. Heat until piping hot; do not let boil. Ladle into bowls; garnish with watercress sprigs.

NUTRITIONAL ANALYSIS PER SERVING

Calories	114
Carbohydrate	18 g
Fiber	3 g
Protein	5 g
Fat, total	3 g
Fat, saturated	1 g
Sodium	390 mg
Cholesterol	2 mg

AMERICA'S EXCHANGES PER SERVING

½	Starch
2	Vegetable
½	Fat

CANADA'S CHOICES PER SERVING

1	Carbohydrate
½	Fat

Creamy Mushroom Soup

Use shiitake mushrooms along with less inexpensive brown mushrooms to create this intensely flavored soup that makes a great starter for a special dinner.

Tip

The stems of shiitake mushrooms are flavorful but very tough. Save them in the freezer and use to flavor soups and stocks.

1 tbsp	soft margarine or butter	15 mL
1	large onion, finely chopped	1
2	cloves garlic, minced	2
8 oz	assorted mushrooms, such as shiitake and cremini, sliced	250 g
1½ tsp	chopped fresh thyme or ½ tsp (2 mL) dried thyme leaves	7 mL
2 tbsp	all-purpose flour	25 mL
4 cups	reduced-sodium chicken broth	1 L
½ tsp	salt	2 mL
¼ tsp	freshly ground black pepper	1 mL
1 cup	half-and-half (10%) cream	250 mL
¼ cup	medium-dry sherry (optional)	50 mL
2 tbsp	chopped fresh chives or parsley	25 mL

1. In a Dutch oven or large saucepan, heat butter over medium-high heat. Cook onion and garlic, stirring, for 2 minutes until softened. Stir in mushrooms and thyme; cook, stirring often, for 5 minutes or until mushrooms are tender.

2. Sprinkle with flour; stir in broth, salt and pepper. Bring to a boil over high heat. Reduce heat to medium-low, cover and simmer for 25 minutes. Let cool slightly.

3. In a food processor or blender, purée soup in batches. Return to saucepan. Place over medium heat; stir in cream and sherry, if using. Add pepper to taste. Heat until piping hot. Ladle into heated bowls and sprinkle with chives.

NUTRITIONAL ANALYSIS PER SERVING	
Calories	113
Carbohydrate	11 g
Fiber	2 g
Protein	4 g
Fat, total	6 g
Fat, saturated	3 g
Sodium	570 mg
Cholesterol	13 mg

AMERICA'S EXCHANGES PER SERVING	
1½	Vegetable
½	Medium-fat Meat
1	Fat

CANADA'S CHOICES PER SERVING	
½	Carbohydrate
½	Meat & Alternatives
1	Fat

**SERVES 6
(1 cup/250 mL per serving)**

Here's a seductive soup with a Caribbean accent to serve for a special dinner. The surprising combination of earthy root vegetables, married with spices like ginger and curry, gives the soup a delicious Island flare. My friends always go home with the recipe.

Tip

The carrots, sweet potato and rutabaga, cut into ½-inch (1 cm) cubes, should total 4 cups (1 L).

Curried Cream of Root Vegetable Soup

I tbsp	vegetable oil	15 mL
I ½ cups	diced, peeled apples	375 mL
I	medium onion, chopped	I
2	cloves garlic, minced	2
I tbsp	minced fresh gingerroot	15 mL
I ½ tsp	mild curry paste or powder	7 mL
½ tsp	ground cumin	2 mL
½ tsp	ground coriander	2 mL
¼ tsp	dried thyme leaves	I mL
Pinch	cayenne pepper	Pinch
2	carrots, peeled and cubed	2
I	sweet potato (about 7 oz/200 g), peeled and cubed	I
I cup	cubed rutabaga	250 mL
4 cups	reduced-sodium chicken broth	I L
I cup	half-and-half (10%) cream	250 mL
¼ cup	chopped fresh cilantro or parsley	50 mL

1. In a large saucepan, heat oil over medium heat. Add apples, onion, garlic, ginger, curry paste, cumin, coriander, thyme and cayenne pepper; cook, stirring, for 5 minutes or until softened.

2. Add carrots, sweet potato, rutabaga and broth. Bring to a boil; reduce heat to medium-low and simmer, covered, for 30 minutes or until vegetables are very tender. Let cool slightly.

3. In a food processor or blender, purée soup in batches until smooth. Return to saucepan; stir in cream and heat through. Do not allow soup to boil or it may curdle. Ladle into bowls; sprinkle with cilantro.

NUTRITIONAL ANALYSIS PER SERVING	
Calories	126
Carbohydrate	19 g
Fiber	3 g
Protein	3 g
Fat, total	4 g
Fat, saturated	1 g
Sodium	395 mg
Cholesterol	3 mg

AMERICA'S EXCHANGES PER SERVING	
½	Starch
I	Vegetable
I	Fat

CANADA'S CHOICES PER SERVING	
I	Carbohydrate
I	Fat

**SERVES 6
(1 cup/250 mL per serving)**

If you have a vegetarian in your family, this is a recipe you can count on. It's no-fuss to prepare, easy to reheat and makes a complete meal.

Tip

Depending on what I have in the fridge, I make variations on this versatile, tasty soup by using other vegetables, such as carrots and cauliflower.

Cheddar Broccoli Chowder

2 tbsp	vegetable oil	25 mL
1	small onion, finely chopped	1
1/4 cup	all-purpose flour	50 mL
3 cups	vegetable broth or reduced-sodium chicken broth	750 mL
2 cups	potatoes, peeled and cut into 1/2-inch (1 cm) cubes	500 mL
1	bay leaf	1
3 cups	finely chopped broccoli florets and peeled stalks	750 mL
1 1/2 cups	low-fat milk	375 mL
1 1/2 cups	shredded light Cheddar cheese	375 mL
	Freshly ground black pepper	

1. In a large saucepan, heat oil over medium heat. Cook onion, stirring, for 2 minutes or until softened. Blend in flour; stir in broth. Bring to a boil, stirring, until thickened.

2. Add potatoes and bay leaf; reduce heat, cover and simmer, stirring occasionally, for 10 minutes.

3. Add broccoli; simmer, stirring occasionally, for 10 minutes more or until vegetables are tender.

4. Stir in milk and cheese; heat just until cheese melts and soup is piping hot. Do not let the soup boil or it may curdle. Remove bay leaf; adjust seasoning with pepper to taste.

NUTRITIONAL ANALYSIS PER SERVING	
Calories	244
Carbohydrate	22 g
Fiber	2 g
Protein	12 g
Fat, total	12 g
Fat, saturated	5 g
Sodium	515 mg
Cholesterol	22 mg

AMERICA'S EXCHANGES PER SERVING	
1	Starch
1/2	Other Carbohydrate
1	High-fat Meat
1/2	Fat

CANADA'S CHOICES PER SERVING	
1 1/2	Carbohydrate
1	Meat & Alternatives
1 1/2	Fat

Corn and Red Pepper Chowder

SERVES 6
(1¼ cups/300 mL per serving)

Sweet, young corn, combined with tender leeks and bell pepper, make a delicately flavored fall soup. Kernels cut from cooked cobs of corn are also ideal for this recipe. You'll need about three cobs.

Tip

To cut kernels from the cob easily, stand the ears on end and use a sharp knife.

1 tbsp	oil	15 mL
2	medium leeks, white and light green part only, finely chopped (see tip, page 43)	2
½ tsp	dried thyme leaves	2 mL
2½ cups	reduced-sodium chicken broth	625 mL
1½ cups	frozen corn kernels	375 mL
1	large red bell pepper, diced	1
3 tbsp	all-purpose flour	45 mL
2 cups	low-fat milk	500 mL
	Freshly ground black pepper	
2 tbsp	chopped fresh parsley or chives	25 mL

1. In a large saucepan, heat oil over medium heat. Add leeks and thyme; cook, stirring often, for 4 minutes or until softened. Do not brown. Stir in broth and corn. Bring to a boil; reduce heat, cover and simmer for 10 minutes. Add red pepper; cover and simmer for 5 minutes or until vegetables are tender.

2. In a bowl, blend flour with ⅓ cup (75 mL) milk to make a smooth paste; stir in remaining milk. Stir into saucepan; bring to a boil, stirring, until thickened. Season with pepper to taste. Ladle into soup bowls; sprinkle with parsley or chives.

NUTRITIONAL ANALYSIS PER SERVING

Calories	124
Carbohydrate	19 g
Fiber	2 g
Protein	6 g
Fat, total	4 g
Fat, saturated	1 g
Sodium	250 mg
Cholesterol	3 mg

AMERICA'S EXCHANGES PER SERVING

½	Milk, Fat-free/Low-fat
1	Other Carbohydrate
½	Fat

CANADA'S CHOICES PER SERVING

1	Carbohydrate
1	Fat

Smoked Salmon Mousse (page 25) ➤
Overleaf: Cheese-Smothered Onion Soup (page 33)

*Looking for a great
opener for a meal? Here
it is. The sweetness of
carrots and orange are
balanced by the tang
of yogurt in this
low-calorie soup.*

Tip

Normally yogurt will curdle
if you add it to a soup or
sauce, but blending it with
cornstarch as a binder
overcomes this problem.

Creamy Carrot Orange Soup

1 tbsp	vegetable oil	15 mL
1	medium onion, chopped	1
1	large clove garlic, finely chopped	1
2 tsp	mild curry paste or powder	10 mL
4 cups	sliced carrots	1 L
4 cups	reduced-sodium chicken broth	1 L
1 cup	orange juice	250 mL
1 cup	plain low-fat yogurt	250 mL
1 tbsp	cornstarch	15 mL
	Freshly ground black pepper	
2 tbsp	chopped fresh parsley or chives	25 mL
	Grated orange zest	

1. In a large saucepan, heat oil over medium heat.
   Add onion, garlic and curry paste; cook, stirring, for
   2 minutes or until softened. Add carrots, broth and
   orange juice. Bring to a boil; cover and simmer for
   45 minutes or until carrots are very tender. Let cool
   10 minutes.

2. In a food processor or blender, purée in batches;
   return to saucepan. In a bowl, blend yogurt with
   cornstarch; stir into soup. Cook over medium heat,
   stirring, for 5 minutes or until heated through.
   Season with pepper to taste. Ladle into bowls;
   sprinkle with parsley and orange zest.

NUTRITIONAL ANALYSIS PER SERVING	
Calories	132
Carbohydrate	20 g
Fiber	3 g
Protein	5 g
Fat, total	4 g
Fat, saturated	1 g
Sodium	470 mg
Cholesterol	2 mg

AMERICA'S EXCHANGES PER SERVING	
2	Vegetable
2	Other Carbohydrate
½	Fat

CANADA'S CHOICES PER SERVING	
1	Carbohydrate
½	Meat & Alternatives
½	Fat

◄ Thyme-Roasted Chicken with Garlic Gravy (page 82)
Overleaf: Quick Bistro-Style Steak (page 78)

SERVES 6
(1⅓ cups/325 mL
per serving)

*Of all dried legumes,
lentils are my favorite.
They're fast and easy to
cook — and healthy too!
With this soup, I bring the
broth to a boil, throw in
some vegetables, sit back,
relax and savor the aroma.
In 40 minutes, I am
ladling out bowlfuls
of wholesome soup.*

Tip

To save time, I chop the
mushrooms, onions, carrots
and celery in batches in the
food processor.

Variation

Add ½ cup (125 mL)
finely chopped baked
ham to the soup along
with the broth.

Super Suppertime Lentil Soup

6 cups	reduced-sodium chicken broth	1.5 L
2 cups	water	500 mL
1 cup	green lentils, rinsed and sorted	250 mL
8 oz	mushrooms, chopped	250 g
2	carrots, peeled and chopped	2
2	stalks celery, including leaves, chopped	2
1	large onion, chopped	1
2	cloves garlic, finely chopped	2
1 tsp	dried thyme or marjoram leaves	5 mL
¼ cup	chopped fresh dill or parsley	50 mL
	Freshly ground black pepper	

1. In a large Dutch oven or stockpot, combine broth, water, lentils, mushrooms, carrots, celery, onion, garlic and thyme.
2. Bring to a boil; reduce heat, cover and simmer 35 to 40 minutes or until lentils are tender. Stir in dill or parsley and pepper to taste.

NUTRITIONAL ANALYSIS PER SERVING

Calories	155
Carbohydrate	26 g
Fiber	7 g
Protein	12 g
Fat, total	1 g
Fat, saturated	0 g
Sodium	520 mg
Cholesterol	0 mg

AMERICA'S EXCHANGES PER SERVING

3	Vegetable
1	Other Carbohydrate
1	Very Lean Meat

CANADA'S CHOICES PER SERVING

| 1½ | Carbohydrate |
| 1½ | Meat & Alternatives |

**SERVES 6
(1 cups/250 mL per
serving)**

*This nourishing soup
makes an ideal lunch or
light supper. Just add some
pita bread or whole-grain
crackers.*

Tips

Cold soups taste best when
refrigerated overnight,
giving the flavors a chance
to blend. Always check
the seasoning of a cold
soup, however. You may
want to add extra salt,
pepper or hot pepper sauce.

To ripen tomatoes, see tip,
page 37.

Spicy Black Bean Gazpacho

1	red bell pepper, coarsely chopped	1
3	green onions, coarsely chopped	3
3	ripe tomatoes, coarsely chopped	3
1	large clove garlic, minced	1
1	can (19 oz/540 mL) black beans, drained and rinsed	1
1	can (19 oz/540 mL) tomato juice	1
2 tbsp	balsamic vinegar	25 mL
1 tbsp	red wine vinegar	15 mL
	Freshly ground black pepper	
1/2 tsp	hot pepper sauce or more to taste	2 mL
1/3 cup	chopped fresh cilantro or parsley	75 mL
6 tbsp	plain low-fat yogurt or light sour cream	90 mL

1. In a food processor, finely chop red pepper and green
   onions, using on-off turns; transfer to a large bowl.
   Add tomatoes to food processor; finely chop, using
   on-off turns. Add to pepper-onion mixture along
   with black beans and tomato juice. Add balsamic
   and red wine vinegars; season with pepper and hot
   pepper sauce to taste. Cover and refrigerate for
   4 hours, preferably overnight.

2. Add about 1/3 cup (75 mL) cold water to thin soup,
   if desired. Adjust seasoning with vinegars, pepper
   and hot pepper sauce to taste. Ladle into chilled
   bowls; sprinkle with cilantro and top each with
   a tablespoonful of yogurt.

NUTRITIONAL ANALYSIS PER SERVING	
Calories	122
Carbohydrate	24 g
Fiber	6 g
Protein	7 g
Fat, total	1 g
Fat, saturated	0 g
Sodium	570 mg
Cholesterol	1 mg

AMERICA'S EXCHANGES PER SERVING	
2	Vegetable
1	Other Carbohydrate
1/2	Very Lean Meat

CANADA'S CHOICES PER SERVING	
1	Carbohydrate
1/2	Meat & Alternatives

*My idea of a no-fuss dinner
is this easy soup served
with warm bread. It's
especially reassuring to
know that when I
come home late from
work, I can reach in my
cupboard and pull out
some convenient canned
products — and dinner is
on the table in no time!*

Tips

Supermarkets are full of
beans these days. With
this recipe, why not try
chickpeas, Romano or
white kidney beans?

Canned products, such
as tomatoes and beans,
contain hefty quantities of
salt, so extra salt is usually
not needed in soups
containing them. Instead,
rely on your pepper mill
for a seasoning boost.

Black Bean and Corn Soup

1 tbsp	olive oil	15 mL
1	medium onion, chopped	1
2	cloves garlic, minced	2
1	green bell pepper, diced	1
1	large stalk celery, diced	1
1 tsp	dried oregano leaves	5 mL
1 tsp	ground cumin	5 mL
½ tsp	dried thyme leaves	2 mL
Pinch	cayenne pepper	Pinch
4 cups	reduced-sodium chicken broth or vegetable broth	1 L
1	can (19 oz/540 mL) tomatoes, including juice, chopped	1
1	can (19 oz/540 mL) black beans, drained and rinsed	1
1 cup	corn kernels (frozen, canned or fresh)	250 mL
¼ cup	chopped fresh cilantro or parsley	50 mL

1. In a large saucepan, heat oil over medium-high heat. Add onion, garlic, green pepper, celery, oregano, cumin, thyme and cayenne pepper; cook, stirring, for 5 minutes or until softened.

2. Add broth and tomatoes with juice; bring to a boil. Reduce heat to medium-low and simmer, covered, for 20 minutes.

3. Stir in beans and corn. Cook 5 minutes more or until vegetables are tender. Stir in cilantro; ladle into warm bowls.

NUTRITIONAL ANALYSIS PER SERVING	
Calories	158
Carbohydrate	26 g
Fiber	7 g
Protein	8 g
Fat, total	3 g
Fat, saturated	0 g
Sodium	680 mg
Cholesterol	0 mg

AMERICA'S EXCHANGES PER SERVING	
1½	Vegetable
1	Other Carbohydrate
1	Lean Meat

CANADA'S CHOICES PER SERVING	
1	Carbohydrate
1	Meat & Alternatives

Loaded with vegetables,
this Vietnamese-style
soup is full of flavor and
takes less than 10 minutes
to cook.

Tips

Assemble and prepare all
of the ingredients before
you begin cooking.

To pull apart rice noodles,
place a bundle of noodles
in a paper bag to prevent
them from flying all over
the kitchen.

Angel hair pasta can be
substituted for the rice
noodles.

Asian Beef Noodle Soup

8 oz	lean tender beef, such as sirloin	250 g
1 tbsp	reduced-sodium soy sauce	15 mL
4 cups	reduced-sodium beef stock	1 L
4 cups	water	1 L
2	thin slices fresh gingerroot, smashed with side of knife	2
2 oz	rice vermicelli, broken into 3-inch (7.5 cm) pieces (about 2 cups/500 mL)	60 g
2	carrots, peeled and shredded	2
2 cups	sliced Napa cabbage or bok choy	500 mL
½ tsp	toasted sesame oil	2 mL
2 cups	mung bean sprouts	500 mL
¼ cup	coarsely chopped fresh cilantro	50 mL
2	green onions, sliced	2

1. Slice beef into very thin strips. In a bowl, combine beef with soy sauce. Set aside.

2. In a large saucepan over high heat, bring stock and gingerroot to a boil. Add vermicelli; boil for 2 minutes or until softened. Add beef, carrots and cabbage.

3. Return to a boil; cook for 2 minutes. Add sesame oil and bean sprouts; cook for 1 minute or until heated through. Ladle into soup bowls; garnish with cilantro and chopped green onions.

NUTRITIONAL ANALYSIS PER SERVING	
Calories	123
Carbohydrate	13 g
Fiber	2 g
Protein	12 g
Fat, total	3 g
Fat, saturated	1 g
Sodium	535 mg
Cholesterol	20 mg

AMERICA'S EXCHANGES PER SERVING	
½	Starch
1	Vegetable
1 ½	Very Lean Meat

CANADA'S CHOICES PER SERVING	
½	Carbohydrate
1 ½	Meat & Alternatives

I can't think of a better combination than thick slices of warm bread from the oven and steaming bowls of soup when you come in from the cold. This tried-and-true soup has a hearty beefy-mushroom taste and lots of old-fashioned appeal.

Tips

Balance the relatively high sodium content of this soup with lower-sodium choices for the rest of your meal.

If I'm going to the trouble of making homemade soup, I like to make a big pot so there are plenty of leftovers for my freezer. Ladle soup into containers and freeze for up to 3 months.

Hearty Beef and Barley Soup

1 tbsp	vegetable oil	15 mL
1½ lbs	meaty beef shanks, trimmed of fat (about 2 or 3)	750 g
1 lb	mushrooms, chopped	500 g
2	large onions, chopped	2
4	cloves garlic, finely chopped	4
2	bay leaves	2
1½ tsp	salt	7 mL
1 tsp	dried thyme leaves	5 mL
¼ tsp	freshly ground black pepper	1 mL
12 cups	water	3 L
¾ cup	pearl or pot barley, rinsed	175 mL
4	carrots, peeled and chopped	4
2	large stalks celery, including leaves, chopped	2

1. In a Dutch oven or stockpot, heat oil over medium-high heat. Add beef and cook until nicely browned on both sides. Transfer to a plate.

2. Reduce heat to medium. Add mushrooms, onions, garlic, bay leaves, salt, thyme and pepper; cook, stirring often, for 5 minutes or until softened. Return beef to pan. Pour in water and bring to a boil. Reduce heat to medium-low and simmer, covered, stirring occasionally, for 1 hour. Skim any fat from surface.

3. Add barley, carrots and celery. Cover and simmer, stirring occasionally, for 1 hour more or until beef is tender.

4. Remove beef with slotted spoon. Discard bones; finely chop the meat and return to soup. Discard bay leaves; adjust seasoning with pepper to taste.

NUTRITIONAL ANALYSIS PER SERVING

Calories	180
Carbohydrate	24 g
Fiber	4 g
Protein	13 g
Fat, total	4 g
Fat, saturated	1 g
Sodium	495 mg
Cholesterol	22 mg

AMERICA'S EXCHANGES PER SERVING

1	Starch
2	Vegetable
1	Lean Meat

CANADA'S CHOICES PER SERVING

1½	Carbohydrate
1	Meat & Alternatives

Harvest Vegetable Barley Soup

SERVES 6
(1 ½ cups/375 mL per serving)

Here's a main course soup to serve with whole-grain bread and a wedge of light Cheddar cheese. Vary the soup according to the kinds of vegetables you have in the fridge. I often add small cauliflower and broccoli florets or a handful of chopped fresh spinach.

Tip

The rutabaga, a traditional winter vegetable, is also known as yellow turnip or Swede.

1 tbsp	vegetable oil	15 mL
1	large onion, chopped	1
3	cloves garlic, finely chopped	3
1 ½ cups	diced peeled rutabaga	375 mL
½ tsp	dried thyme or marjoram leaves	2 mL
6 cups	reduced-sodium chicken broth or vegetable broth	1.5 L
2 cups	water	500 mL
½ cup	pearl barley, rinsed	125 mL
1 ½ cups	diced peeled sweet potatoes	375 mL
1 ½ cups	diced zucchini	375 mL
	Freshly ground black pepper	

1. In a large Dutch oven or stockpot, heat oil over medium heat. Add onion, garlic, rutabaga and thyme; cook, stirring often, for 5 minutes or until vegetables are lightly colored.

2. Stir in broth, water and barley; bring to a boil. Reduce heat, cover and simmer for 20 minutes. Add sweet potatoes and zucchini; simmer, covered, for 15 minutes or until barley is tender. Season with pepper to taste.

NUTRITIONAL ANALYSIS PER SERVING

Calories	148
Carbohydrate	26 g
Fiber	4 g
Protein	5 g
Fat, total	3 g
Fat, saturated	0 g
Sodium	580 mg
Cholesterol	0 mg

AMERICA'S EXCHANGES PER SERVING

1	Starch
1 ½	Vegetable
½	Fat

CANADA'S CHOICES PER SERVING

1 ½	Carbohydrate
½	Fat

*Serve cupfuls of this
colorful soup as an
elegant starter to a fall
menu. I turn to it when
fresh-picked squash are
plentiful in the market.
I often make extra purée
and freeze it in containers.
It takes no time at all to
make the soup if you have
the purée on hand in the
freezer. The finished soup
also freezes well.*

Tip

To make squash purée,
cut one small butternut or
large acorn squash (about
2 lbs/1 kg) into quarters;
remove seeds. Place in large
casserole dish with ½ cup
(125 mL) water. Cover and
microwave at High for 15 to
20 minutes or until squash
is tender when pierced
with a fork. (Cooking time
varies with size and type
of squash.) Let stand
15 minutes or until cool
enough to handle. Scoop out
pulp; place in food processor
and purée. Makes about
2 cups (500 mL).

Gingery Squash Soup

1 tbsp	vegetable oil	15 mL
1	large onion, chopped	1
2	cloves garlic, finely chopped	2
4 tsp	minced fresh gingerroot	20 mL
2 tbsp	all-purpose flour	25 mL
2 cups	reduced-sodium chicken broth	750 mL
2 cups	cooked squash purée (such as butternut or acorn)	500 mL
½ cup	light (5%) cream	125 mL
1 tsp	grated orange zest	5 mL
	Freshly ground black pepper and freshly grated nutmeg	
2 tbsp	chopped fresh chives or parsley	25 mL

1. In a large saucepan, heat oil over medium-low heat. Add onion, garlic and ginger; cook, stirring often, for 5 minutes or until onion is softened. Blend in flour; stir in broth and squash. Bring to a boil and cook, stirring, until thickened. Reduce heat, cover and simmer for 10 minutes.

2. In a food processor or blender, purée in batches until smooth. Return to saucepan. Add cream and orange zest; season with pepper and nutmeg to taste. Heat just until piping hot; do not boil or soup will curdle. Ladle into bowls; sprinkle with chives.

NUTRITIONAL ANALYSIS PER SERVING

Calories	151
Carbohydrate	22 g
Fiber	4 g
Protein	6 g
Fat, total	6 g
Fat, saturated	2 g
Sodium	390 mg
Cholesterol	6 mg

AMERICA'S EXCHANGES PER SERVING

1½	Starch
½	Vegetable
½	Fat

CANADA'S CHOICES PER SERVING

1	Carbohydrate
½	Meat & Alternatives
1	Fat

Sandwiches and Light Suppers

**MAKES 2 WRAPS
(1 wrap per serving)**

This versatile egg salad is great as a filling for a wrap, on a whole-grain roll or tucked into pita pockets with shredded lettuce or sprouts and tomato wedges.

Tips

To hard-cook eggs, place in saucepan and add cold water to cover eggs by 1 inch (2.5 cm). Place over medium-high heat and bring to a boil. Boil for 2 minutes; cover and remove from heat. Let stand for 10 minutes. Drain and chill eggs in cold water.

Wraps can be prepared up to 1 day ahead. Wrap each roll in plastic wrap and refrigerate.

Variation

Egg Salad Tortilla Spirals
To make easy pick-up sandwiches for kids' lunches, cut wraps into 1-inch (2.5 cm) pieces.

NUTRITIONAL ANALYSIS PER SERVING	
Calories	330
Carbohydrate	31 g
Fiber	3 g
Protein	17 g
Fat, total	14 g
Fat, saturated	5 g
Sodium	470 mg
Cholesterol	289 mg

Egg Salad Wraps

2 tbsp	light cream cheese, softened	25 mL
2 tbsp	plain low-fat yogurt	25 mL
1 tsp	Dijon mustard	5 mL
1/4 tsp	freshly ground black pepper	1 mL
3	hard-cooked eggs, finely chopped (see tip, at left)	3
1	small green onion, finely chopped	1
2	whole wheat flour tortillas (9 inches/23 cm)	2
	Leaf or romaine lettuce	
6	thin slices tomato	6

1. In a bowl, combine cream cheese, yogurt, mustard and pepper. Stir in eggs and green onion.

2. Spread egg salad on flour tortillas, leaving a 1-inch (2.5 cm) border. Layer with lettuce and tomato. Fold bottom over filling, then sides; roll up tightly.

AMERICA'S EXCHANGES PER SERVING	
2	Starch
1/2	Vegetable
1 1/2	Medium-fat Meat
1	Fat

CANADA'S CHOICES PER SERVING	
2	Carbohydrate
2	Meat & Alternatives
1	Fat

**MAKES
4 SANDWICHES
(1 sandwich per
serving)**

*I like to add inexpensive
eggs to help stretch more
costly canned salmon or
solid white tuna when
making sandwiches.*

Tips

Whole-grain breads add
extra flavor to sandwiches,
and the glycemic index is
lower than for more refined
breads. A 1-ounce (30 g)
slice of bread generally
contains about 150 mg of
sodium, but some breads
are higher.

To prevent cucumber from
turning soggy, assemble
sandwiches the same day
they are served.

The salmon and egg salad
can be prepared up to
2 days ahead. Cover
and refrigerate.

Dilled Salmon and Egg Salad on 12-Grain Bread

3	hard-cooked eggs, finely chopped (see tip, page 58)	3
1	can (7½ oz/213 g) sockeye salmon, drained and flaked	1
3 tbsp	light mayonnaise	45 mL
1	large green onion, finely chopped	1
2 tbsp	chopped fresh dill or parsley	25 mL
1 tsp	grated lemon zest	5 mL
¼ tsp	freshly ground black pepper	1 mL
8	slices 12-grain bread (about 1 oz/30 g each)	8
½	seedless cucumber, thinly sliced	½

1. In a bowl, combine eggs, salmon, mayonnaise, green onion, dill, lemon zest and pepper.
2. Divide salad among 8 bread slices, spreading evenly. Layer with cucumber slices. Serve open-faced or sandwich together. Cut in half.

NUTRITIONAL ANALYSIS PER SERVING

Calories	310
Carbohydrate	30 g
Fiber	5 g
Protein	20 g
Fat, total	13 g
Fat, saturated	3 g
Sodium	605 mg
Cholesterol	162 mg

AMERICA'S EXCHANGES PER SERVING

2	Starch
2	Lean Meat
1	Fat

CANADA'S CHOICES PER SERVING

1½	Carbohydrate
2	Meat & Alternatives
1½	Fat

**MAKES
4 SANDWICHES
(1 sandwich per
serving)**

*Chicken salad sandwiches
have never been the same
in my house since I added
some pizzazz to the old
standby with apples and
a hint of curry.*

Tip

Simmer 2 small boneless
chicken breasts (8 oz/250 g
total) in lightly salted water
or chicken broth for
10 minutes; remove from
heat. Let cool in broth for
15 minutes.

Curried Chicken Salad Sandwiches

1/3 cup	light mayonnaise	75 mL
2 tbsp	plain low-fat yogurt	25 mL
2 tbsp	bottled mango chutney	25 mL
1 tsp	mild curry paste or powder	5 mL
1 1/2 cups	finely diced cooked chicken (see tip, at left)	375 mL
1/2 cup	finely diced unpeeled apple	125 mL
1	stalk celery, finely chopped	1
1	large green onion, finely chopped	1
8	slices whole-grain bread	8
	Red leaf or Boston lettuce	

1. In a bowl, blend mayonnaise, yogurt, chutney and curry paste. Stir in chicken, apple, celery and green onions.
2. Spread 4 bread slices with chicken mixture; top with lettuce and remaining bread. Cut into halves and serve.

**NUTRITIONAL ANALYSIS
PER SERVING**

Calories	353
Carbohydrate	39 g
Fiber	5 g
Protein	22 g
Fat, total	12 g
Fat, saturated	2 g
Sodium	650 mg
Cholesterol	53 mg

**AMERICA'S EXCHANGES
PER SERVING**

2	Starch
1/2	Other Carbohydrate
2	Medium-fat Meat

**CANADA'S CHOICES
PER SERVING**

2	Carbohydrate
2 1/2	Meat & Alternatives

When I'm too busy to cook dinner, I often rely on this simple satisfying sandwich instead of ordering take-out.

Tips

Light Cheddar is just one of the growing number of light (reduced-fat) cheeses available. A light cheese contains at least 25% less fat than the full-fat version.

Tuna filling can be prepared up to 1 day ahead. Cover and refrigerate.

Tuna Cheddar Melts

● *Preheat broiler* ● *Baking sheet*

1	can (6 oz/170 g) tuna, drained and flaked	1
¼ cup	light mayonnaise	50 mL
¼ cup	finely chopped celery	50 mL
1	green onion, finely chopped	1
1 tsp	freshly squeezed lemon juice	5 mL
4	slices whole-grain bread	4
8	thin tomato slices	8
	Freshly ground black pepper	
4 oz	light Cheddar cheese, thinly sliced or shredded	125 g

1. In a bowl, combine tuna, mayonnaise, celery, green onion and lemon juice.

2. Spread bread slices with tuna mixture. Layer with tomato slices; season with pepper. Top with cheese.

3. Arrange on baking sheet; place under broiler for about 3 minutes or until cheese is melted. Serve immediately.

NUTRITIONAL ANALYSIS PER SERVING	
Calories	255
Carbohydrate	18 g
Fiber	3 g
Protein	18 g
Fat, total	12 g
Fat, saturated	5 g
Sodium	605 mg
Cholesterol	34 mg

AMERICA'S EXCHANGES PER SERVING	
1	Starch
1	Vegetable
2	Medium-fat Meat

CANADA'S CHOICES PER SERVING	
1	Carbohydrate
2	Meat & Alternatives
½	Fat

Grilled Italian Sandwiches

*The classic grilled
cheese sandwich takes
on a Mediterranean spin
with basil pesto and
Italian cheese.*

4	slices crusty Italian multigrain or seed bread	4
3 tbsp	store-bought or homemade Basil Pesto (see recipe, page 157)	45 mL
4	slices (about 3 oz/85 g total) light provolone or part-skim mozzarella cheese	4
6	thin tomato slices	6
	Freshly ground black pepper	
4 tsp	olive oil	20 mL

1. Lightly spread bread slices with pesto. Layer 2 bread slices with 1 slice of cheese. Layer with tomato slices; season with pepper to taste. Top with remaining cheese and bread slices. Brush top bread slices lightly with olive oil.

2. Place oiled-side down in a large nonstick skillet over medium heat; brush sandwich tops with remaining olive oil. Grill, for 2 to 3 minutes per side, or until nicely toasted and cheese is melted. Cut into quarters and serve.

NUTRITIONAL ANALYSIS PER SERVING

Calories	396
Carbohydrate	32 g
Fiber	5 g
Protein	20 g
Fat, total	21 g
Fat, saturated	6 g
Sodium	550 mg
Cholesterol	15 mg

AMERICA'S EXCHANGES PER SERVING

2	Starch
½	Vegetable
2	Medium-fat Meat
1½	Fat

CANADA'S CHOICES PER SERVING

2	Carbohydrate
2	Meat & Alternatives
2½	Fat

MAKES 4 SLICES
(1 slice per serving)

Bruschetta is an Italian open-faced sandwich. It can be served unadorned, with garlic and olive oil, or with a myriad of popular toppings such as juicy ripe tomatoes, fresh basil and Parmesan. When summer tomatoes and fresh basil beckon, make bruschettas for a simple light lunch or as an appetizer for a barbecue.

Classic Bruschetta with Tomato and Parmesan

● *Preheat broiler*

2	large ripe tomatoes, seeded and diced	2
2 tbsp	coarsely chopped fresh basil	25 mL
1	clove garlic, minced	1
2 tsp	balsamic vinegar	10 mL
	Freshly ground black pepper	
4	slices crusty Italian bread	4
1 tbsp	olive oil	15 mL
	Shaved Parmesan cheese	

1. In a small bowl, combine tomatoes, basil and balsamic vinegar; season with pepper to taste. Gently toss and let stand for up to 1 hour.

2. Toast bread in a grill pan over medium heat or under broiler, for about 2 minutes per side, or until golden brown. Brush bread tops lightly with oil. Arrange on a serving plate.

3. Spoon tomato mixture over warm toast and top with a few shavings of Parmesan cheese. Serve immediately.

NUTRITIONAL ANALYSIS PER SERVING	
Calories	267
Carbohydrate	40 g
Fiber	4 g
Protein	7 g
Fat, total	9 g
Fat, saturated	2 g
Sodium	370 mg
Cholesterol	0 mg

AMERICA'S EXCHANGES PER SERVING	
2	Starch
1½	Vegetable
1½	Fat

CANADA'S CHOICES PER SERVING	
2½	Carbohydrate
2	Fat

*These huge sandwiches
are stuffed to overflowing
with lots of great things.
Grill extra flank or round
steak or use store-bought
sliced roast beef in this
family favorite.*

Tip

Look for thinly sliced
cooked roast beef at the
deli counter.

Hot Roast Beef Heroes

● *Preheat broiler* ● *Baking sheet*

4	crusty whole-grain rolls (each about 2 oz/60 g)	4
1/4 cup	light cream cheese, softened (see tip, page 24)	50 mL
2 tbsp	plain low-fat yogurt or light sour cream	25 mL
2 tbsp	Dijon mustard	25 mL
2	tomatoes, thinly sliced	2
2 tsp	olive oil	10 mL
1/2	large green bell pepper, cut into thin strips	1/2
1	small onion, thinly sliced	1
1	large clove garlic, minced	1
1 cup	sliced mushrooms	250 mL
1/2 tsp	dried oregano leaves	2 mL
4 oz	thinly sliced cooked lean roast beef	125 mL
	Freshly ground black pepper	

1. Split rolls along one side and open like a book. (Do not cut all the way through.) Place on baking sheet and broil cut side until toasted.

2. In a bowl, combine cream cheese, yogurt and mustard; spread over cut sides of rolls. Line bottom halves with tomato slices.

3. In a large nonstick skillet, heat oil over high heat; cook green pepper, onion, garlic, mushrooms and oregano, stirring occasionally, for 5 minutes. Add beef; cook, stirring, 1 minute more or until hot. Season with pepper to taste. Spoon into rolls and serve immediately.

NUTRITIONAL ANALYSIS PER SERVING	
Calories	290
Carbohydrate	32 g
Fiber	5 g
Protein	17 g
Fat, total	11 g
Fat, saturated	4 g
Sodium	610 mg
Cholesterol	25 mg

AMERICA'S EXCHANGES PER SERVING	
1 1/2	Starch
1/2	Other Carbohydrate
1 1/2	Medium-fat Meat
1/2	Fat

CANADA'S CHOICES PER SERVING	
2	Carbohydrate
1 1/2	Meat & Alternatives
1	Fat

*Why order out when it's so
easy to prepare these pizza-
style sandwiches at home?*

Tip

Prepare sandwich filling
ahead, cover and
refrigerate. Layer rolls with
cheese; spoon in vegetable
filling. Wrap in paper
towels and microwave at
Medium-High (70%) for
2½ to 3 minutes for 2 rolls,
or 1½ minutes for 1 roll,
or until heated through.

Veggie Pizza Buns

● *Preheat broiler* ● *Baking sheet*

2 tsp	olive oil	10 mL
2 cups	sliced mushrooms	500 mL
1	large green bell pepper, cut into thin strips	1
1	medium onion, cut into thin wedges	1
1	large clove garlic, minced	1
1 tsp	dried basil or oregano leaves	5 mL
¼ tsp	hot pepper flakes	1 mL
¾ cup	pizza sauce or tomato pasta sauce	175 mL
	Freshly ground black pepper	
4	whole-grain panini rolls (each about 2 oz/60 g)	4
4 oz	thinly sliced light provolone or part-skim mozzarella cheese	125 g

1. In a large nonstick skillet, heat oil over medium-high
heat. Add mushrooms, green pepper, onion, garlic,
basil and hot pepper flakes; cook, stirring, for
5 minutes or until softened. Stir in pizza sauce; cook
until heated through. Remove from heat; season with
pepper to taste.

2. Cut rolls along one side and open like a book; layer
with cheese slices. Place on baking sheet under
preheated broiler for 1 minute or until cheese melts.
Watch carefully. Spoon vegetable mixture into rolls
and serve immediately.

NUTRITIONAL ANALYSIS PER SERVING	
Calories	289
Carbohydrate	38 g
Fiber	6 g
Protein	16 g
Fat, total	9 g
Fat, saturated	3 g
Sodium	635 mg
Cholesterol	10 mg

AMERICA'S EXCHANGES PER SERVING	
1½	Starch
1	Other Carbohydrate
1½	Medium-fat Meat

CANADA'S CHOICES PER SERVING	
2	Carbohydrate
1½	Meat & Alternatives
½	Fat

"Let's order pizza!" The next time you hear this request from your kids, assemble the ingredients here and get them cooking. Why order out, when making pizza at home using store-bought bread bases and sauces is such a breeze? It's more economical, too.

Tips

This recipe is the perfect way to deal with the odd bits of vegetables and cheese left in my fridge by week's end. Vary the toppings according to what you have on hand, including sliced tomatoes or chopped broccoli.

Four 7-inch (18 cm) pitas or 6 split English muffins can also be used. If necessary, arrange on 2 baking sheets; rotate halfway during baking so breads bake evenly. Reduce baking time to 10 minutes.

Vegetarian Pizza

● *Preheat oven to 400°F (200°C)* ● *Baking sheet*

2 tsp	vegetable or olive oil	10 mL
I	small onion, thinly sliced	I
I	large clove garlic, minced	I
I ½ cups	sliced mushrooms	375 mL
I	green or red bell pepper, cut into thin strips	I
½ tsp	dried basil leaves	2 mL
½ tsp	dried oregano leaves	2 mL
I	12-inch (30 cm) prebaked pizza shell or 9- by 12-inch (23 by 30 cm) focaccia	I
½ cup	pizza sauce (approx.)	125 mL
I ½ cups	shredded light cheese, such as mozzarella, Fontina or provolone	375 mL

1. In a large nonstick skillet, heat oil over medium-high heat. Add onion, garlic, mushrooms, pepper, basil and oregano; cook, stirring, for 4 minutes or until softened.

2. Arrange pizza shell on baking sheet; spread with pizza sauce. Top with vegetables and shredded cheese.

3. Bake in preheated oven for 20 to 25 minutes or until cheese is melted.

NUTRITIONAL ANALYSIS PER SERVING	
Calories	391
Carbohydrate	46 g
Fiber	4 g
Protein	20 g
Fat, total	14 g
Fat, saturated	5 g
Sodium	700 mg
Cholesterol	15 mg

AMERICA'S EXCHANGES PER SERVING	
2 ½	Starch
½	Other Carbohydrate
I ½	Medium-fat Meat
I	Fat

CANADA'S CHOICES PER SERVING	
3	Carbohydrate
2	Meat & Alternatives
I	Fat

**MAKES 4 WRAPS
(1 wrap per serving)**

*Adding fresh basil to the
mayonnaise gives this
sandwich a thoroughly
modern twist.*

Tip

Smoked turkey contains
about 25% less salt than
ham but is still high in
sodium. This easy wrap
can also be prepared with
leftover skinless turkey
or chicken.

It's a Wrap!

¼ cup	light mayonnaise	50 mL
2 tbsp	chopped fresh basil (or ½ tsp/2 mL dried)	25 mL
4	9-inch (23 cm) flour tortillas	4
2	large tomatoes	2
6 oz	thinly sliced smoked turkey	175 g
4 cups	shredded romaine lettuce	1 L

1. In a bowl, combine mayonnaise and basil. Spread over tortillas, leaving a 1-inch (2.5 cm) border around edges. Cut tomatoes in half crosswise and gently squeeze out seeds; slice thinly. Layer tortillas with tomato slices, turkey and lettuce. Fold 1 inch (2.5 cm) of the right and left sides of tortilla over filling. Starting from the bottom, roll up tortillas around filling. Serve immediately or cover in plastic wrap and store in the refrigerator for up to 1 day.

NUTRITIONAL ANALYSIS PER SERVING	
Calories	302
Carbohydrate	31 g
Fiber	4 g
Protein	19 g
Fat, total	10 g
Fat, saturated	2 g
Sodium	740 mg
Cholesterol	37 mg

AMERICA'S EXCHANGES PER SERVING	
1½	Starch
1	Vegetable
2	Medium-fat Meat

CANADA'S CHOICES PER SERVING	
2	Carbohydrate
2	Meat & Alternatives
½	Fat

MAKES 6 FAJITAS
(1 fajita per serving)

I love this recipe because it's a quick and easy main dish, yet it calls for only a few ingredients. It's ideal to serve for an impromptu dinner. I set out bowls of the cheese, sour cream and salsa, and let everyone help themselves.

Turkey Fajitas

1 lb	boneless skinless turkey breast, or chicken breast, thinly sliced	500 g
1 tbsp	freshly squeezed lime juice	15 mL
1	clove garlic, minced	1
1/2 tsp	dried oregano leaves	2 mL
1/2 tsp	ground cumin	2 mL
1/2 tsp	ground coriander	2 mL
1/2 tsp	salt	2 mL
Pinch	cayenne pepper	Pinch
1 tbsp	olive oil	15 mL
1	medium red onion, thinly sliced	1
1	small red bell pepper, cut into thin 2-inch (5 cm) strips	1
1	small green bell pepper, cut into thin 2-inch (5 cm) strips	1
6	9-inch (23 cm) flour tortillas, warmed	6
	Salsa, light sour cream, shredded lettuce and shredded light Cheddar cheese for garnishes	

1. In a bowl, toss turkey with lime juice, garlic, oregano, cumin, coriander, salt and cayenne pepper. Marinate for 15 minutes at room temperature, or longer in the refrigerator.

2. In a large nonstick skillet, heat 1 tbsp (15 mL) oil over high heat; cook turkey for 2 to 3 minutes per side, or until lightly browned and no longer pink in center. Transfer to plate; keep warm.

3. Add onion and peppers to skillet; cook, stirring, for 3 minutes or until tender-crisp. Remove from heat. Cut turkey into thin diagonal strips; toss with onion-pepper mixture. Spoon turkey mixture down center of each tortilla; add a small spoonful of salsa and sour cream, if desired, and sprinkle with shredded lettuce and cheese. Roll up.

NUTRITIONAL ANALYSIS PER SERVING

Calories	307
Carbohydrate	30 g
Fiber	3 g
Protein	23 g
Fat, total	9 g
Fat, saturated	2 g
Sodium	445 mg
Cholesterol	45 mg

AMERICA'S EXCHANGES PER SERVING

2	Starch
2 1/2	Lean Meat

CANADA'S CHOICES PER SERVING

2	Carbohydrate
2 1/2	Meat & Alternatives

**MAKES
4 QUESADILLAS
(1 quesadilla per
serving)**

*Here's my modern
rendition of grilled cheese:
thin flour tortillas replace
sliced bread, mozzarella
substitutes for processed
cheese and chunky salsa
stands in for the ketchup.
And the beans? They're
optional, but make a
wholesome addition.*

Tips

I often serve these warm
cheesy wedges with soup
for an easy dinner.
They're also great as a
snack that both kids and
grownups applaud.

Use mild salsa to appease
those with timid taste buds,
but add a dash of hot
pepper sauce to the filling
for those who like a burst
of heat.

Cheese and Salsa Quesadillas

½ cup	salsa, plus additional for serving	125 mL
4	9-inch (23 cm) flour tortillas	4
1 cup	canned black or pinto beans, drained and rinsed	250 mL
1 cup	shredded part-skim mozzarella or light Cheddar cheese	250 mL

1. Spread 2 tbsp (25 mL) salsa on half of each tortilla. Sprinkle with ¼ cup (50 mL) each of the beans and the cheese. Fold tortillas over and press down lightly.

2. In a large nonstick skillet over medium heat, cook tortillas, two at a time, pressing down lightly with the back of a metal spatula, for about 2 minutes per side, until lightly toasted and cheese is melted. Or place directly on barbecue grill over medium heat until lightly toasted on both sides.

3. Cut into wedges and serve warm with additional salsa, if desired.

NUTRITIONAL ANALYSIS PER SERVING

Calories	305
Carbohydrate	37 g
Fiber	6 g
Protein	16 g
Fat, total	9 g
Fat, saturated	4 g
Sodium	625 mg
Cholesterol	20 mg

AMERICA'S EXCHANGES PER SERVING

1½	Starch
2	Other Carbohydrate
1½	Medium-fat Meat

CANADA'S CHOICES PER SERVING

2	Carbohydrate
1½	Meat & Alternatives
½	Fat

MAKES 6 ENCHILADAS (1 enchilada per serving)

Instead of turning chicken leftovers into a week's worth of cold sandwiches, whip up this fast-fix dinner with loads of family appeal.

Tips

You can assemble this dish a day ahead of baking; just top with salsa and cheese prior to popping in the oven.

Replace the chicken with an equal amount of cooked turkey.

Variation

Shrimp Enchiladas
$1\frac{1}{2}$ cups (375 mL) small cooked shrimp can be used instead of chicken.

Amazing Chicken Enchiladas

- *Preheat oven to 350°F (180°C)*
- *13- by 9-inch (3 L) baking dish, sprayed with vegetable cooking spray*

4 oz	light cream cheese	125 g
$\frac{1}{2}$ cup	plain low-fat yogurt or light sour cream	125 mL
2 cups	cooked chicken, cut into thin strips	500 mL
3	green onions, finely chopped	3
2	tomatoes, seeded and diced	2
$\frac{1}{4}$ cup	chopped fresh cilantro or parsley	50 mL
6	9-inch (23 cm) flour tortillas	6
1 cup	mild or medium salsa	250 mL
$\frac{3}{4}$ cup	shredded light Cheddar cheese	175 mL

1. Place cream cheese in a large bowl; microwave at Medium (50%) for 1 minute to soften. Stir well. Stir in yogurt, chicken, green onions, tomatoes and cilantro.

2. Spread about $\frac{1}{2}$ cup (125 mL) of the chicken mixture down center of each tortilla and roll up. Arrange tortillas in single layer, seam side down, in prepared baking dish. Spread each tortilla with salsa and sprinkle with cheese. Bake for 30 to 35 minutes or until heated through. Sprinkle with extra chopped cilantro, if desired.

Microwave Method

1. Do not sprinkle with the cheese. Cover dish with waxed paper; microwave at Medium-High (70%) for 7 to 9 minutes or until heated through. Sprinkle with cheese; microwave at High for 1 minute or until cheese melts.

NUTRITIONAL ANALYSIS PER SERVING

Calories	374
Carbohydrate	33 g
Fiber	4 g
Protein	26 g
Fat, total	14 g
Fat, saturated	6 g
Sodium	700 mg
Cholesterol	64 mg

AMERICA'S EXCHANGES PER SERVING

2	Starch
$\frac{1}{2}$	Vegetable
$2\frac{1}{2}$	Medium-fat Meat

CANADA'S CHOICES PER SERVING

2	Carbohydrate
2	Meat & Alternatives
$\frac{1}{2}$	Fat

MAKES 8 PITA POCKETS
(1 pita pocket per serving)

Aside from being lower in fat, I find pitas make much better containers than taco shells, which tend to crumble when you bite into them and cause the filling to spill out.

Tip

To heat pitas, wrap in foil and place in a 350°F (180°C) oven for 15 to 20 minutes. Or wrap 4 at a time in paper towels and microwave at High for 1 to 1½ minutes.

Variation

Sloppy Joe Pitas
Increase beef to 1 lb (500 g). Omit beans and add 1 can (7½ oz/ 213 mL) tomato sauce; cook 3 minutes more or until sauce is slightly thickened.

Taco Pitas

8 oz	lean ground beef	250 g
1	small onion, finely chopped	1
1	large clove garlic, minced	1
2 tsp	chili powder	10 mL
2 tsp	all-purpose flour	10 mL
½ tsp	dried oregano leaves	2 mL
½ tsp	ground cumin	2 mL
Pinch	cayenne pepper	Pinch
½ cup	reduced-sodium beef broth	125 mL
1	can (19 oz/540 mL) pinto, black or red kidney beans, drained and rinsed	1
4	7-inch (18 cm) whole wheat pitas, halved to form pockets, warmed	4
	Salsa, shredded lettuce, tomato wedges, pepper strips, shredded part-skim mozzarella or light Cheddar cheese	

1. In a large nonstick skillet over medium-high heat, cook beef, breaking up with the back of a wooden spoon, for 4 minutes or until no longer pink. Place beef in colander and drain fat.

2. Return to pan and reduce heat to medium. Add onion, garlic, chili powder, flour, oregano, cumin and cayenne pepper. Cook, stirring often, for 5 minutes or until onions are softened.

3. Pour in broth; cook, stirring, until slightly thickened. Stir in beans; cook 2 minutes more or until heated through.

4. Divide mixture evenly into pita pockets; top with salsa, lettuce, tomato, pepper and cheese.

NUTRITIONAL ANALYSIS PER SERVING	
Calories	217
Carbohydrate	33 g
Fiber	7 g
Protein	13 g
Fat, total	4 g
Fat, saturated	1 g
Sodium	425 mg
Cholesterol	14 mg

AMERICA'S EXCHANGES PER SERVING	
1	Starch
1	Other Carbohydrate
1½	Lean Meat

CANADA'S CHOICES PER SERVING	
1½	Carbohydrate
1½	Meat & Alternatives

**MAKES
4 BURRITOS
(1 burrito per
serving)**

*Forget forks and knives
when serving this tasty
pick-up sandwich that
has all the appeal of a
traditional breakfast of
ham and scrambled eggs.*

Scrambled Eggs
and Ham Burritos

● *Preheat oven to 350°F (180°C)* ● *Baking sheet*

4	7-inch (18 cm) flour tortillas	4
1/2 cup	shredded light Cheddar cheese	125 mL
4	eggs	4
2 tsp	low-fat milk	10 mL
Pinch	freshly ground black pepper	Pinch
1 tsp	butter	5 mL
1/3 cup	finely diced lean smoked ham	75 mL
1	green onion, sliced	1
1/4 cup	mild or medium salsa	50 mL

1. Place tortillas on cookie sheet; sprinkle with cheese. Place in oven for 5 minutes or until cheese melts.

2. Meanwhile, in a bowl, beat together eggs, milk and pepper. In a large nonstick skillet, melt butter over medium heat; cook ham and green onion, stirring, for 1 minute or until onion is softened. Add eggs; cook, stirring often, for about 2 minutes or until eggs are just set.

3. Spoon egg mixture along bottom third of tortillas; top with salsa. Fold 1 inch (2.5 cm) of right and left sides of tortilla over filling, starting from the bottom, and roll up tortillas around filling. Serve immediately.

**NUTRITIONAL ANALYSIS
PER SERVING**

Calories	251
Carbohydrate	19 g
Fiber	2 g
Protein	15 g
Fat, total	12 g
Fat, saturated	5 g
Sodium	520 mg
Cholesterol	205 mg

**AMERICA'S EXCHANGES
PER SERVING**

1	Starch
1	Other Carbohydrate
1 1/2	Lean Meat

**CANADA'S CHOICES
PER SERVING**

1	Carbohydrate
2	Meat & Alternatives
1	Fat

*Mexican dishes are a big
hit with teens — and their
parents. It makes a
nourishing snack or
supper. For a meat version,
add strips of ham, cooked
turkey or chicken.*

Tip

Make a batch of burritos,
wrap each in a paper towel,
then in plastic wrap. Keep
handy in the fridge ready to
microwave for school
lunches or after-school
snacks. Remove plastic
wrap before microwaving.

Black Bean Vegetable Burritos

1 tbsp	vegetable oil	15 mL
3	green onions, chopped	3
1	large clove garlic, minced	1
1 cup	diced zucchini	250 mL
1	red or green bell pepper, chopped	1
1 tsp	dried oregano leaves	5 mL
1 tsp	ground cumin	5 mL
1	can (19 oz/540 mL) black beans or kidney beans, drained and rinsed	1
8	large 9-inch (23 cm) whole wheat tortillas	8
1 cup	shredded part-skim mozzarella or light Cheddar cheese	250 mL
1 cup	mild or medium salsa	250 mL
1/2 cup	light sour cream	125 mL

1. In a large nonstick skillet, heat oil over medium heat. Add green onions, garlic, zucchini, bell pepper, oregano and cumin; cook, stirring, for 5 minutes or until vegetables are tender-crisp. Stir in beans; cook 1 to 2 minutes or until heated through.

2. Spoon 1/4 cup (50 mL) of the bean mixture down the middle of each tortilla. Top each with 2 tbsp (25 mL) shredded cheese, 2 tbsp (25 mL) salsa and 1 tbsp (15 mL) sour cream. Roll to enclose filling. Wrap each burrito in a paper towel. Place four at a time on a plate; microwave at Medium-High (70%) for 3 to 4 minutes or until heated through. To heat a single burrito, microwave at Medium-High (70%) for 1 minute.

NUTRITIONAL ANALYSIS PER SERVING	
Calories	310
Carbohydrate	42 g
Fiber	7 g
Protein	14 g
Fat, total	9 g
Fat, saturated	3 g
Sodium	565 mg
Cholesterol	10 mg

AMERICA'S EXCHANGES PER SERVING	
1 1/2	Starch
1	Vegetable
1	Other Carbohydrate
1	Medium-fat Meat
1/2	Fat

CANADA'S CHOICES PER SERVING	
2 1/2	Carbohydrate
1	Meat & Alternatives
1	Fat

Ham and Potato Frittata

Nothing beats a delicious egg dish like this frittata for a special occasion breakfast or brunch, or for an easy supper dish. A frittata is an Italian version of an omelette. Unlike its finicky cousin, which needs careful flipping and turning, a frittata doesn't require any major cooking skills other than stirring — so it's almost impossible to ruin this dish.

Tip

Bake or microwave 2 large potatoes the day before and refrigerate so cubes keep their shape during cooking.

● *Preheat oven to 375°F (190°C)*

2 tsp	vegetable oil	10 mL
I	small onion, finely chopped	I
2 cups	peeled cooked potatoes, cut into ¹/₂-inch (1 cm) cubes	500 mL
I	small red bell pepper, finely diced (optional)	I
³/₄ cup	diced lean smoked ham (about 4 oz/125 g)	175 mL
	Freshly ground black pepper	
8	eggs	8
2 tbsp	low-fat milk	25 mL
2 tbsp	finely chopped fresh parsley	25 mL
I cup	shredded light Cheddar or light Havarti cheese	250 mL

1. In a large nonstick skillet, heat oil over medium-high heat. Add onion, potatoes, red pepper and ham; cook, stirring often, for 5 minutes or until vegetables are tender. Reduce heat to medium-low.

2. Meanwhile, in a large bowl, beat together eggs, milk and parsley; season with pepper. Pour over potato mixture in skillet; cook, stirring gently, for about 1 minute or until eggs start to set. (The eggs will appear semi-scrambled.) Stir in cheese.

3. If skillet handle is not ovenproof, wrap in double layer of foil to shield it from oven heat. Place skillet in preheated oven for 15 to 20 minutes or until eggs are just set in center. Let cool 5 minutes. Turn out onto large serving plate and cut into wedges.

NUTRITIONAL ANALYSIS PER SERVING

Calories	244
Carbohydrate	13 g
Fiber	I g
Protein	17 g
Fat, total	13 g
Fat, saturated	5 g
Sodium	440 mg
Cholesterol	271 mg

AMERICA'S EXCHANGES PER SERVING

I	Starch
2	Medium-fat Meat
¹/₂	Fat

CANADA'S CHOICES PER SERVING

I	Carbohydrate
2	Meat & Alternatives
I	Fat

SERVES 6

You can always count on eggs for an economical meal. This oven-baked crustless quiche is perfect for brunch or an easy supper, served with juicy sliced tomatoes and good bread.

Tip

Wrap grated zucchini in a clean dry kitchen towel to remove excess moisture.

Crustless Zucchini Quiche

- Preheat oven to 325°F (160°C)
- 10-inch (25 cm) pie plate or quiche dish, buttered

2 tsp	vegetable oil	10 mL
3 cups	grated zucchini (unpeeled), squeezed dry	750 mL
4	green onions, chopped	4
1	red bell pepper, diced	1
6	eggs	6
¾ cup	shredded light Cheddar cheese	175 mL
½ cup	soft fresh bread crumbs	125 mL
¼ tsp	salt	1 mL
¼ tsp	freshly ground black pepper	1 mL

1. In a large nonstick skillet, heat oil over medium-high heat. Add zucchini, green onions and red pepper; cook, stirring often, for 5 minutes or until softened. Let cool slightly.

2. In a large bowl, beat eggs; stir in zucchini mixture, cheese, bread crumbs, salt and pepper. Pour into pie plate. Bake for 35 to 40 minutes or until set in center.

NUTRITIONAL ANALYSIS PER SERVING

Calories	157
Carbohydrate	7 g
Fiber	2 g
Protein	11 g
Fat, total	10 g
Fat, saturated	4 g
Sodium	300 mg
Cholesterol	196 mg

AMERICA'S EXCHANGES PER SERVING

1	Vegetable
1½	Medium-fat Meat
½	Fat

CANADA'S CHOICES PER SERVING

½	Carbohydrate
1½	Meat & Alternatives
1	Fat

Versatile mushrooms star in this terrific dish that's perfect to serve for brunch or a light supper.

Tips

Use a variety of white and exotic mushrooms such as shiitake, portobello and oyster.

Herbed soft goat cheese can replace the cream cheese, if desired.

Cheese and Mushroom Oven Omelette

- Preheat oven to 350°F (180°C)
- Well-buttered 9- or 10-inch (23 or 25 cm) pie plate, sprinkled with 1 tbsp (15 mL) fine dry bread crumbs

4	eggs, separated	4
2 tbsp	low-fat milk	25 mL
	Freshly ground black pepper	
2 tsp	butter or soft margarine	10 mL
3 cups	sliced assorted mushrooms	750 mL
3	green onions, chopped	3
1/4 cup	light cream cheese	50 mL
1/3 cup	shredded light Cheddar cheese	75 mL
2 oz	lean smoked ham, cut into thin strips	60 g

1. In a small bowl, beat egg yolks with milk; season with pepper. In a bowl, using an electric mixer, beat egg whites until stiff peaks form. Slowly beat in yolk mixture on low speed until blended into egg whites. Pour into prepared pie plate. Bake for 15 minutes or until just set in the center.

2. Meanwhile, in a large nonstick skillet, melt butter over medium-high heat. Cook mushrooms and green onions, stirring, for 5 minutes or until tender and liquid is evaporated. Remove from heat; stir in cream cheese until smooth.

3. Spoon evenly over omelette; sprinkle with cheese and ham. Bake for 8 minutes more or until cheese is melted.

NUTRITIONAL ANALYSIS PER SERVING	
Calories	253
Carbohydrate	7 g
Fiber	2 g
Protein	18 g
Fat, total	17 g
Fat, saturated	8 g
Sodium	570 mg
Cholesterol	286 mg

AMERICA'S EXCHANGES PER SERVING	
1	Vegetable
2 1/2	Medium-fat Meat
1	Fat

CANADA'S CHOICES PER SERVING	
2 1/2	Meat & Alternatives
1 1/2	Fat

Main Dishes

Quick Bistro-Style Steak

SERVES 4

Dressed up with wine, garlic and herbs, this steak recipe becomes a special dish when you're entertaining friends.

Tips

Serve with Roasted Garlic Potatoes (see recipe, page 197).

Herbes de Provence is a blend of French herbs that often includes thyme, rosemary, basil and sage. If you can't find this blend in your supermarket, substitute a generous pinch of each of these herbs.

2	boneless striploin steaks, each 8 oz (250 g), well trimmed	2
1/2 tsp	coarsely ground black pepper	2 mL
2 tsp	olive oil	10 mL
2 tsp	butter	10 mL
1/4 cup	finely chopped shallots	50 mL
1	large clove garlic, finely chopped	1
1/4 tsp	dried herbes de Provence (see tip, at left)	1 mL
1/3 cup	red wine or additional beef broth	75 mL
1/2 cup	reduced-sodium beef broth	125 mL
1 tbsp	Dijon mustard	15 mL
2 tbsp	chopped fresh parsley	25 mL

1. Remove steaks from refrigerator 30 minutes before cooking. Season with pepper.

2. Heat a large heavy nonstick skillet over medium heat until hot; add oil and butter. Increase heat to high; brown steaks about 1 minute on each side. Reduce heat to medium; cook to desired degree of doneness. Transfer to a heated serving platter; keep warm.

3. Add shallots, garlic and herbes to skillet; cook, stirring, for 1 minute. Stir in red wine; cook, scraping up any brown bits from bottom of pan, until liquid has almost evaporated.

4. Stir in broth, mustard and parsley; season with salt and pepper to taste. Cook, stirring, until slightly reduced. Spoon sauce over steaks. Serve immediately.

NUTRITIONAL ANALYSIS PER SERVING	
Calories	207
Carbohydrate	5 g
Fiber	1 g
Protein	21 g
Fat, total	11 g
Fat, saturated	4 g
Sodium	255 mg
Cholesterol	46 mg

AMERICA'S EXCHANGES PER SERVING	
1	Vegetable
2	Lean Meat

CANADA'S CHOICES PER SERVING	
3	Meat & Alternatives

SERVES 6

*Here's my favorite way
to prepare beef on the
barbecue. Flank steak
is easy to marinate ahead,
and leftovers make great-
tasting sandwiches.*

Tip

Flank steak becomes more
tender the longer it's
marinated. Thick-cut round
steak can also be prepared
in the same way.

Easy Asian Flank Steak

● *Preheat barbecue grill or broiler*

1/4 cup	hoisin sauce	50 mL
2 tbsp	reduced-sodium soy sauce	25 mL
2 tbsp	freshly squeezed lime juice	25 mL
1 tbsp	vegetable oil	15 mL
4	cloves garlic, minced	4
2 tsp	Oriental chili paste or 1 tsp (5 mL) hot pepper flakes	10 mL
1 1/2 lbs	flank steak	750 g

1. In a shallow glass dish, whisk together hoisin sauce, soy sauce, lime juice, oil, garlic and chili paste; add steak, turning to coat both sides with marinade. Refrigerate, covered, at least 8 hours or up to 24 hours. Remove meat from refrigerator 30 minutes before cooking.

2. Place steak on a grill sprayed with vegetable cooking spray over medium-high heat and brush with marinade. Cook for 7 to 8 minutes per side or until medium-rare. (Alternatively, place steak on foil-lined baking sheet; broil 4 inches/10 cm below preheated broiler for 7 to 8 minutes on each side.) Transfer to cutting board, cover loosely with foil; let stand for 5 minutes. Thinly slice at right angles to the grain of meat.

NUTRITIONAL ANALYSIS PER SERVING	
Calories	214
Carbohydrate	3 g
Fiber	0 g
Protein	26 g
Fat, total	10 g
Fat, saturated	4 g
Sodium	230 mg
Cholesterol	46 mg

AMERICA'S EXCHANGES PER SERVING	
3 1/2	Lean Meat

CANADA'S CHOICES PER SERVING	
3 1/2	Meat & Alternatives

Beef and Broccoli Stir-Fry

SERVES 4

Here's a fast stir-fry that doesn't require a lot of chopping. Serve with steamed rice, cooked rice vermicelli or a string pasta such as linguine.

Variation

Substitute boneless skinless chicken breast or pork tenderloin for the beef.

1 lb	boneless sirloin steak, well trimmed, cut into thin strips	500 g
2 tbsp	hoisin sauce	25 mL
2	cloves garlic, minced	2
1 tbsp	minced fresh gingerroot	15 mL
1 tsp	grated orange zest	5 mL
1/2 cup	orange juice	125 mL
2 tbsp	reduced-sodium soy sauce	25 mL
2 tsp	cornstarch	10 mL
1/4 tsp	hot pepper flakes	1 mL
1 tbsp	vegetable oil	15 mL
6 cups	small broccoli florets and chopped peeled stems (about 1 large bunch)	1.5 L
4	green onions, chopped	4

1. In a bowl, toss beef strips with hoisin sauce, garlic and ginger. Let marinate at room temperature for 15 minutes. (Cover and refrigerate if preparing ahead.)

2. In a glass measuring cup, combine orange zest and juice, soy sauce, cornstarch and hot pepper flakes.

3. In a large nonstick skillet, heat oil over high heat; cook beef, stirring, for 2 minutes or until no longer pink. Transfer to a plate.

4. Add broccoli and soy sauce mixture to skillet; reduce heat to medium, cover and cook for 2 to 3 minutes or until broccoli is tender-crisp. Add beef strips with any accumulated juices and green onions; cook, stirring, for 1 minute or until heated through.

NUTRITIONAL ANALYSIS PER SERVING	
Calories	288
Carbohydrate	17 g
Fiber	4 g
Protein	23 g
Fat, total	8 g
Fat, saturated	2 g
Sodium	440 mg
Cholesterol	45 mg

AMERICA'S EXCHANGES PER SERVING	
1 1/2	Vegetable
1/2	Other Carbohydrate
3	Lean Meat

CANADA'S CHOICES PER SERVING	
1	Carbohydrate
3	Meat & Alternatives

*When I was growing up,
Sunday dinner in my
home was often a standing
rib roast seasoned simply
with salt and pepper and
served with pan gravy.
This recipe, with its
thyme-pepper rub and red
wine to enhance the gravy,
makes salt unnecessary.*

Sunday Roast Beef with Wine Gravy

● *Preheat oven to 450°F (230°C)* ● *Roasting pan*

3 lbs	standing rib roast	1.5 kg
1	large clove garlic, cut in small slivers	1
2 tbsp	Dijon mustard	25 mL
1 tsp	dried thyme leaves	5 mL
1/2 tsp	salt	2 mL
1 tsp	coarsely ground black pepper	5 mL

WINE GRAVY

1/2 cup	red wine	125 mL
1 1/2 cups	reduced-sodium beef broth	375 mL
1 tbsp	cornstarch	15 mL
2 tbsp	water	25 mL
1 tbsp	Worcestershire sauce	15 mL
	Freshly ground black pepper	

1. Make small slits in roast and insert garlic slivers. Let roast stand for 1 hour. In a bowl, combine mustard, thyme, salt and pepper. Spread over roast.

2. Place rib-side down in shallow roasting pan. Roast in preheated oven for 15 minutes; reduce heat to 350°F (180°C) and continue to roast for 1 1/4 to 1 1/2 hours or until meat thermometer registers 140°F (60°C) for medium-rare. Transfer to carving board, covered loosely with foil, for 15 minutes.

3. *Wine Gravy:* Skim fat from drippings in pan. Place over medium heat; add wine. Cook, scraping up brown bits from bottom, until reduced by half. Stir in beef broth; strain sauce through a fine sieve into a saucepan. Bring to a boil; cook for 5 minutes or until slightly reduced.

4. In a small bowl, blend cornstarch with water and Worcestershire sauce. Add to pan, stirring constantly, until sauce boils and thickens. Season with pepper to taste. Cut beef into thin slices and accompany with sauce.

NUTRITIONAL ANALYSIS PER SERVING	
Calories	257
Carbohydrate	2 g
Fiber	0 g
Protein	32 g
Fat, total	12 g
Fat, saturated	5 g
Sodium	585 mg
Cholesterol	73 mg

AMERICA'S EXCHANGES PER SERVING	
4 1/2	Lean Meat

CANADA'S CHOICES PER SERVING	
4 1/2	Meat & Alternatives

SERVES 4
(4 oz/125 g, no
skin, per serving,
with ¼ cup/50 mL
gravy)

*I feel like it's a special
occasion when I have a
roast chicken in the oven.
It conjures up a homey
smell and feel. In my
opinion, it's one of the
most satisfying dishes on
earth. Here I place herbs
and seasonings under the
bird's skin to produce a
succulent, flavorful
chicken. Slow roasting
with lots of garlic creates
a wonderful aroma — yet,
surprisingly, imparts only a
subtle flavor to the gravy.*

Thyme-Roasted Chicken with Garlic Gravy

● *Preheat oven to 325°F (160°C)* ● *Roasting pan with rack*

1	chicken (about 3½ lbs/1.75 kg)	1
10	cloves garlic, peeled	10
1 tsp	dried thyme leaves	5 mL
¼ tsp	salt	1 mL
¼ tsp	freshly ground black pepper	1 mL
1⅓ cups	reduced-sodium chicken broth (approx.), divided	325 mL
½ cup	white wine or additional chicken broth	125 mL
1 tbsp	all-purpose flour	15 mL

1. Remove giblets and neck from chicken. Rinse and pat chicken dry inside and out. Place 2 cloves garlic inside cavity. Starting at cavity opening, gently lift skin and rub thyme, salt and pepper over breasts and legs. Tie legs together with string; tuck wings under back.

2. Add remaining garlic, ⅔ cup (150 mL) chicken broth and wine to roasting pan; place chicken, breast side up, on rack in pan.

3. Roast in preheated oven, basting every 30 minutes, adding additional broth if pan juices evaporate, for 1¾ to 2 hours or until pan juices run clear when chicken is pierced and meat thermometer inserted in thigh registers 185°F (85°C).

4. Transfer to a platter; tent with foil and let stand for 10 minutes before carving. Meanwhile, strain pan juices into measure, pressing down firmly to mash garlic into juices; skim off fat. Add enough of the remaining broth to make ¾ cup (175 mL).

5. In a small saucepan, stir together 2 tbsp (25 mL) of pan juices and flour; cook, stirring, over medium heat for 1 minute. Gradually whisk in remaining pan juices; cook, stirring, until boiling and thickened. Serve with chicken.

NUTRITIONAL ANALYSIS PER SERVING

Calories	264
Carbohydrate	4 g
Fiber	1 g
Protein	38 g
Fat, total	9 g
Fat, saturated	3 g
Sodium	420 mg
Cholesterol	112 mg

AMERICA'S EXCHANGES PER SERVING

5	Very Lean Meat
1	Fat

CANADA'S CHOICES PER SERVING

5	Meat & Alternatives

One-Hour Roast Chicken with Sage and Garlic

SERVES 4
(4 oz/125 g, no skin, per serving)

Who has time to wait around for a chicken to roast when you're in a hurry? I take an hour off the roasting time by doing two things: I cut the bird open along the backbone, place it flat on the broiler pan and then boost the oven temperature. The result? A golden, succulent bird in about half the time.

Tip

In this recipe, the chicken is "butterflied," or "spatchcocked." Cooking time is reduced when the bird is cut along the backbone and flattened.

- Preheat oven to 400°F (200°C)
- Broiler pan, sprayed with vegetable cooking spray

1	chicken (about 3½ lbs/1.75 kg)	1
1 tbsp	butter, softened	15 mL
2	cloves garlic, minced	2
1 tbsp	minced fresh sage or 1 tsp (5 mL) dried sage leaves	15 mL
1½ tsp	grated lemon zest	7 mL
½ tsp	salt	2 mL
½ tsp	freshly ground black pepper	2 mL
2 tsp	olive oil	10 mL
¼ tsp	paprika	1 mL

1. Remove giblets and neck from chicken. Rinse and pat chicken dry inside and out with paper towels. Using heavy-duty kitchen scissors, cut chicken open along backbone; press down on breast bone to flatten slightly and arrange skin-side up on rack of a broiler pan.

2. In a bowl, blend butter with garlic, sage, lemon zest, salt and pepper. Gently lift breast skin; using a knife or spatula, spread butter mixture under skin to coat breasts and part of legs. Press down on outside skin to smooth and spread butter mixture.

3. In a small bowl, combine olive oil and paprika; brush over chicken.

4. Roast chicken for 1 hour or until juices run clear and a meat thermometer inserted in the thickest part of the thigh registers 185°F (85°C). Transfer chicken to a platter. Tent with foil; let rest 5 minutes before carving.

NUTRITIONAL ANALYSIS PER SERVING	
Calories	256
Carbohydrate	1 g
Fiber	0 g
Protein	36 g
Fat, total	11 g
Fat, saturated	3 g
Sodium	415 mg
Cholesterol	116 mg

AMERICA'S EXCHANGES PER SERVING	
5	Very Lean Meat
1	Fat

CANADA'S CHOICES PER SERVING	
5	Meat & Alternatives

**SERVES 4
(2 pieces per serving)**

Kids love simple dishes like this one, with its straightforward flavors. And this chicken dish is simple enough that even young cooks can make it.

Tip

This recipe also works well with a whole cut-up chicken or bone-in chicken breasts. With its tang of lemon and sweetness of honey, this dish is sure to become a family favorite.

Just-for-Kids Honey Lemon Chicken

- Preheat oven to 350°F (180°C)
- 13- by 9-inch (3 L) baking dish

8	chicken thighs, skin removed	8
2 tbsp	liquid honey	25 mL
2 tsp	grated lemon zest	10 mL
1 tsp	freshly squeezed lemon juice	5 mL
1	large clove garlic, minced	1
1/4 tsp	salt	1 mL
1/4 tsp	freshly ground black pepper	1 mL

1. Arrange chicken in baking dish. In a bowl, combine honey, lemon zest, lemon juice, garlic, salt and pepper; spoon over chicken.

2. Bake in oven, basting once, for 45 to 55 minutes or until juices run clear when chicken is pierced.

NUTRITIONAL ANALYSIS PER SERVING

Calories	192
Carbohydrate	6 g
Fiber	0 g
Protein	25 g
Fat, total	7 g
Fat, saturated	2 g
Sodium	185 mg
Cholesterol	95 mg

AMERICA'S EXCHANGES PER SERVING

1/2	Other Carbohydrate
3 1/2	Very Lean Meat
1/2	Fat

CANADA'S CHOICES PER SERVING

| 1/2 | Carbohydrate |
| 3 1/2 | Meat & Alternatives |

My Favorite Chicken Dish

**SERVES 4
(3 pieces of chicken per serving)**

Boneless chicken breasts are a staple in my weekly grocery cart. Everyone needs an all-purpose chicken dish to whip up on the spur of the moment. This is one of mine. It's a breeze to cook and always a hit with my family. Serve alongside noodles or rice. Add a salad and you've got dinner ready in 30 minutes.

Tip

Vary the flavors by using different herbs such as tarragon or herbes de Provence.

1 lb	boneless skinless chicken breasts (about 3)	500 g
2 tbsp	all-purpose flour	25 mL
½ tsp	salt	2 mL
½ tsp	freshly ground black pepper	2 mL
1 tbsp	butter	15 mL
½ cup	reduced-sodium chicken broth	125 mL
½ cup	orange juice or mixture of juice and part dry white wine	125 mL
1	large clove garlic, finely chopped	1
½ tsp	dried Italian herbs or basil leaves	2 mL
¼ tsp	granulated sugar	1 mL
1 tbsp	chopped fresh parsley or chives	15 mL

1. On a cutting board using a sharp knife, cut each breast lengthwise into 4 thin pieces. Place flour in a shallow bowl; season with salt and pepper. Coat chicken in flour mixture, shaking off excess.

2. Heat a large nonstick skillet over medium-high heat. Add butter; when foamy, add chicken pieces. Cook 2 minutes per side or until lightly browned. Transfer to a plate.

3. Reduce heat to medium; add broth, orange juice, garlic, Italian herbs and sugar to skillet. Bring to a boil; cook for 1 minute or until slightly reduced. Season sauce with pepper to taste. Return chicken to skillet; reduce heat, cover and simmer for 5 minutes or until no longer pink inside and sauce is slightly thickened. Serve sprinkled with parsley.

NUTRITIONAL ANALYSIS PER SERVING

Calories	163
Carbohydrate	7 g
Fiber	0 g
Protein	23 g
Fat, total	4 g
Fat, saturated	2 g
Sodium	420 mg
Cholesterol	66 mg

AMERICA'S EXCHANGES PER SERVING

½	Starch
3	Very Lean Meat

CANADA'S CHOICES PER SERVING

½	Carbohydrate
3	Meat & Alternatives

What a relief to know when you come home frazzled from a day at work, you can count on these tasty chicken fingers stashed away in your freezer. Round out the meal with rice and a steamed vegetable, such as broccoli, for a dinner that's on the table in 30 minutes.

Tips

Buy boneless chicken breasts when they're featured as a supermarket special and make batches of chicken fingers to freeze ahead. Use fresh (not defrosted) chicken breasts; prepare recipe as directed, placing unbaked strips on a rack set on baking sheet. Freeze until firm; transfer to a storage container. Can be frozen for up to 2 months. No need to defrost before baking.

You can also make extra batches of the crumb mixture and store in the freezer.

Yummy Parmesan Chicken Fingers

- Preheat oven to 400°F (200°C)
- Baking sheet with rack, rack sprayed with vegetable cooking spray

1/2 cup	finely crushed soda cracker crumbs (about 16 crackers)	125 mL
1/3 cup	freshly grated Parmesan cheese	75 mL
1/2 tsp	dried basil leaves	2 mL
1/2 tsp	dried marjoram leaves	2 mL
1/2 tsp	paprika	2 mL
1/2 tsp	salt	2 mL
1/4 tsp	freshly ground black pepper	1 mL
4	boneless skinless chicken breasts	4
1	egg	1
1	clove garlic, minced	1

1. In a food processor, combine cracker crumbs, Parmesan cheese, basil, marjoram, paprika, salt and pepper. Process to make fine crumbs. Place in a shallow bowl.

2. Cut chicken breasts into 4 strips each. In a bowl, beat egg and garlic; add chicken strips. Using a fork, dip chicken strips in crumb mixture until evenly coated. Arrange on rack set on baking sheet.

3. Bake in preheated oven for 14 to 18 minutes or until no longer pink in center. (If frozen, bake for up to 25 minutes.)

NUTRITIONAL ANALYSIS PER SERVING	
Calories	115
Carbohydrate	3 g
Fiber	0 g
Protein	18 g
Fat, total	3 g
Fat, saturated	1 g
Sodium	245 mg
Cholesterol	59 mg

AMERICA'S EXCHANGES PER SERVING	
2 1/2	Very Lean Meat
1/2	Fat

CANADA'S CHOICES PER SERVING	
2 1/2	Meat & Alternatives

In the time it takes to cook rice or pasta, this streamlined dish is ready to serve.

Chicken Curry with Red Peppers

I cup	reduced-sodium chicken broth	250 mL
2 tsp	cornstarch	10 mL
¼ tsp	salt	I mL
4 tsp	vegetable oil, divided	20 mL
I lb	boneless skinless chicken breasts, cut into thin strips	500 g
2	cloves garlic, minced	2
I tbsp	minced fresh gingerroot	15 mL
I tbsp	mild curry paste or powder	15 mL
2	large red bell peppers, cut into thin strips	2
4	green onions, sliced	4

1. In a liquid glass measure, combine broth, cornstarch and salt; set aside.

2. In a large nonstick skillet, heat 2 tsp (10 mL) oil over medium-high heat; cook chicken, stirring often, for 5 minutes or until no longer pink inside. Transfer to a plate.

3. Reduce heat to medium; add remaining oil. Cook garlic, ginger and curry paste, stirring, for 1 minute. Add peppers; cook, stirring, for 2 minutes. Stir reserved broth mixture and pour into skillet; bring to a boil. Cook, stirring, until thickened. Add chicken and green onions; cook, stirring, for 2 minutes or until heated through.

NUTRITIONAL ANALYSIS PER SERVING

Calories	234
Carbohydrate	9 g
Fiber	2 g
Protein	29 g
Fat, total	8 g
Fat, saturated	I g
Sodium	460 mg
Cholesterol	71 mg

AMERICA'S EXCHANGES PER SERVING

1½	Vegetable
3½	Lean Meat

CANADA'S CHOICES PER SERVING

½	Carbohydrate
3½	Meat & Alternatives

SERVES 10, PLUS LEFTOVERS
(4 oz/125 g, no skin,
per serving,
with ¼ cup/50 mL
gravy and ⅓ cup/
75 mL stuffing)

Turkey always has the place of honor when my family and friends gathers for holiday meals. It's perfect when serving a crowd. It's economical, too, and everyone loves it. Best of all are the leftovers that get wrapped and placed in the fridge for hearty sandwiches the next day — or even later that night.

Tips

See Turkey Tips, page 90.

Toast bread cubes on a baking sheet in a 350°F (180°C) oven for 15 minutes.

NUTRITIONAL ANALYSIS PER SERVING	
Calories	275
Carbohydrate	13 g
Fiber	2 g
Protein	37 g
Fat, total	8 g
Fat, saturated	3 g
Sodium	430 mg
Cholesterol	89 mg

Roast Turkey with Sage-Bread Stuffing

- *Preheat oven to 325°F (160°C)*
- *12-cup (3 L) casserole dish, sprayed with vegetable cooking spray*
- *Shallow roasting pan or broiler pan with rack, rack sprayed with vegetable cooking spray*

STUFFING

2 tbsp	butter	25 mL
2 cups	chopped onions	500 mL
2 cups	chopped celery	500 mL
8 oz	mushrooms, chopped	250 g
4	cloves garlic, minced	4
1 tbsp	dried rubbed sage	15 mL
1 tsp	dried thyme leaves	5 mL
1 tsp	dried marjoram leaves	5 mL
1 tsp	salt	5 mL
½ tsp	freshly ground black pepper	2 mL
12 cups	whole wheat or white bread cubes, toasted (see tip, at left)	3 L
½ cup	chopped fresh parsley	125 mL
1 cup	turkey stock or reduced-sodium chicken broth (approx.)	250 mL

TURKEY

1	turkey (about 12 to 14 lbs/6 to 7 kg)	1
2 tbsp	melted butter	25 mL
6	cloves garlic, unpeeled	6
1	large onion, cut into 8 wedges	1
2	carrots, cut into chunks	2
1	large stalk celery, cut into chunks	1
1 tsp	dried rosemary leaves, crumbled	5 mL
½ tsp	dried thyme leaves	2 mL
½ tsp	dried marjoram leaves	2 mL
	Freshly ground black pepper	

AMERICA'S EXCHANGES PER SERVING	
½	Starch
½	Vegetable
5	Very Lean Meat
½	Fat

CANADA'S CHOICES PER SERVING	
1	Carbohydrate
4½	Meat & Alternatives

GRAVY

¼ cup	all-purpose flour	50 mL
½ cup	white wine or additional stock	125 mL
3 cups	turkey gravy stock or reduced-sodium chicken broth	750 mL

1. *Stuffing:* In a large nonstick skillet, melt butter over medium heat; cook onions, celery, mushrooms, garlic, sage, thyme, marjoram, salt and pepper, stirring often, for 15 minutes or until tender.

2. In a large bowl, combine onion mixture, bread cubes and parsley. Spoon into casserole dish.

3. To bake, add enough turkey stock to moisten stuffing and toss. (If you plan to stuff the bird, omit stock.) Cover with lid or foil and place in oven for the last hour of roasting turkey, uncovering for last 30 minutes to brown and crisp the top.

4. *Turkey:* Remove neck and giblets from bird; reserve to make stock. Rinse turkey with cold water; pat dry. Secure legs by tying with string or tuck under skin around the tail; fold wings back and secure neck skin with skewer.

5. Place turkey, breast side up, on rack in roasting pan. Brush bird with melted butter. Lightly crush garlic with side of knife; scatter garlic, onion, carrots and celery in pan. Season turkey and vegetables with rosemary, thyme, marjoram and pepper.

6. Insert meat thermometer into thickest part of inner turkey thigh, being careful not to touch bone. Roast turkey for 3¼ to 3½ hours; no need to baste. (If turkey starts to brown too quickly, tent bird loosely with heavy-duty foil, shiny side down.) Turkey is done when meat thermometer registers 170°F (80°C) for unstuffed bird; 180°F (82°C) if stuffed.

7. Remove from oven; cover with foil and let stand for 15 minutes for easy carving.

8. *Gravy:* Skim fat from roasting pan; place over medium heat. Stir in flour; cook, stirring, for 1 minute. Add wine; cook, stirring, until reduced by half. Stir in stock; bring to boil, scraping up brown bits from bottom of pan, until gravy thickens. Strain through a fine sieve into a saucepan, pressing down on vegetables; discard the vegetables. Season gravy with pepper to taste.

continued on next page

Turkey Gravy Stock

Pat neck and giblets dry. (Do not use liver.) In a large saucepan, heat 1 tbsp (15 mL) vegetable oil over medium-high heat; cook neck and giblets, stirring, for 8 minutes or until nicely browned. Add 1 each chopped onion, carrot and celery stalk including leaves along with 1 tsp (5 mL) dried thyme; cook, stirring, for 3 minutes or until vegetables are lightly colored. Add 1 cup (250 mL) white wine, if desired. Stir in 6 cups (1.5 L) water; season with up to ¾ tsp (4 mL) salt, and pepper to taste. Bring to a boil, cover and simmer over medium-low heat for 3 hours. Strain stock through cheesecloth-lined or fine sieve; discard solids. Skim fat from surface. Makes about 4 cups (1 L) stock.

Turkey Tips

- I prefer to roast a fresh turkey rather than a frozen bird, which is less moist and juicy. To streamline the preparations, I've done away with stuffing the turkey. Instead, the stuffing is packed into a casserole dish and baked in the oven for the last hour of roasting the bird.
- Not sure what size turkey to buy? Estimate 1 lb (500 g) per person.
- Wash hands well before and after handling turkey. Wash and disinfect work surface and utensils with hot soapy water and dry thoroughly.
- Cook turkey thoroughly. Never slow roast at low temperatures or partially cook a bird, then continue roasting later on in day or next day.
- Roast in a 325°F (160°C) oven until a meat thermometer, inserted in the thickest portion of inner thigh, reaches an internal temperature of 170°F (80°C) for unstuffed bird; 180°F (82°C) for stuffed bird.
- Chill leftovers promptly. Do not leave cooked turkey at room temperature for more than 2 hours. Place cooked turkey meat in a casserole or wrap in foil or plastic and refrigerate immediately. Leftovers will keep in the fridge for up to 4 days or in the freezer for up to 1 month.

Quick Defrosting Method

Place frozen turkey (in original wrapping) in cold water and change water frequently. Allow 1 hour per pound (2 hours per kg). Once defrosted, cook turkey within 2 days.

Whole Turkey Roasting Times

Today's leaner turkeys take less time to cook than in the past. Don't rely on outdated information from old cookbooks and recipes. Here are newly revised roasting times:

COOKING TIME (HOURS) IN 325°F (160°C) OVEN		
WEIGHT	STUFFED	UNSTUFFED
6 to 8 lbs (3 to 3.5 kg)	3 to 3$\frac{1}{4}$	2$\frac{1}{2}$ to 2$\frac{3}{4}$
8 to 10 lbs (3.5 to 4.5 kg)	3$\frac{1}{4}$ to 3$\frac{1}{2}$	2$\frac{3}{4}$ to 3
10 to 12 lbs (4.5 to 5.5 kg)	3$\frac{1}{2}$ to 3$\frac{3}{4}$	3 to 3$\frac{1}{4}$
12 to 16 lbs (5.5 to 7 kg)	3$\frac{3}{4}$ to 4	3$\frac{1}{4}$ to 3$\frac{1}{2}$
16 to 22 lbs (7 to 10 kg)	4 to 4$\frac{1}{2}$	3$\frac{1}{2}$ to 4

This recipe will make you want to roast a turkey just so you have some leftovers on hand. But, if time does not permit, buy a roasted chicken from the deli section of the supermarket and use the diced meat in this no-fuss dish.

Tip

Mango chutney is called for in this recipe, but any type, whether store-bought or homemade, can be used; add according to taste. Serve over basmati rice and sprinkle with chopped cilantro, if desired.

Quick Turkey Curry

2 tsp	vegetable oil	10 mL
1	small onion, chopped	1
1	large clove garlic, minced	1
2 tsp	minced fresh gingerroot	10 mL
1	apple, peeled and chopped	1
1/2 cup	finely diced celery	125 mL
2 tsp	mild curry paste or powder	10 mL
1 tbsp	all-purpose flour	15 mL
1 1/3 cups	reduced-sodium chicken broth	325 mL
3 tbsp	mango chutney	45 mL
2 cups	diced cooked turkey or chicken	500 mL
1/4 cup	raisins	50 mL
	Freshly ground black pepper	

1. In a large nonstick skillet, heat oil over medium heat. Add onion, garlic, ginger, apple, celery and curry paste; cook, stirring, for 5 minutes or until softened.

2. Blend in flour; add chicken broth and chutney. Cook, stirring, until sauce comes to a boil and thickens. Stir in turkey and raisins; season with pepper to taste. Cook for 3 minutes or until heated through.

NUTRITIONAL ANALYSIS PER SERVING	
Calories	266
Carbohydrate	28 g
Fiber	2 g
Protein	23 g
Fat, total	7 g
Fat, saturated	1 g
Sodium	510 mg
Cholesterol	53 mg

AMERICA'S EXCHANGES PER SERVING	
1	Fruit
1/2	Other Carbohydrate
1/2	Vegetable
3	Lean Meat

CANADA'S CHOICES PER SERVING	
1 1/2	Carbohydrate
3	Meat & Alternatives

SERVES 6
(1 chop per serving)

Sweet potato or winter squash can replace the rutabaga in this mellow ginger-and-spice-infused dish.

Tip

The taste of freshly grated nutmeg is so much better than the pre-ground variety. Whole nutmeg can be found in the spice section of your supermarket or bulk food store. Look for inexpensive nutmeg graters in kitchenware shops.

Pork Chop Bake with Rutabaga and Apples

- Preheat oven to 350°F (180°C)
- 13- by 9-inch (3 L) baking dish

1	rutabaga (1 1/2 lbs/750 g)	1
1/4 cup	all-purpose flour	50 mL
1 lb	thin boneless pork loin chops, trimmed (about 6)	500 g
2 tbsp	vegetable oil, divided	25 mL
2	large apples, peeled, cored and sliced	2
1	onion, halved lengthwise, sliced into thin wedges	1
2 tbsp	minced fresh gingerroot	25 mL
1 tsp	ground cumin	5 mL
1 tsp	ground coriander	5 mL
1/2 tsp	salt	2 mL
1/4 tsp	freshly ground black pepper	1 mL
1/4 tsp	ground cinnamon	1 mL
1/4 tsp	freshly grated nutmeg	1 mL
1 cup	apple juice	250 mL
1 tbsp	packed brown sugar	15 mL

1. Peel and quarter rutabaga; cut into 1/4-inch (0.5 cm) slices; layer in baking dish.

2. Place flour in a heavy plastic bag; shake pork in batches in flour to coat, shaking off excess; reserve remaining flour.

3. In a large nonstick skillet, heat 1 tbsp (15 mL) oil over medium-high heat; brown pork lightly on both sides. Arrange over rutabaga; top with apple slices.

NUTRITIONAL ANALYSIS PER SERVING	
Calories	284
Carbohydrate	30 g
Fiber	4 g
Protein	18 g
Fat, total	11 g
Fat, saturated	2 g
Sodium	245 mg
Cholesterol	45 mg

AMERICA'S EXCHANGES PER SERVING	
1	Starch
1	Fruit
2	Medium-fat Meat

CANADA'S CHOICES PER SERVING	
2	Carbohydrate
2	Meat & Alternatives

4. Add remaining oil to skillet; reduce heat to medium. Add onion, ginger, cumin, coriander, salt, pepper, cinnamon and nutmeg; cook, stirring, for 3 minutes or until onion is softened. Sprinkle with reserved flour. Add apple juice and brown sugar; bring to a boil. Pour over apples in baking dish.

5. Cover and bake in oven for 1 hour or until rutabaga is tender.

Tip

The rutabaga, a traditional winter vegetable, is also known as yellow turnip or Swede.

*I love the way the
sweetness of dried fruit
accents the delicate taste
of pork in this recipe. And
when you stuff the loin
with a fruit-and-spice
mixture, you ensure that
the meat will be extra
moist and flavorful.*

Tip

It may appear that you have
too much stuffing when you
first tie the pork. But once
all the strings are in place,
it's easy to enclose the
meat completely around
the fruit mixture.

Company Pork Roast with Fruit Stuffing

- *Preheat oven to 350°F (180°C)*
- *Roasting pan with rack, rack sprayed with vegetable cooking spray*

STUFFING

1 tbsp	butter	15 mL
1/3 cup	chopped green onions	75 mL
1 tsp	ground cumin	5 mL
1 tsp	mild curry paste or powder	5 mL
1	egg	1
1 cup	chopped mixed dried fruits, such as apricots, prunes, apples, cranberries	250 mL
1/2 cup	soft fresh bread crumbs	125 mL
1 tsp	finely grated orange zest	5 mL
1/4 tsp	salt	1 mL
	Freshly ground black pepper	

PORK ROAST

3 lbs	boneless pork loin roast	1.5 kg
2 tsp	vegetable oil	10 mL
1	large clove garlic, minced	1
1 tsp	dried sage leaves	5 mL
1/2 tsp	dried thyme leaves	2 mL
	Freshly ground black pepper	

GRAVY

1 tbsp	all-purpose flour	15 mL
1/2 cup	white wine or reduced-sodium chicken broth	125 mL
3/4 cup	reduced-sodium chicken broth	175 mL
	Freshly ground black pepper	

1. In a small nonstick skillet, melt butter over medium heat. Add green onions, cumin and curry paste; cook, stirring, for 2 minutes or until softened.

2. In a bowl, beat egg; add onion mixture, dried fruits, bread crumbs and orange zest; season with salt and pepper.

3. *Pork Roast:* Remove strings from pork roast; unfold roast and trim excess fat. Place pork roast, trimmed fat layer down, on work surface. Cover with plastic wrap and pound using a meat mallet to flatten slightly. Season with pepper; spread stuffing down center of meat. Roll the pork around the stuffing and tie securely at six intervals with butcher's string.

4. Place roast on rack in roasting pan. In a small bowl, combine oil, garlic, sage and thyme; spread over pork roast and season with pepper.

5. Roast in preheated oven for $1\frac{1}{2}$ to $1\frac{3}{4}$ hours or until meat thermometer registers 160°F (70°C).

6. Transfer roast to cutting board; tent with foil and let stand for 10 minutes before carving.

7. *Gravy:* Skim fat from pan and discard. Place roasting pan over medium heat; sprinkle with flour. Cook, stirring, for 1 minute or until lightly colored. Add wine; cook until partially reduced. Add broth and bring to a boil, scraping any brown bits from bottom of pan. Season with pepper to taste. Strain sauce through a fine sieve into a warm sauceboat. Cut pork into thick slices and serve accompanied with gravy.

Tip

Pork today is much leaner than it used to be. All trimmed pork cuts except ribs contain less than 10 g of fat per 3 oz (90 g) cooked meat, and several contain less than 7 grams. Spareribs, regardless of cooking method, are much higher in fat and should be considered a special occasion treat.

Simple and tasty — this is my favorite way to cook fast-fry pork chops. Serve with rice and steamed broccoli.

Pork Chops with Honey and Thyme

½ cup	reduced-sodium chicken broth	125 mL
1 tbsp	liquid honey	15 mL
1 tbsp	cider vinegar	15 mL
1 tsp	cornstarch	5 mL
1 lb	thin boneless loin pork chops, trimmed (about 6)	500 g
2 tsp	vegetable oil	10 mL
	Freshly ground black pepper	
3	green onions, sliced	3
½ tsp	dried thyme leaves	2 mL

1. In a bowl, combine broth, honey, vinegar and cornstarch. Set aside.

2. Blot pork chops dry with paper towels. In a large nonstick skillet, heat oil over high heat; cook pork for 1 to 2 minutes per side or until lightly browned. Season with pepper. Transfer to a plate.

3. Reduce heat to medium. Stir in green onions and thyme; cook, stirring for 30 seconds. Stir reserved chicken broth mixture and add to skillet; cook, stirring, for 1 minute or until sauce boils and thickens. Return pork and any juices to skillet; cover and cook for 2 minutes or until pork is no longer pink in center. Season sauce, if necessary, with additional pepper to taste.

NUTRITIONAL ANALYSIS PER SERVING	
Calories	135
Carbohydrate	4 g
Fiber	0 g
Protein	15 g
Fat, total	6 g
Fat, saturated	2 g
Sodium	110 mg
Cholesterol	41 mg

AMERICA'S EXCHANGES PER SERVING	
½	Other Carbohydrate
2	Lean Meat

CANADA'S CHOICES PER SERVING	
2	Meat & Alternatives

Yummy Parmesan Chicken Fingers (page 86) ➤
Overleaf: Zesty Barbecue Spareribs (page 97)

"You've got to put your rib recipe in your cookbook," advised my son, whose favorite dinner request is a plate of these succulent ribs. So here it is. And since the only way to eat ribs is with your fingers, be sure to have plenty of napkins handy.

Tips

While today's pork, including ribs, is much leaner than in the past, it's still important to eat these in moderation, as much of the fat is saturated.

Ribs are great on the barbecue, too. Partially cook ribs in oven for 30 minutes as directed in recipe. Complete cooking on grill over medium-low flame, basting often with the sauce.

Zesty Barbecued Spareribs

- Preheat oven to 375°F (190°C)
- Shallow roasting pan or broiler pan, with rack

3 lbs	pork back ribs	1.5 kg
	Freshly ground black pepper	
1 cup	ketchup or prepared chili sauce	250 mL
1/3 cup	liquid honey	75 mL
1	small onion, finely chopped	1
2	cloves garlic, minced	2
2 tbsp	Worcestershire sauce	25 mL
2 tbsp	freshly squeezed lemon juice	25 mL
1 tbsp	Dijon mustard	15 mL
1 tsp	hot pepper sauce or to taste	5 mL
1	lemon, cut into wedges	1

1. Place ribs on rack in roasting pan; season with pepper. Cover with foil. Roast in preheated oven for 30 minutes.

2. In a small saucepan, combine chili sauce, honey, onion, garlic, Worcestershire sauce, lemon juice, mustard and hot pepper sauce. Bring to a boil; reduce heat and simmer, stirring occasionally, for 10 to 15 minutes or until slightly thickened.

3. Remove foil; brush ribs generously on both sides with sauce. Roast, uncovered, for 25 to 30 minutes, brushing generously every 10 minutes with the sauce, until spareribs are nicely glazed and tender.

4. Cut into serving portions; serve with any remaining sauce and lemon wedges.

NUTRITIONAL ANALYSIS PER SERVING

Calories	325
Carbohydrate	20 g
Fiber	1 g
Protein	29 g
Fat, total	15 g
Fat, saturated	5 g
Sodium	410 mg
Cholesterol	66 mg

AMERICA'S EXCHANGES PER SERVING

1 1/2	Other Carbohydrate
4	Lean Meat
1/2	Fat

CANADA'S CHOICES PER SERVING

1	Carbohydrate
4	Meat & Alternatives

◄ Chicken-Vegetable Cobbler (page 116)
Overleaf: Old-Fashioned Beef Stew (page 110)

Rosemary Roast Lamb with New Potatoes

- *Preheat oven to 350°F (180°C)*
- *Large shallow roasting pan, sprayed with vegetable cooking spray*

Lamb is often my first choice when planning a special dinner. It's always a crowd pleaser. I love the heavenly aroma of garlic and rosemary in this recipe — it fills my house and makes an especially warm welcome for friends as they come through the door.

Tips

Take the lamb out of the fridge about 30 minutes before roasting.

Choose potatoes that are the same size so they roast evenly.

If you don't want to open a bottle of white wine, a good substitute is dry white vermouth. Keep a bottle handy in the cupboard for those recipes that call for white wine.

1	leg of lamb (about 5 to 6 lbs/2.5 to 3 kg)	1
8	cloves garlic	8
	Grated zest and juice of 1 lemon	
2 tbsp	olive oil	25 mL
2 tbsp	chopped fresh rosemary leaves or 1 tbsp (15 mL) dried rosemary leaves, crumbled	25 mL
1/2 tsp	salt	2 mL
1/2 tsp	freshly ground black pepper	2 mL
12	whole new potatoes, scrubbed (about 3 lbs/1.5 kg)	12
1 tbsp	all-purpose flour	15 mL
1/2 cup	white wine	125 mL
1 cup	reduced-sodium chicken broth	250 mL

1. Cut 6 cloves garlic into 8 to 10 slivers each. Using the tip of a knife, cut shallow slits all over lamb and insert a garlic sliver into each.
2. Finely chop remaining 2 garlic cloves. In a bowl, combine garlic, lemon zest and juice, oil, rosemary, salt and pepper. Place lamb in prepared roasting pan; surround with potatoes. Brush lamb and potatoes generously with lemon-garlic mixture. Insert meat thermometer into thickest part of leg.
3. Roast in preheated oven for about 1 1/2 hours, turning potatoes over halfway through roasting, until meat thermometer registers 135°F (57°C) for medium-rare. (For medium, remove the potatoes and continue to roast lamb for 15 to 20 minutes more or to your liking.)

NUTRITIONAL ANALYSIS PER SERVING	
Calories	374
Carbohydrate	31 g
Fiber	3 g
Protein	35 g
Fat, total	12 g
Fat, saturated	4 g
Sodium	325 mg
Cholesterol	113 mg

AMERICA'S EXCHANGES PER SERVING	
2	Starch
4 1/2	Very Lean Meat
1	Fat

CANADA'S CHOICES PER SERVING	
2	Carbohydrate
4	Meat & Alternatives

4. Remove lamb to a platter; tent with foil and let rest 10 minutes before carving. Transfer potatoes to a dish; keep warm.

5. Skim fat in pan; place over medium heat. Stir in flour and cook, stirring, until lightly colored. Pour in wine; cook, scraping up any brown bits, until wine is reduced by half. Stir in broth; bring to a boil, stirring, until thickened. Strain through a fine sieve into a warm sauceboat.

6. Carve the lamb. Arrange slices on serving plate and moisten with some of the sauce; surround with roasted potatoes. Serve with remaining sauce.

Tip

In the past it was customary to cook lamb to well-done, but this does it a disservice. For the best flavor and juiciness, be sure at least a hint of pink remains. Trimmed lean lamb, whether domestic or imported, is lower in fat than many people think— about 6 g per 3 oz (90 g) lean roast leg of lamb.

*Tender milk-fed veal is
preferred over grain-fed in
this classic pan-fried recipe
with flavorful herbs. This
schnitzel goes well with a
salad of vibrant mesclun
mix or watercress greens.*

Tip

Make sure cutlets are thin;
if necessary, pound meat
thin between sheets of
plastic wrap using a meat
mallet or rolling pin.

Herb Wiener Schnitzel

1 lb	thin veal or turkey cutlets (8 cutlets)	500 g
1/2 tsp	salt	2 mL
1/2 tsp	freshly ground black pepper	2 mL
1 cup	plain dry bread crumbs	250 mL
1/3 cup	lightly packed fresh parsley	75 mL
3/4 tsp	dried herbes de Provence (see tip, page 78) or thyme leaves	4 mL
1/3 cup	all-purpose flour	75 mL
2	eggs, beaten	2
2 tbsp	butter, divided	25 mL
2 tbsp	vegetable oil, divided (approx.)	25 mL
	Lemon wedges	

1. Blot veal dry with paper towels. Season with salt and pepper.

2. In a food processor, process bread crumbs, parsley and herbes de Provence.

3. Place flour, beaten eggs and bread crumb mixture in 3 separate shallow bowls. Just before cooking, dredge veal in flour, shaking off excess; dip in egg and then coat well in bread crumb mixture.

4. In a large nonstick skillet, heat 1 1/2 tsp (7 mL) each butter and oil over medium-high heat. Cook veal in batches for 1 1/2 minutes per side or until golden. Wipe skillet clean with paper towels before second batch. Transfer to a baking sheet; place in warm oven while cooking remaining schnitzel. Serve accompanied with lemon wedges.

NUTRITIONAL ANALYSIS PER SERVING	
Calories	300
Carbohydrate	19 g
Fiber	1 g
Protein	29 g
Fat, total	11 g
Fat, saturated	3 g
Sodium	570 mg
Cholesterol	158 mg

AMERICA'S EXCHANGES PER SERVING	
1	Starch
3 1/2	Lean Meat

CANADA'S CHOICES PER SERVING	
1	Carbohydrate
3 1/2	Meat & Alternatives

Veal Paprikash

4 tsp	vegetable oil, divided	20 mL
I lb	grain-fed veal scallops or boneless trimmed beef sirloin, cut into thin strips	500 g
4 cups	quartered mushrooms (about 12 oz/375 g)	I L
I	large onion, halved lengthwise and thinly sliced	I
2	cloves garlic, minced	2
4 tsp	paprika	20 mL
$1/2$ tsp	dried marjoram leaves	2 mL
$1/2$ tsp	salt	2 mL
$1/4$ tsp	freshly ground black pepper	I mL
I tbsp	all-purpose flour	15 mL
$3/4$ cup	reduced-sodium chicken broth	175 mL
$1/2$ cup	light sour cream	125 mL
	Freshly ground black pepper	

1. In a large nonstick skillet, heat 1 tbsp (15 mL) oil over high heat; stir-fry veal in two batches, each for 3 minutes or until browned but still pink inside. Transfer to a plate along with pan juices; keep warm.

2. Reduce heat to medium. Add remaining oil. Add mushrooms, onion, garlic, paprika, marjoram, salt and pepper; cook, stirring often, for 7 minutes or until lightly colored.

3. Sprinkle mushroom mixture with flour; pour in broth. Cook, stirring, for 2 minutes or until thickened. Stir in sour cream. Return veal and accumulated juices to pan; cook 1 minute more or until heated through. Adjust seasoning with pepper to taste; serve immediately.

NUTRITIONAL ANALYSIS PER SERVING	
Calories	207
Carbohydrate	14 g
Fiber	3 g
Protein	29 g
Fat, total	4 g
Fat, saturated	I g
Sodium	545 mg
Cholesterol	89 mg

AMERICA'S EXCHANGES PER SERVING	
2	Vegetable
$3^{1}/_{2}$	Very Lean Meat

CANADA'S CHOICES PER SERVING	
$1/2$	Carbohydrate
$3^{1}/_{2}$	Meat & Alternatives

SERVES 8
(4½ oz/130 g per
serving, with gravy)

*You will be delighted by
the tantalizing aromas
of rosemary and garlic
wafting through your
kitchen whenever you
prepare this distinctive
roast — ideal for a Sunday
or other special occasion.*

Tip

Pancetta is unsmoked
Italian bacon that is
available in supermarket
deli counters.

Tuscan Roast Veal with Rosemary and White Wine

● *Preheat oven to 350°F (180°C)* ● *Roasting pan*

2 oz	pancetta, finely diced, or bacon (see tip, at left)	60 g
¼ cup	finely chopped fresh parsley	50 mL
2	cloves garlic, minced	2
1 tsp	grated lemon zest	5 mL
	Freshly ground black pepper	
3 lbs	boneless leg of veal roast, well trimmed, tied	1.5 kg
2 tbsp	olive oil	25 mL
1 tbsp	chopped fresh rosemary leaves or 1½ tsp (7 mL) dried rosemary leaves, crumbled	15 mL
1 cup	dry white wine, divided	250 mL
1 cup	chicken broth or veal stock, divided	250 mL

1. In a bowl, combine pancetta, parsley, garlic and zest; season with pepper. Stuff into cavity of roast, as evenly as possible. (Prepare earlier in the day and refrigerate to allow flavors to penetrate veal.)

2. Place veal in pan. Brush with oil; season with rosemary and pepper. Place in oven and roast, uncovered, for 30 minutes. Add ½ cup (125 mL) each wine and broth to roasting pan. Tent loosely with foil and continue to roast for 1½ hours more, adding more wine and broth to the pan as necessary, until meat thermometer registers 170°F (80°C).

3. Transfer meat to serving platter and keep warm. Pour remaining wine and broth into roasting pan and place on stovetop over high heat. Bring to a boil, scraping up any brown bits from bottom of pan. Strain into a saucepan and boil until partially reduced. Slice veal into slices and drizzle with some of the pan juices. Serve remainder in a sauceboat.

NUTRITIONAL ANALYSIS PER SERVING

Calories	255
Carbohydrate	1 g
Fiber	0 g
Protein	37 g
Fat, total	10 g
Fat, saturated	3 g
Sodium	270 mg
Cholesterol	135 mg

AMERICA'S EXCHANGES PER SERVING

5	Very Lean Meat
1	Fat

CANADA'S CHOICES PER SERVING

5	Meat & Alternatives

This easy-to-make saucy veal is one of my all-time favorite dishes to serve when I'm entertaining. Delicious served with noodles and a green vegetable such as asparagus.

Veal Scaloppini with Marsala

1 lb	thin veal or pork cutlets	500 g
½ tsp	salt	2 mL
¼ tsp	freshly ground black pepper	1 mL
¼ cup	all-purpose flour	50 mL
2 tsp	butter, divided	10 mL
2 tsp	olive oil, divided	10 mL
⅓ cup	minced shallots	75 mL
¾ lb	assorted mushrooms, such as shiitake, oyster and button mushrooms, sliced	375 g
1 tbsp	chopped fresh thyme or 1 tsp (5 mL) dried thyme leaves	15 mL
½ cup	dry Marsala or white wine	125 mL
½ cup	reduced-sodium chicken broth	125 mL

1. Blot veal dry with paper towels. Season with salt and pepper; dredge in flour, shaking off excess.

2. In a large nonstick skillet, heat 1 tsp (5 mL) each butter and oil over high heat; cook veal in two batches, 1 minute per side or until lightly browned. Add remaining butter and oil for second batch. Transfer to a plate.

3. Reduce heat to medium; cook shallots, mushrooms and thyme, stirring, for 5 minutes or until softened. Add Marsala and broth; cook for 2 minutes or until slightly reduced. Return veal to skillet. Cook for 2 to 3 minutes, turning occasionally, until heated through and coated in sauce. Adjust seasoning with pepper to taste.

NUTRITIONAL ANALYSIS PER SERVING	
Calories	238
Carbohydrate	13 g
Fiber	2 g
Protein	27 g
Fat, total	7 g
Fat, saturated	2 g
Sodium	450 mg
Cholesterol	94 mg

AMERICA'S EXCHANGES PER SERVING	
2	Vegetable
3½	Very Lean Meat
½	Fat

CANADA'S CHOICES PER SERVING	
½	Carbohydrate
3½	Meat & Alternatives

SERVES 4

Fresh gingerroot gives such a sparkling flavor to salmon — or any fish, for that matter. Dried ground ginger just doesn't come close to imparting the same crisp taste as fresh gingerroot, available in most supermarkets and produce stores.

Tips

To store gingerroot, peel it, place in glass jar and add white wine or sherry to cover. As an added bonus, you can use the ginger-infused wine or sherry to flavor other fish or chicken dishes, or stir-fries.

One of the best uses for the microwave is for quickly cooking fish. Arrange fish and sauce in a shallow baking dish and cover with microwave-safe plastic wrap; turn back one corner to vent. Microwave at Medium (50%) for 4 minutes. Turn fish over and re-cover; microwave at Medium (50%) for 3 to 5 minutes more or until salmon turns opaque.

Salmon with Lemon-Ginger Sauce

● *Preheat oven to 425°F (220°C)* ● *Shallow baking dish*

4	salmon fillets, each 5 oz (150 g)	4
MARINADE		
2	green onions	2
1½ tsp	minced fresh gingerroot	7 mL
1	clove garlic, minced	1
2 tbsp	reduced-sodium soy sauce	25 mL
1 tsp	grated lemon zest	5 mL
1 tbsp	freshly squeezed lemon juice	15 mL
1 tsp	granulated sugar	5 mL
1 tsp	sesame oil	5 mL

1. Place salmon fillets in a single layer in baking dish.

2. *Marinade:* Chop green onions; set aside chopped green tops for garnish. In a bowl, combine white part of green onions, ginger, garlic, soy sauce, lemon zest and juice, sugar and sesame oil. Pour marinade over salmon; let stand at room temperature for 15 minutes or in the refrigerator for up to 1 hour.

3. Bake, uncovered, in preheated oven for 13 to 15 minutes or until salmon turns opaque. Arrange on serving plates, spoon sauce over and sprinkle with reserved green onion tops.

NUTRITIONAL ANALYSIS PER SERVING

Calories	286
Carbohydrate	3 g
Fiber	0 g
Protein	29 g
Fat, total	17 g
Fat, saturated	3 g
Sodium	320 mg
Cholesterol	80 mg

AMERICA'S EXCHANGES PER SERVING

4	Lean Meat
1	Fat

CANADA'S CHOICES PER SERVING

4	Meat & Alternatives

What to do with fresh cod from the market and ripe tomatoes plucked from your garden? Add some briny olives and pungent capers, and make this delicious fish dish that bursts with the sunny flavors of the Mediterranean.

Cod Provençal

● *Preheat oven to 425°F (220°C)* ● *Shallow baking dish*

I lb	cod or halibut, cut into 4 pieces	500 g
	Freshly ground black pepper	
2	ripe tomatoes, diced	2
2	green onions, sliced	2
I	clove garlic, minced	I
¼ cup	Kalamata olives, rinsed, cut into slivers	50 mL
2 tbsp	chopped fresh parsley or basil leaves	25 mL
I tbsp	capers, drained and rinsed	I5 mL
Pinch	hot pepper flakes (optional)	Pinch
I tbsp	olive oil	I5 mL

1. Arrange cod in a single layer in baking dish. Season with pepper.

2. In a bowl, combine tomatoes, green onions, garlic, olives, parsley, capers and hot pepper flakes, if using; season with pepper. Spoon tomato-olive mixture over fish fillets; drizzle with oil.

3. Bake in preheated oven for 15 to 20 minutes or until fish flakes when tested with a fork. Serve in warmed wide shallow bowls and spoon pan juices over top.

NUTRITIONAL ANALYSIS PER SERVING

Calories	I40
Carbohydrate	4 g
Fiber	I g
Protein	2I g
Fat, total	4 g
Fat, saturated	I g
Sodium	I40 mg
Cholesterol	49 mg

AMERICA'S EXCHANGES PER SERVING

I	Vegetable
3	Very Lean Meat

CANADA'S CHOICES PER SERVING

3	Meat & Alternatives

No trip to the fish market is required to make this quick main course dish. Packaged frozen fish fillets work just fine. And here's an extra bonus — even with a small amount of half-and-half cream added, this dish is low in fat.

Cod with Mushrooms and Tomato

- Preheat oven to 375°F (190°C)
- 8-inch (2 L) square baking dish

1	package (14 oz/400 g) frozen cod, sole, turbot or haddock fillets, defrosted (see tip, page 108)	1
	Freshly ground black pepper	
1½ cups	sliced mushrooms	375 mL
1	large tomato, seeded and diced	1
2	green onions, sliced	2
2 tbsp	chopped fresh dill or parsley	25 mL
⅓ cup	dry white wine or fish broth	75 mL
1 tbsp	cornstarch	15 mL
⅓ cup	half-and-half (10%) cream	75 mL

1. Arrange fish fillets in a single layer in baking dish; season with pepper. Layer with mushrooms, tomato, green onions and dill. Pour wine over top. Bake for 20 to 25 minutes or until fish is opaque and flakes when tested with a fork.

2. Remove from oven; carefully pour juices from dish into small saucepan. (Place a large plate or lid over dish.) Return fish to turned-off oven to keep warm.

3. In a bowl, blend cornstarch with 2 tbsp (25 mL) cold water; stir in cream. Add to saucepan. Place over medium heat; cook, whisking, until sauce comes to a boil and thickens. Season with pepper to taste. (Sauce will be thick.) Pour over fish and serve.

NUTRITIONAL ANALYSIS PER SERVING

Calories	135
Carbohydrate	6 g
Fiber	1 g
Protein	19 g
Fat, total	3 g
Fat, saturated	1 g
Sodium	240 mg
Cholesterol	49 mg

AMERICA'S EXCHANGES PER SERVING

½	Other Carbohydrate
2½	Very Lean Meat

CANADA'S CHOICES PER SERVING

½	Carbohydrate
2½	Meat & Alternatives

Want to wow your guests? Put this on your menu. Tender sole fillets with vibrant red pepper stuffing marry well in a light wine and cream sauce. It makes an attractive fish dish that never fails to impress.

Tip

In the past, fish dishes were adorned with silky rich sauces loaded with cream and butter. Adding only a small amount of cream still gives this sauce its luxurious and creamy appeal, but keeps the calorie count way down.

Stuffed Sole

- Preheat oven to 425°F (220°C)
- 8-inch (2 L) square baking dish

1 tbsp	butter	15 mL
1/4 cup	chopped green onions	50 mL
1 cup	chopped mushrooms	250 mL
1	red bell pepper, cut into very thin 1-inch (2.5 cm) strips	1
1 tsp	dried tarragon	5 mL
	Freshly ground white pepper	
6	sole fillets (about 1 1/2 pounds/750 g)	8
1/3 cup	white wine or fish broth	75 mL
2 tsp	cornstarch	10 mL
1/3 cup	half-and-half (10%) cream	75 mL

1. In a nonstick skillet, heat butter over medium heat. Add green onions, mushrooms, red pepper and tarragon; cook, stirring, for 3 minutes or until softened. Let cool.

2. Lay sole fillets, skinned side down, on work surface with smaller tapered ends closest to you; season with white pepper. Spoon a generous tablespoonful (15 mL) on bottom ends of fillets. Roll up and place fillets seam-side down in baking dish. Pour wine over top. (Recipe can be prepared up to this point earlier in day, then covered and refrigerated.)

3. To bake, cover with lid or foil; place in preheated oven for 16 to 20 minutes or until fish turns opaque.

4. Using a slotted spoon, remove fillets and arrange on serving plate; cover and keep warm.

5. Strain fish juices through a fine sieve into a medium saucepan; bring to a boil over high heat and reduce to about 1/2 cup (125 mL). In a bowl, blend cornstarch with 1 tbsp (15 mL) cold water; stir in cream. Pour into saucepan, whisking constantly, until sauce comes to a boil and thickens. Adjust seasoning with white pepper to taste. Spoon sauce over fish and serve.

NUTRITIONAL ANALYSIS PER SERVING	
Calories	154
Carbohydrate	4 g
Fiber	1 g
Protein	22 g
Fat, total	5 g
Fat, saturated	2 g
Sodium	120 mg
Cholesterol	70 mg

AMERICA'S EXCHANGES PER SERVING	
1/2	Vegetable
3	Very Lean Meat
1/2	Fat

CANADA'S CHOICES PER SERVING	
3	Meat & Alternatives

Crispy Almond Baked Fish

SERVES 4

This easy, practical method is my preferred way to cook white fish fillets, such as sole, haddock or turbot. Unlike many stovetop methods, where fish must be cooked in more than one batch, all the fish is cooked (and ready) at the same time.

Tip

To defrost package of frozen fish fillets, remove package wrapping; place fish on plate. Microwave at Medium (50%) for 3 minutes. Shield ends with thin strips of foil to prevent them from cooking before the rest of the fish has defrosted. Microwave at Defrost for 3 minutes more or until fish separates into fillets. Let stand for 10 minutes to complete defrosting. Pat dry with paper towels to absorb excess moisture.

- Preheat oven to 425°F (220°C)
- Baking sheet, sprayed with vegetable cooking spray

½ cup	soft fresh bread crumbs	125 mL
⅓ cup	sliced blanched almonds	75 mL
½ tsp	dried tarragon or basil leaves	2 mL
½ tsp	grated orange or lemon zest	2 mL
I lb	fish fillets, such as sole, haddock or turbot	500 g
	Freshly ground black pepper	
	Lemon wedges	

1. In a food processor, combine bread crumbs, almonds, tarragon and orange zest. Process, using on-off turns, until almonds are finely chopped.

2. Wrap fish in paper towels to absorb excess moisture. Arrange fillets on sheet in single layer. Season with pepper. Sprinkle crumb mixture over fish and pat lightly.

3. Bake in preheated oven for 8 to 10 minutes or until fish flakes when tested with a fork. (Time depends on thickness of fish; increase time accordingly.) Serve with lemon wedges.

NUTRITIONAL ANALYSIS PER SERVING

Calories	166
Carbohydrate	4 g
Fiber	I g
Protein	24 g
Fat, total	6 g
Fat, saturated	I g
Sodium	125 mg
Cholesterol	60 mg

AMERICA'S EXCHANGES PER SERVING

| 2½ | Very Lean Meat |
| I | Lean Meat |

CANADA'S CHOICES PER SERVING

| 3 | Meat & Alternatives |

Stews, Pot Roasts and One-Pot Simmers

Old-Fashioned Beef Stew

SERVES 6

What's more comforting than a satisfying stew? You start feeling good the minute you set this one-pot dish to simmer on the stovetop. As the herb-infused aroma wafts through your kitchen, the good feeling grows. The first forkful confirms that this stew is comfort food at its best. What's more, it can comfort you all over again the next day with easy-to-reheat leftovers. Delicious served with crusty bread to mop up the flavorful sauce.

Tip

A word about parsley. Use either the curly leaf variety or the more strongly flavored flat-leaf type. Wash well in plenty of water to remove dirt; dry parsley in a salad spinner or wrap in clean towel. The drier the parsley, the longer it lasts in your refrigerator. Wrap in paper towels, then in a plastic bag and refrigerate.

1/4 cup	all-purpose flour	50 mL
1 tsp	salt	5 mL
1/2 tsp	freshly ground black pepper	2 mL
1 1/2 lbs	lean stewing beef, cut into 1 1/2-inch (4 cm) cubes	750 g
2 tbsp	vegetable oil (approx.), divided	25 mL
2	medium onions, chopped	2
3	cloves garlic, finely chopped	3
1 tsp	dried thyme leaves	5 mL
1 tsp	dried marjoram leaves	5 mL
1	bay leaf	1
1 cup	red wine or additional beef broth	250 mL
3 tbsp	tomato paste	45 mL
3 cups	reduced-sodium beef broth (approx.)	750 mL
5	carrots	5
2	stalks celery	2
4 to 5	potatoes (about 1 1/2 lbs/750 g)	4 to 5
12 oz	green beans	375 g
1/4 cup	chopped fresh parsley (see tip, at left)	50 mL

1. Combine flour, salt and pepper in a heavy plastic bag. In batches, add beef to flour mixture and toss to coat. Transfer to a plate. Reserve remaining flour mixture.

2. In a Dutch oven or large saucepan, heat 1 tbsp (15 mL) oil over medium-high heat; cook beef in batches, adding more oil as needed, until browned all over. Transfer to a plate.

3. Reduce heat to medium-low. Add onions, garlic, thyme, marjoram, bay leaf and remaining flour to pan; cook, stirring, for 4 minutes or until softened. Add wine and tomato paste; cook, stirring, to scrape up brown bits. Return beef and any accumulated juices to pan; pour in broth.

NUTRITIONAL ANALYSIS PER SERVING	
Calories	362
Carbohydrate	35 g
Fiber	5 g
Protein	27 g
Fat, total	12 g
Fat, saturated	3 g
Sodium	815 mg
Cholesterol	47 mg

AMERICA'S EXCHANGES PER SERVING	
1 1/2	Starch
3	Vegetable
2 1/2	Very Lean Meat
1 1/2	Fat

CANADA'S CHOICES PER SERVING	
2	Carbohydrate
3	Meat & Alternatives

4. Bring to a boil, stirring, until slightly thickened. Reduce heat, cover and simmer over medium-low heat, stirring occasionally, for 1 hour.

5. Meanwhile, peel carrots and halve lengthwise. Cut carrots and celery into 1½-inch (4 cm) chunks. Peel potatoes and quarter. Add vegetables to pan. Cover and simmer for 30 minutes.

6. Trim ends of beans and cut into 2-inch (5 cm) lengths. Stir into stew mixture, adding more broth if necessary until vegetables are just covered. Cover and simmer for 30 minutes more or until vegetables are tender. Remove bay leaf and stir in parsley. Adjust seasoning with pepper to taste.

Freezing and Reheating Soups, Stews and Casseroles

Label and date containers and casseroles before refrigerating or freezing.

Meat- and chicken-based soups, stews and casseroles can be kept safely for up to 3 days in the refrigerator; vegetable-based dishes can be kept refrigerated for 5 days.

To reheat, place in saucepan over medium heat, stirring occasionally, until piping hot; or place in covered casserole and bake in 350°F (180°C) oven for 30 to 45 minutes or until piping hot; or microwave, covered with lid or microwave-safe plastic wrap, at Medium-High (70%) for 9 to 15 minutes, stirring occasionally, or until heated through to center. For single servings, microwave, covered, at Medium-High (70%) for 3 to 5 minutes.

Stews, soups and casseroles can be frozen for up to 3 months. Defrost in refrigerator overnight and reheat as directed above.

Tip

To save time, every few weeks I finely chop a few bunches of parsley, pack into a container and freeze. Though not suitable for fresh salads, the frozen parsley is perfect to add to soups, stews, meat loaves and casseroles.

SERVES 8
(2½ oz/75 g lean meat only per serving, with gravy and vegetables)

When I was growing up, pot roasts were a staple in my house. I can remember coming home from school to the tantalizing smell of a roast slowly braising in the oven. This recipe features a richly colored sauce from caramelized onions and a subtle sweet-sour taste from the beer and brown sugar. It's delicious served with creamy mashed potatoes or egg noodles.

Tip

Use a light-colored beer, or an amber one, such as pale ale. For a robust-flavored stew, try a dark beer, such as porter or stout.

Pot Roast with Beer and Caramelized Onions

● Preheat oven to 325°F (160°C)

I	beef pot roast, such as cross-rib, rump or brisket (about 3 lbs/1.5 kg)	I
¼ cup	all-purpose flour	50 mL
2 tbsp	vegetable oil (approx.), divided	25 mL
4	medium onions, halved lengthwise and thinly sliced (about 1¼ lbs/625 g)	4
2 tbsp	packed brown sugar	25 mL
2	bay leaves	2
I tsp	salt	5 mL
½ tsp	ground cinnamon	2 mL
½ tsp	ground ginger	2 mL
½ tsp	freshly ground black pepper	2 mL
3	large cloves garlic, finely chopped	3
2 tbsp	balsamic vinegar	25 mL
I	bottle (12 oz/341 mL) beer	I
I	can (7½ oz/213 mL) tomato sauce	I
1½ lbs	carrots (about 8)	750 g
I	small rutabaga (about 1 lb/500 g)	I

1. On a large plate, roll meat in flour to coat. Shake off excess; reserve.

2. In a Dutch oven or large saucepan, heat 1 tbsp (15 mL) oil over medium-high heat. Brown meat on all sides, about 6 minutes. Transfer to a plate.

3. Reduce heat to medium. Add remaining oil to Dutch oven. Add onions, brown sugar, bay leaves, salt, cinnamon, ginger and pepper; cook, stirring often, for 12 to 15 minutes or until onions are softened and nicely colored. (Add more oil, if needed, to prevent onions from burning.)

NUTRITIONAL ANALYSIS PER SERVING

Calories	339
Carbohydrate	27 g
Fiber	4 g
Protein	30 g
Fat, total	12 g
Fat, saturated	3 g
Sodium	570 mg
Cholesterol	63 mg

AMERICA'S EXCHANGES PER SERVING

3½	Vegetable
½	Other Carbohydrate
3½	Lean Meat
½	Fat

CANADA'S CHOICES PER SERVING

1½	Carbohydrate
4	Meat & Alternatives

4. Add reserved flour and garlic; cook, stirring, for 30 seconds. Add vinegar; cook until evaporated. Pour in beer and tomato sauce; bring to a boil, stirring, until thickened. Return meat and accumulated juices to pan. Cover and roast in preheated oven for 2 hours.

5. Meanwhile, peel carrots and rutabaga; cut into 2- by $\frac{1}{2}$-inch (5 by 1 cm) strips. Add to beef. Cover and cook 1 to $1\frac{1}{2}$ hours more or until meat is tender.

6. Remove roast from pan; cut into thin slices. Arrange on serving platter; surround with vegetables. Skim any fat from sauce; remove bay leaves and spoon some sauce over meat and pour the rest into a warmed sauceboat to serve on the side.

Tip

To reduce the amount of fat used, when browning meat, pat meat dry with paper towels before cooking. Add a bit of the oil to the pan and heat until hot but not smoking. Add a small amount of the meat at a time until nicely colored; remove. Add a bit more oil to pan if necessary and reheat before adding next batch of meat.

Braised Beef Short Ribs

When it comes to favorite recipes, these slowly braised short ribs in a rich herb-orange-flavored sauce served with creamy mashed potatoes are the quintessence of comfort food.

Tip

For maximum flavor, braise meat the day before. Let cool, cover and refrigerate. Skim fat before reheating.

3 lbs	boneless beef short ribs	1.5 kg
2 tbsp	olive oil, divided	25 mL
2	onions, chopped	2
3	cloves garlic, finely chopped	3
1 tsp	dried rosemary or thyme leaves, crumbled	5 mL
1 tsp	salt	5 mL
½ tsp	freshly ground black pepper	2 mL
1½ cups	reduced-sodium beef broth (approx.)	375 mL
1 cup	canned tomatoes, including juice, chopped	250 mL
2 tbsp	Worcestershire sauce	25 mL
3	strips orange peel (3 inch/8 cm in length)	3

1. Pat short ribs dry with paper towels. In a Dutch oven or large saucepan, heat 1 tbsp (15 mL) oil over medium-high heat; brown short ribs in batches, adding remaining oil as needed, until nicely browned on all sides. Transfer to a plate.

2. Reduce heat to medium; cook onions, garlic, rosemary, salt and pepper, stirring often, for 5 minutes or until softened.

3. Add broth, tomatoes with juice, Worcestershire sauce and orange peel. Return beef and accumulated juices to pan; bring to a boil. Cover and reduce heat; simmer for 2 hours, adding additional broth to keep beef covered while braising, until beef is fork-tender. Remove meat and skim fat from pan juices before serving.

NUTRITIONAL ANALYSIS PER SERVING

Calories	352
Carbohydrate	6 g
Fiber	1 g
Protein	33 g
Fat, total	21 g
Fat, saturated	8 g
Sodium	730 mg
Cholesterol	77 mg

AMERICA'S EXCHANGES PER SERVING

1	Vegetable
4½	Medium-fat Meat

CANADA'S CHOICES PER SERVING

½	Carbohydrate
4½	Meat & Alternatives

SERVES 5
(2 pieces per
serving, with sauce)

To survive the six o'clock weeknight rush, batch-cook stews and sauce-based meals on weekends and keep in fridge for up to 3 days or freeze for easy reheating. When you breeze through the door at night, you simply have to decide whether you'll serve the stew with pasta or rice — and dinner's on the table.

Tip

Sun-dried tomatoes sold dry in packages are more economical than those packed in oil. To reconstitute, place in a bowl and cover with boiling water. Or cover with cold water and microwave at High for 2 minutes or until just boiling. Let stand for 10 minutes or until softened; drain and chop.

Everyone's Favorite Chicken Cacciatore

3 tbsp	all-purpose flour	45 mL
1/2 tsp	salt	2 mL
1/2 tsp	freshly ground black pepper	2 mL
2 lbs	skinless chicken thighs (about 10)	1 kg
4 tsp	olive oil, divided	20 mL
1	small onion, chopped	1
2	cloves garlic, finely chopped	2
3 cups	sliced mushrooms	750 mL
1/2 cup	white wine or reduced-sodium chicken broth	125 mL
1	can (19 oz/540 mL) tomatoes, including juice, chopped	1
1/3 cup	chopped sun-dried tomatoes	75 mL
1/4 cup	chopped fresh basil leaves or parsley or a mixture of both	50 mL

1. In a heavy plastic bag, shake together flour, salt and pepper. In batches, toss chicken to coat, shaking off excess.

2. In a Dutch oven or large saucepan, heat 1 tbsp (15 mL) oil over medium-high heat. Brown chicken on all sides. Transfer to a plate. Add remaining oil; cook onion, garlic and mushrooms, stirring, for 5 minutes or until softened.

3. Add wine; return chicken and any juices to pan along with tomatoes with juice and sun-dried tomatoes. Bring to a boil; reduce heat, cover and simmer for 35 minutes or until chicken is tender. Stir in basil; season with pepper to taste.

NUTRITIONAL ANALYSIS PER SERVING	
Calories	274
Carbohydrate	14 g
Fiber	3 g
Protein	28 g
Fat, total	11 g
Fat, saturated	3 g
Sodium	580 mg
Cholesterol	95 mg

AMERICA'S EXCHANGES PER SERVING	
2 1/2	Vegetable
3 1/2	Lean Meat

CANADA'S CHOICES PER SERVING	
1	Carbohydrate
3 1/2	Meat & Alternatives

SERVES 6

Some dishes never lose their appeal — like this old-fashioned favorite, which is perfect to make on a lazy Sunday afternoon. It requires a little time to prepare, but once the creamy chicken mixture and its golden biscuit crust is bubbling away in the oven, you'll be glad you made the effort. And so will your family.

Tips

I've chosen a biscuit crust for this cobbler, but you can omit the topping altogether and serve over rice or noodles.

Fines herbes, available in the spice section of your grocery store, contains dried parsley, chives, tarragon and chervil. You can also use an Italian herb mix of basil, oregano and marjoram.

Chicken-Vegetable Cobbler

● *12-cup (3 L) deep casserole dish*

2 lbs	chicken legs, with skin and excess fat removed	1 kg
3½ cups	water	875 mL
1 tsp	salt	5 mL
	Freshly ground black pepper	
1	bay leaf	1
2 tsp	butter	10 mL
2 cups	quartered mushrooms	500 mL
1	medium onion, chopped	1
1	large clove garlic, minced	1
2 tsp	dried fines herbes (see tip, at left) or dried basil	10 mL
⅓ cup	all-purpose flour	75 mL
3	carrots, peeled and sliced	3
2	stalks celery, chopped	2
½ cup	half-and-half (10%) cream	125 mL
1 cup	frozen peas	250 mL
¼ cup	chopped fresh parsley	50 mL
	Cheddar Biscuit Crust (see recipe, opposite)	

1. In a large saucepan, combine chicken, water, salt, pepper and bay leaf. Bring to a boil; reduce heat to medium-low, cover and simmer for 1 hour. Let stand until chicken is cool enough to handle. Pull chicken meat from bones; cut into bite-size pieces. Strain stock and skim off any fat; there should be 2½ cups (625 mL) of stock. Add water, if necessary. Discard bay leaf. Set aside.

2. In a large saucepan, melt butter over medium heat; cook mushrooms, onion, garlic and fines herbes, stirring often, for 5 minutes or until softened.

NUTRITIONAL ANALYSIS PER SERVING (with crust)

Calories	353
Carbohydrate	30 g
Fiber	4 g
Protein	25 g
Fat, total	15 g
Fat, saturated	7 g
Sodium	730 mg
Cholesterol	85 mg

AMERICA'S EXCHANGES PER SERVING	
1½	Starch
1	Vegetable
2½	Medium-fat Meat

CANADA'S CHOICES PER SERVING	
2	Carbohydrate
3½	Meat & Alternatives
½	Fat

3. Blend flour with a small amount of stock until smooth; add remaining stock. Stir into mushroom mixture; bring to a boil, stirring, until thickened and smooth. Preheat oven to 400°F (200°C).

4. Add carrots and celery to saucepan; cover and simmer over low heat, stirring occasionally, for 15 minutes or until vegetables are just tender.

5. Add chicken, cream, peas and parsley; season with additional pepper to taste. Heat through. Spoon hot chicken mixture into casserole dish.

6. Meanwhile, prepare Cheddar Biscuit Crust. Spoon dough over top of hot chicken mixture. (If making chicken mixture ahead, cover and refrigerate; microwave at Medium-High (70%), or reheat in saucepan on stovetop until piping hot before topping with crust.)

7. Bake in preheated oven for 25 to 30 minutes or until crust is golden and filling is bubbly.

Tip

The chicken-vegetable mixture without the crust freezes well for up to 2 months.

Cheddar Biscuit Crust

¾ cup	all-purpose flour	175 mL
⅓ cup	shredded Cheddar cheese	75 mL
I tsp	baking powder	5 mL
¼ tsp	baking soda	I mL
2 tbsp	butter, melted	25 mL
½ cup	plain low-fat yogurt	125 mL

1. In a bowl, combine flour, cheese, baking powder and baking soda.

2. Stir butter into yogurt; stir into flour mixture just until combined.

Even if you don't have a lot of time to spend in the kitchen, you can rustle up a great-tasting stew using boneless chicken thighs and convenient frozen vegetables. This satisfying dish does away with browning the chicken. You'll save time but not lose any flavor. Serve over noodles.

Tip

Use 5 cups (1.25 L) fresh vegetables instead of frozen, if you wish. Cut them into bite-size pieces. For slower-cooking vegetables, such as carrots and celery, add them along with the chicken. For faster-cooking ones, such as broccoli and zucchini, add in the last 10 minutes of cooking.

Streamlined Chicken and Vegetable Stew

2 tsp	vegetable oil	10 mL
I	large onion, chopped	I
2	cloves garlic, finely chopped	2
I tsp	dried Italian herbs or fines herbes	5 mL
I lb	boneless skinless chicken thighs (about 8), cut into 1-inch (2.5 cm) cubes	500 g
3 tbsp	all-purpose flour	45 mL
2 cups	reduced-sodium chicken broth	500 mL
I	package (I lb/500 g) frozen mixed vegetables	I
	Freshly ground black pepper	

1. In a Dutch oven or large saucepan, heat oil over medium heat. Add onion, garlic and Italian herbs; cook, stirring, for 4 minutes or until lightly colored.

2. In a bowl, toss chicken with flour until well-coated. Add to pan along with any remaining flour; stir in broth. Bring to a boil and cook, stirring, until sauce thickens. Reduce heat, cover and simmer, stirring occasionally, for 20 minutes.

3. Add frozen vegetables; return to a boil. Season with pepper to taste. Reduce heat, cover and simmer for 10 minutes or until chicken and vegetables are tender.

NUTRITIONAL ANALYSIS PER SERVING	
Calories	275
Carbohydrate	25 g
Fiber	5 g
Protein	26 g
Fat, total	8 g
Fat, saturated	2 g
Sodium	360 mg
Cholesterol	75 mg

AMERICA'S EXCHANGES PER SERVING	
2	Vegetable
I	Other Carbohydrate
3	Lean Meat

CANADA'S CHOICES PER SERVING	
I ½	Carbohydrate
3	Meat & Alternatives

SERVES 6

*Economical chicken
thighs make a comforting
weeknight supper. Here
they star in a full-bodied
stew with chunks of
wholesome sweet potatoes.
It's equally good when
made with a winter squash,
such as butternut, instead.*

Tips

Replace sweet potatoes, if
desired, with 4 potatoes,
peeled and cubed, and
4 sliced carrots.

To prepare ahead, cover
and refrigerate for up to
3 days or freeze for up to
1 month.

Chicken and Sweet Potato Stew

3 tbsp	all-purpose flour	45 mL
1 tsp	salt	5 mL
1/2 tsp	freshly ground black pepper	2 mL
2 1/2 lbs	skinless chicken thighs (12 thighs)	1.25 kg
2 tbsp	vegetable oil, divided	25 mL
1	large onion, chopped	1
2	cloves garlic, finely chopped	2
1 1/2 tsp	mild curry paste or powder	7 mL
1 tsp	dried thyme leaves	5 mL
1/2 tsp	dried marjoram leaves	2 mL
1 1/2 cups	reduced-sodium chicken broth	375 mL
3	sweet potatoes (about 2 lbs/1 kg)	3
1/4 cup	chopped fresh parsley	50 mL

1. In a heavy plastic bag, shake together flour, salt and pepper. In batches, add chicken; shake to coat.

2. In a Dutch oven or large saucepan, heat 1 tbsp (15 mL) oil over medium-high heat; brown chicken on all sides. Transfer to a plate.

3. Add remaining oil to pan; reduce heat to medium. Cook onion, garlic, curry paste, thyme and marjoram, stirring, for 5 minutes or until softened.

4. Add broth; bring to a boil. Return chicken and any juices to pan; cover and simmer for 20 minutes. Peel and quarter sweet potatoes; cut into 2-inch (5 cm) chunks. Add to pan; simmer, covered, for 20 minutes or until tender. Stir in parsley.

NUTRITIONAL ANALYSIS PER SERVING	
Calories	362
Carbohydrate	33 g
Fiber	3 g
Protein	28 g
Fat, total	13 g
Fat, saturated	2 g
Sodium	660 mg
Cholesterol	95 mg

AMERICA'S EXCHANGES PER SERVING	
2	Starch
1/2	Vegetable
3 1/2	Lean Meat

CANADA'S CHOICES PER SERVING	
2	Carbohydrate
3 1/2	Meat & Alternatives

One-Pot Italian Sausages Braised with Potatoes

This rustic dish is perfect with a glass of red wine on a wind-down Friday night. Do give the fennel a try; when raw, this vegetable has an assertive anise taste. However, when cooked, it's much more mellow and inviting.

Tip

Consumers today are asking for leaner sausages. Look for both fresh and frozen sausages, made from turkey and other meats, that contain no more than 10 g of fat per 3½ ounces (100 g). Lower-fat sausages still contain significant amounts of sodium, so keep your portion to one.

Variation

Instead of fennel, use about 3 cups (750 mL) shredded cabbage.

1 lb	lean mild or hot Italian-style turkey sausages (see tip, at left)	500 g
2 tbsp	water (approx.)	25 mL
2 tsp	olive oil	10 mL
1	large onion, halved lengthwise, sliced	1
1	large bulb fennel, trimmed, cored and cut into strips	1
2	cloves garlic, finely chopped	2
1 tsp	dried oregano leaves	5 mL
4	medium potatoes, peeled and cubed (about 1½ lbs/750 g)	4
1	can (14 oz/398 mL) tomatoes, including juice, chopped	1
½ cup	reduced-sodium beef broth	125 mL
½ tsp	salt	2 mL
¼ tsp	freshly ground black pepper	1 mL
2 tbsp	chopped fresh parsley	25 mL

1. With a fork, prick sausages all over and place in large saucepan over medium-high heat. Add water and cook, turning often and adding more water as needed (to prevent sausages from sticking), for 10 to 12 minutes or until browned and no longer pink in center. Transfer to a cutting board. Let cool slightly; cut into slices.

2. Drain fat from pan; add oil, onion, fennel, garlic and oregano; cook, stirring, for 3 minutes or until softened. Add potatoes, tomatoes with juice, broth, salt and pepper; bring to a boil. Reduce heat, cover and cook for 15 minutes or until potatoes are almost tender. Return sausage to pan; cover and cook for 8 minutes or until potatoes are tender. Sprinkle with parsley.

NUTRITIONAL ANALYSIS PER SERVING	
Calories	222
Carbohydrate	25 g
Fiber	4 g
Protein	16 g
Fat, total	6 g
Fat, saturated	2 g
Sodium	725 mg
Cholesterol	81 mg

AMERICA'S EXCHANGES PER SERVING	
1	Starch
½	Other Carbohydrate
2	Lean Meat

CANADA'S CHOICES PER SERVING	
1½	Carbohydrate
2	Meat & Alternatives

Greek Lamb and Bean Stew

SERVES 6

Oregano-scented tomato sauce with a burst of heat from hot pepper flakes is the perfect foil for buttery lima beans and lamb.

Tips

Canned tomatoes are a great timesaver, but they do contain significant amounts of sodium. One 19-oz (540 mL) can of tomatoes contains about 800 mg of sodium, as compared to 50 mg in the same quantity of diced fresh tomatoes. If you are concerned about sodium, replace the canned tomatoes in this recipe with 3 large ripe tomatoes, peeled and chopped.

Stew can be cooked ahead and stored in a tightly covered container in the refrigerator for up to 3 days or frozen for up to 1 month.

● *Preheat oven to 350°F (180°C)*

4 tsp	olive oil, divided	20 mL
I lb	lean boneless lamb, cut into 1-inch (2.5 cm) pieces	500 g
I	Spanish onion (I lb/500 g), chopped	I
4	cloves garlic, finely chopped	4
I tbsp	dried oregano	15 mL
½ tsp	hot pepper flakes	2 mL
I	can (19 oz/540 mL) tomatoes, including juice, chopped	I
½ tsp	salt	2 mL
½ tsp	freshly ground black pepper	2 mL
3 cups	frozen lima beans	750 mL
I	large red bell pepper, seeded and cubed	I
I	large green bell pepper, seeded and cubed	I
½ cup	reduced-sodium chicken broth (approx.)	125 mL
¼ cup	chopped fresh parsley	50 mL

1. In a Dutch oven or large saucepan, heat 2 tsp (10 mL) oil over high heat; brown lamb, in batches if necessary. Transfer to a plate.

2. Add remaining oil to pan; reduce heat to medium. Add onion, garlic, oregano and hot pepper flakes; cook, stirring, for 5 minutes or until softened. Return meat to pan along with any juices. Add tomatoes with juice, salt and pepper; bring to boil. Reduce heat, cover and simmer for 45 minutes.

3. Add beans, red and green peppers and enough chicken broth to make a sauce-like consistency. Cover and bake in preheated oven for 40 minutes or until lamb is tender. Stir in parsley.

NUTRITIONAL ANALYSIS PER SERVING	
Calories	350
Carbohydrate	32 g
Fiber	7 g
Protein	27 g
Fat, total	12 g
Fat, saturated	4 g
Sodium	445 mg
Cholesterol	70 mg

AMERICA'S EXCHANGES PER SERVING	
I	Starch
3	Vegetable
2½	Medium-fat Meat
I	Fat

CANADA'S CHOICES PER SERVING	
2	Carbohydrate
3	Meat & Alternatives

SERVES 6

Sometimes you crave a dish that explodes with spicy flavors. The ginger and hot pepper flakes used here will satisfy that craving — and soothe your soul, too. I like to serve this spice-infused stew with basmati rice.

Tip

Buy a 3-lb (1.5 kg) leg of lamb or shoulder roast to get 1½ lbs (750 g) boneless lamb.

Variation

Spicy Beef Stew
Substitute an equal amount of lean stewing beef for the lamb; increase cooking time to 1½ hours or until meat is tender.

Spicy Lamb Stew

2 tbsp	vegetable oil (approx.), divided	25 mL
1½ lbs	lean boneless lamb, (cut into 1-inch/2.5 cm cubes)	750 g
1	large onion, chopped	1
2	cloves garlic, finely chopped	2
1 tbsp	minced fresh gingerroot	15 mL
1 tsp	ground cumin	5 mL
1 tsp	ground coriander	5 mL
½ tsp	ground cinnamon	2 mL
½ tsp	salt	2 mL
¼ tsp	hot pepper flakes, or to taste	1 mL
Pinch	ground cloves	Pinch
1 tbsp	all-purpose flour	15 mL
½ cup	plain low-fat yogurt	125 mL
1	large tomato, chopped	1
½ cup	reduced-sodium chicken broth or lamb stock	125 mL
¼ cup	chopped fresh cilantro or parsley	50 mL

1. In a large saucepan, heat 1 tbsp (15 mL) oil over medium-high heat; cook lamb in batches, adding more oil as needed, until browned on all sides. Remove from pan and set aside.

2. Reduce heat to medium. Add onion, garlic, ginger, cumin, coriander, cinnamon, salt, hot pepper flakes and cloves; cook, stirring, for 2 minutes or until softened.

3. Sprinkle with flour; stir in yogurt. Cook for 1 minute or until thickened. Add lamb with any accumulated juices, tomato and broth; bring to a boil. Reduce heat and simmer, covered, for 45 minutes or until lamb is tender. Sprinkle with cilantro or parsley before serving.

NUTRITIONAL ANALYSIS PER SERVING	
Calories	316
Carbohydrate	7 g
Fiber	1 g
Protein	30 g
Fat, total	18 g
Fat, saturated	6 g
Sodium	340 mg
Cholesterol	107 mg

AMERICA'S EXCHANGES PER SERVING	
½	Other Carbohydrate
4	Lean Meat
1	Fat

CANADA'S CHOICES PER SERVING	
½	Carbohydrate
4	Meat & Alternatives

SERVES 6

Richly flavored braised meats like veal are always a welcome choice for a family meal. I make them in advance, since their flavor improves when refrigerated and reheated the next day.

Tips

When a recipe calls for broth or stock, always use reduced-sodium or salt-free products. In this recipe, replacing the reduced-sodium broth with regular broth would increase the sodium by about 120 mg per serving. If you do need to use regular broth, remember to omit or cut down the salt in the recipe.

Serve this simple dish with noodles or creamy mashed potatoes.

Veal Braised with Onions

2 tbsp	olive oil, divided	25 mL
2 lbs	lean stewing veal, cut into ¾-inch (2 cm) cubes	1 kg
2	large onions, chopped	2
2	cloves garlic, finely chopped	2
2 tbsp	all-purpose flour	25 mL
1½ cups	reduced-sodium chicken broth	375 mL
½ cup	dry white wine or additional broth	125 mL
2 tbsp	tomato paste	25 mL
½ tsp	salt	2 mL
½ tsp	freshly ground black pepper	2 mL
¼ cup	chopped fresh parsley	50 mL
1 tsp	grated lemon zest	5 mL

1. In a Dutch oven or large saucepan, heat 1 tbsp (15 mL) oil over high heat; brown veal in batches. Transfer to a plate.

2. Reduce heat to medium; add remaining oil. Cook onions and garlic, stirring, for 5 minutes or until lightly colored. Blend in flour; stir in broth, wine and tomato paste. Add veal along with accumulated juices; season with salt and pepper. Bring to a boil.

3. Reduce heat, cover and simmer, stirring occasionally, for 50 minutes. Stir in parsley and lemon zest; cook, covered, for 10 minutes or until veal is tender.

NUTRITIONAL ANALYSIS PER SERVING	
Calories	250
Carbohydrate	9 g
Fiber	2 g
Protein	33 g
Fat, total	9 g
Fat, saturated	2 g
Sodium	410 mg
Cholesterol	127 mg

AMERICA'S EXCHANGES PER SERVING	
1½	Vegetable
4	Very Lean Meat
1	Fat

CANADA'S CHOICES PER SERVING	
½	Carbohydrate
4	Meat & Alternatives

SERVES 8

I like to make this delicious comfort stew ahead and have it tucked away in the freezer ready for company. Adding the peppers at the end of cooking helps keep their shape and lends a slightly smoky taste that lingers in your memory long after the last bite.

Tips

Use a combination of green, red and yellow peppers for maximum color effect.

The recipe can be prepared through Step 3 up to 48 hours ahead, then covered and refrigerated — or freeze for up to 3 months. Before reheating, let defrost in fridge overnight. Bring to a boil; cover and simmer for 20 minutes or until veal is thoroughly heated.

Veal Ragout with Sweet Peppers

3 lbs	lean stewing veal, cut into 1-inch (2.5 cm) cubes	1.5 kg
2 tbsp	all-purpose flour	25 mL
4 tbsp	olive oil (approx.), divided	60 mL
1	Spanish onion, chopped (about 1 lb/500 g)	1
4	large cloves garlic, finely chopped	4
1 tsp	dried thyme leaves	5 mL
1 tsp	paprika	5 mL
1	bay leaf	1
1 tsp	salt	5 mL
1/2 tsp	freshly ground black pepper	2 mL
1 cup	red wine or reduced-sodium beef broth	250 mL
4	tomatoes, chopped	4
4	bell peppers (any color), cubed	4
1/3 cup	chopped fresh parsley	75 mL

1. In a bowl, toss veal cubes with flour until well-coated. In a Dutch oven or large heavy saucepan, heat 1 tbsp (15 mL) oil over high heat. In small batches, add veal and cook until nicely browned on all sides, adding more oil as needed. Remove and set aside.

2. Reduce heat to medium. Add 1 tbsp (15 mL) more oil. Add onion, garlic, thyme, paprika, bay leaf, salt and pepper; cook, stirring often, for 5 minutes or until softened.

3. Add wine and bring to a boil. Stir in veal along with accumulated juices; add tomatoes. Bring to boil; reduce heat to medium-low and simmer, covered, for 1 1/4 to 1 1/2 hours or until veal is tender.

NUTRITIONAL ANALYSIS PER SERVING	
Calories	311
Carbohydrate	14 g
Fiber	3 g
Protein	37 g
Fat, total	11 g
Fat, saturated	2 g
Sodium	395 mg
Cholesterol	143 mg

AMERICA'S EXCHANGES PER SERVING	
2 1/2	Vegetable
4 1/2	Lean Meat

CANADA'S CHOICES PER SERVING	
1	Carbohydrate
4 1/2	Meat & Alternatives

4. Shortly before serving, heat 1 tbsp (15 mL) oil in a large nonstick skillet over high heat; cook pepper cubes, stirring, for 2 to 3 minutes or until lightly colored. Reduce heat to medium-low, cover and simmer for 8 to 10 minutes or until tender-crisp.

5. Add peppers to veal; stir in parsley and simmer for 5 minutes to let the flavors blend. Adjust seasoning with pepper to taste. Remove bay leaf.

Variation

Beef Ragout with Sweet Peppers Substitute an equal amount of lean stewing beef for the veal.

Do you pine for the days when elegant luncheons were in fashion? Here's a special dish reminiscent of white-gloved ladies at lunch. Serve this richly flavored sauce over rice, or toss with pasta.

Tips

Cooked lobster can replace part of the shellfish.

For a less expensive version, omit scallops and shrimp; increase the amount of sole, haddock or cod to 1 ½ lbs (750 g).

The moisture content of fresh and frozen seafood differs and may result in a finished sauce being too thick or too thin. To eliminate this problem, poach the uncooked seafood first in wine and stock.

Seafood Supreme

1 cup	fish broth or reduced-sodium chicken broth (approx.)	250 mL
½ cup	dry white wine or vermouth	125 mL
8 oz	sole or other white fish, cut into 1-inch (2.5 cm) cubes	250 g
8 oz	small scallops	250 g
8 oz	small cooked, peeled shrimp	250 g
3 tbsp	butter	45 mL
⅓ cup	finely chopped green onions	75 mL
¾ cup	diced red bell pepper	175 mL
¼ cup	all-purpose flour	50 mL
½ cup	half-and-half (10%) cream	125 mL
	Freshly ground white pepper	
2 tbsp	chopped fresh dill or parsley	25 mL

1. In a saucepan, bring broth and wine to a boil over medium heat. Add sole cubes; poach 2 minutes (start timing when fish is added to broth). Add scallops; poach 1 to 2 minutes more or until seafood is opaque. Remove using a slotted spoon; place in a bowl along with shrimp and set aside.

2. Strain liquid into glass measure; there should be 2 cups (500 mL). Add water, if necessary; reserve.

3. In a saucepan, melt butter over medium heat. Add green onions and red peppers; cook, stirring, for 3 minutes or until softened. Blend in flour; pour in reserved liquid. Bring to a boil, stirring, until sauce is very thick and smooth. Stir in cream; bring to a boil.

4. Just before serving, add seafood and heat through. Season with white pepper to taste; stir in dill. Serve immediately.

SERVES 4

Gingerroot adds a vibrant flavor to this stew. Serve steaming bowls with chunks of crusty whole-grain bread. It's a complete meal!

Easy Curried Fish Stew

2 tsp	vegetable oil	10 mL
1	small onion, finely chopped	1
1 tbsp	minced fresh gingerroot	15 mL
2 tsp	mild curry paste or powder	10 mL
2 cups	diced peeled potatoes	500 mL
1 1/2 cups	thinly sliced carrots	375 mL
2 1/4 cups	fish broth or reduced-sodium chicken broth	550 mL
1 tbsp	cornstarch	15 mL
	Freshly ground black pepper	
1 1/2 cups	snow peas, ends trimmed, halved	375 mL
1 lb	fresh or frozen haddock or cod fillets, cut into chunks	500 g

1. In a large saucepan, heat oil over medium heat. Add onion, ginger and curry paste; cook, stirring, for 2 minutes or until softened. Add potatoes, carrots and fish broth. Bring to a boil; reduce heat, cover and simmer for 10 to 12 minutes or until vegetables are just tender.

2. In a bowl, blend cornstarch with 2 tbsp (25 mL) water. Add to stew and cook, stirring, until thickened. Season with pepper to taste. Stir in snow peas and fish; cover and cook for 2 to 3 minutes or until snow peas are tender-crisp and fish is opaque.

NUTRITIONAL ANALYSIS PER SERVING

Calories	258
Carbohydrate	26 g
Fiber	5 g
Protein	26 g
Fat, total	5 g
Fat, saturated	1 g
Sodium	470 mg
Cholesterol	65 mg

AMERICA'S EXCHANGES PER SERVING

1	Starch
2	Vegetable
3	Very Lean Meat

CANADA'S CHOICES PER SERVING

1 1/2	Carbohydrate
3	Meat & Alternatives

Jambalaya

Jambalaya is the perfect party dish. A one-pot wonder originating from New Orleans, it pleases all palates with its piquant flavors and mix of chicken, sausage and shrimp. Set this dish on the table and watch it disappear.

Tips

Try not to stir the jambalaya or the rice will turn sticky.

If using chicken thighs with the bone in, increase cooking time by 5 to 10 minutes.

For the sausage, try andouille or chorizo.

Variation

Try replacing the sausage with 4 oz (125 g) cubed smoked ham.

- Preheat oven to 350°F (180°C)
- 12-cup (3 L) baking dish or ovenproof serving dish

4 tsp	olive oil	20 mL
1½ lbs	boneless skinless chicken thighs (about 12), halved	750 g
4 oz	smoked sausage, thinly sliced	125 g
1	large onion, chopped	1
3	cloves garlic, finely chopped	3
2	stalks celery, diced	2
2	bell peppers, any color, diced	2
1 tsp	dried thyme leaves	5 mL
1 tsp	paprika	5 mL
½ tsp	salt	2 mL
¼ tsp	ground allspice	1 mL
¼ tsp	cayenne pepper	1 mL
1½ cups	long-grain rice	375 mL
1	can (14 oz/398 mL) tomatoes, including juice, chopped	1
1¾ cups	reduced-sodium chicken broth	425 mL
8 oz	medium raw shrimp, in the shell	250 g
⅓ cup	chopped fresh parsley	75 mL
3	green onions, finely chopped	3

1. In a Dutch oven, heat oil over medium-high heat. Add chicken and cook for 5 minutes or until browned on both sides. Transfer to a plate.

2. Add sausage, onion, garlic, celery, bell peppers, thyme, paprika, salt, allspice and cayenne to Dutch oven; cook, stirring often, for 5 minutes or until vegetables are softened. Return chicken to dish along with accumulated juices. Stir in rice, tomatoes with juice and broth; bring to a boil.

3. Transfer to baking dish. Cover and bake for 30 minutes or until rice and chicken are just tender. Stir in shrimp, parsley and green onions; cover and bake for 5 to 8 minutes or until shrimp turns pink.

NUTRITIONAL ANALYSIS PER SERVING

Calories	371
Carbohydrate	35 g
Fiber	2 g
Protein	28 g
Fat, total	13 g
Fat, saturated	4 g
Sodium	630 mg
Cholesterol	115 mg

AMERICA'S EXCHANGES PER SERVING

2	Starch
1	Vegetable
3½	Lean Meat

CANADA'S CHOICES PER SERVING

2	Carbohydrate
3½	Meat & Alternatives

A Pound
of Ground

Best-Ever Meat Loaf

SERVES 6

I could make this juicy meat loaf with Fluffy Garlic Mashed Potatoes (see recipes, page 192) every week and never hear a complaint from my family that it's served too often.

Tips

I like to use oatmeal as a binder, since it gives a coarser texture to the meat loaf (bread crumbs produce a finer one).

I always double the recipe and wrap the extra cooked meat loaf in plastic wrap, then in foil, for the freezer. Defrost overnight in the fridge. To reheat, cut into slices and place in saucepan. Moisten with about ½ cup (125 mL) reduced-sodium beef broth; set over medium heat until piping hot. Or place meat loaf and broth in casserole dish and microwave at Medium (50%) until heated through.

- Preheat oven to 350°F (180°C)
- 9- by 5-inch (2 L) loaf pan

2 tsp	vegetable oil	10 mL
1	medium onion, chopped	1
2	cloves garlic, minced	2
1 tsp	dried basil leaves	5 mL
1 tsp	dried marjoram leaves	5 mL
¾ tsp	salt	4 mL
¼ tsp	freshly ground black pepper	1 mL
1	egg	1
¼ cup	chili sauce or ketchup	50 mL
1 tbsp	Worcestershire sauce	15 mL
2 tbsp	chopped fresh parsley	25 mL
1½ lbs	lean ground beef	750 g
½ cup	quick-cooking rolled oats	125 mL

1. In a large nonstick skillet, heat oil over medium heat. Add onion, garlic, basil, marjoram, salt and pepper; cook, stirring, for 3 minutes or until softened. (Or place in microwave-safe bowl; microwave, covered, at High for 3 minutes.) Let cool slightly.

2. In a large bowl, beat egg; stir in onion mixture, chili sauce, Worcestershire sauce and parsley. Crumble beef over mixture and sprinkle with oats. Using a wooden spoon, gently mix until evenly combined.

3. Press mixture lightly into loaf pan. Bake in preheated oven for 1 hour or until meat thermometer registers 170°F (80°C). Let stand for 5 minutes. Drain pan juices; turn out onto a plate and cut into thick slices.

NUTRITIONAL ANALYSIS PER SERVING

Calories	264
Carbohydrate	10 g
Fiber	2 g
Protein	24 g
Fat, total	14 g
Fat, saturated	5 g
Sodium	540 mg
Cholesterol	90 mg

AMERICA'S EXCHANGES PER SERVING

½	Starch
3	Medium-fat Meat

CANADA'S CHOICES PER SERVING

½	Carbohydrate
3	Meat & Alternatives
1	Fat

Turkey Meat Loaf

I serve this family favorite meat loaf accompanied with fluffy mashed potatoes and Lemon-Glazed Baby Carrots (see recipe, page 211) for a delicious, economical supper.

Variation

Mini Turkey Meat Loaves
Divide into 12 balls; lightly press into muffin cups. Bake at 400°F (200°C) for 20 minutes or until no longer pink in center. Drain off juice.

- Preheat oven to 350°F (180°C)
- 9- by 5-inch (2 L) loaf pan

2 tsp	olive oil	15 mL
I	onion, finely chopped	I
I	large clove garlic, finely chopped	I
1/2 tsp	dried thyme or marjoram leaves	2 mL
I tsp	salt	5 mL
1/4 tsp	freshly ground black pepper	I mL
I	egg	I
1/4 cup	reduced-sodium chicken broth	50 mL
I tsp	grated lemon zest	5 mL
1/2 cup	dry seasoned bread crumbs	125 mL
2 tbsp	finely chopped fresh parsley	25 mL
1 1/2 lbs	lean ground turkey or chicken	750 g

1. In a large nonstick skillet, heat oil over medium heat; cook onion, garlic, thyme, salt and pepper, stirring often, for 3 minutes or until softened. Let cool slightly.

2. In a bowl, beat together egg, broth and lemon zest. Stir in onion mixture, bread crumbs, parsley and turkey. Using a wooden spoon, gently mix until evenly combined.

3. Press mixture lightly into loaf pan. Bake in preheated oven for 1 hour or until meat thermometer registers 170°F (80°C). Let stand for 5 minutes. Drain pan juices; turn out onto a plate and cut into thick slices.

NUTRITIONAL ANALYSIS PER SERVING	
Calories	219
Carbohydrate	9 g
Fiber	I g
Protein	25 g
Fat, total	9 g
Fat, saturated	3 g
Sodium	580 mg
Cholesterol	99 mg

AMERICA'S EXCHANGES PER SERVING	
1/2	Starch
3 1/2	Very Lean Meat
I	Fat

CANADA'S CHOICES PER SERVING	
1/2	Carbohydrate
3	Meat & Alternatives

Everyone loves meat loaf and mashed potatoes. Here's a creative way to prepare this favorite combo.

Tips

Can be prepared up to 1 day ahead; cover and refrigerate. Add 10 minutes to the baking time.

Make a double batch of meat loaf. Press into two pie plates; bake according to recipe until no longer pink in center. Top one meat loaf with mashed potatoes; let the other one cool, wrap well and freeze for another meal.

Meat Loaf and Mashed Potato Pie

- Preheat oven to 375°F (190°C)
- Deep 9- or 10-inch (23 or 25 cm) pie plate, sprayed with vegetable cooking spray

MASHED POTATO TOPPING

6	medium Russet or Yukon Gold potatoes, peeled and cubed (about 2 lbs/1 kg)	6
½ cup	light sour cream	125 mL
	Freshly ground black pepper	

MEAT LOAF

1	egg	1
¼ cup	chili sauce or ketchup	50 mL
¼ cup	minced onion	50 mL
1	clove garlic, minced	1
1 tsp	Worcestershire sauce	5 mL
½ tsp	salt	2 mL
¼ tsp	freshly ground black pepper	1 mL
¼ cup	dry seasoned bread crumbs	50 mL
1 lb	lean ground beef or veal	500 g
½ cup	shredded light Cheddar cheese	125 mL

1. *Mashed Potato Topping:* In a large saucepan, cook potatoes in boiling salted water until tender. Drain well and return to saucepan; place over low heat for 1 minute to dry. Mash until smooth. Beat in sour cream; season with pepper to taste. Keep warm over low heat.

2. *Meat Loaf:* In a bowl, beat egg; stir in chili sauce, onion, garlic, Worcestershire sauce, salt and pepper. Mix in bread crumbs and beef. Press evenly into pie plate. Bake for 25 to 30 minutes or until no longer pink in center; drain juice.

3. Spread mashed potatoes over meat; sprinkle with cheese. Bake for 20 to 25 minutes or until cheese is melted.

NUTRITIONAL ANALYSIS PER SERVING	
Calories	309
Carbohydrate	29 g
Fiber	2 g
Protein	21 g
Fat, total	11 g
Fat, saturated	5 g
Sodium	525 mg
Cholesterol	77 mg

AMERICA'S EXCHANGES PER SERVING	
2	Starch
2	Medium-fat Meat

CANADA'S CHOICES PER SERVING	
2	Carbohydrate
2	Meat & Alternatives
1	Fat

Instead of ketchup, serve salsa (see tip, below) with this oregano-and-cumin-flavored meat loaf.

Tip

Driven by the popularity of Tex-Mex foods, salsa sales now rival those of ketchup. Salsa usually contains little or no salt and is much lower in sodium than ketchup. As always, check labels for sodium content.

Variation

Instead of all beef, use ¾ lb (375 g) each ground pork and ground beef, if desired.

Southwest Meat Loaf

- Preheat oven to 350°F (180°C)
- 9- by 5-inch (2 L) loaf pan

2 tsp	olive oil	10 mL
1	small green bell pepper, finely chopped	1
2	jalapeño peppers, minced (optional)	2
1	onion, finely chopped	1
2	cloves garlic, finely chopped	2
1 tsp	dried oregano leaves	5 mL
1 tsp	ground cumin	5 mL
1 tsp	salt	5 mL
¼ tsp	freshly ground black pepper	1 mL
1	egg	1
2 tsp	Dijon mustard	10 mL
1 cup	soft fresh bread crumbs	250 mL
1½ lbs	lean ground beef or veal	750 g

1. In a large nonstick skillet, heat oil over medium heat; cook green pepper, jalapeño peppers, if using, onion, garlic, oregano, cumin, salt and pepper, stirring often, for 5 minutes or until softened. Let cool slightly.

2. In a bowl, beat egg and mustard. Stir in vegetable mixture, bread crumbs and beef. Using a wooden spoon, gently mix until evenly combined.

3. Press mixture lightly into loaf pan. Bake in preheated oven for 1 hour or until meat thermometer registers 170°F (80°C). Let stand for 5 minutes. Drain pan juices; turn out onto a plate and cut into thick slices.

NUTRITIONAL ANALYSIS PER SERVING	
Calories	247
Carbohydrate	7 g
Fiber	1 g
Protein	23 g
Fat, total	13 g
Fat, saturated	5 g
Sodium	545 mg
Cholesterol	89 mg

AMERICA'S EXCHANGES PER SERVING	
1	Vegetable
3	Medium-fat Meat

CANADA'S CHOICES PER SERVING	
½	Carbohydrate
3	Meat & Alternatives

Mushrooms add a depth of flavor to this dish and help cut down on the amount of meat used. When my children were young and didn't like the sight of mushrooms in their favorite supper dish, I would finely chop the mushrooms in a food processor and they never knew the difference.

Tip

To speed preparation, the lean ground beef in this recipe is not drained after browning. If drained, the fat per serving would be reduced by 3 g. If you plan not to drain fat from ground beef, look for a package that is 85% or more lean (U.S.) or lean or extra-lean (Canada).

Shepherd's Pie

- Preheat oven to 375°F (190°C)
- Shallow 12- by 8-inch (2.5 L) baking dish

MASHED POTATO TOPPING

6	potatoes, peeled and cubed (about 2 lbs/1 kg)	6
¾ cup	low-fat milk or buttermilk	175 mL
	Freshly ground black pepper	

MEAT LAYER

1 lb	lean ground beef or veal	500 g
8 oz	mushrooms, sliced or chopped	250 g
1	medium onion, finely chopped	1
2	cloves garlic, minced	2
½ tsp	dried thyme leaves	2 mL
½ tsp	dried marjoram leaves	2 mL
3 tbsp	all-purpose flour	45 mL
1½ cups	reduced-sodium beef broth	375 mL
2 tbsp	tomato paste (see tip, page 139)	25 mL
2 tsp	Worcestershire sauce	10 mL
	Freshly ground black pepper	
1	can (12 oz/341 mL) corn kernels, drained	1

BREAD CRUMB TOPPING

2 tbsp	dry bread crumbs	25 mL
2 tbsp	freshly grated Parmesan cheese	25 mL
¼ tsp	paprika	1 mL

1. *Mashed Potato Topping:* In a large saucepan of boiling salted water, cook potatoes until tender. Drain and mash using a potato masher or electric mixer; beat in milk until smooth. Season with pepper to taste.

2. *Meat Layer:* In a large nonstick skillet, cook beef over medium-high heat, breaking up with a wooden spoon, for 5 minutes or until no longer pink.

NUTRITIONAL ANALYSIS PER SERVING

Calories	320
Carbohydrate	40 g
Fiber	4 g
Protein	22 g
Fat, total	9 g
Fat, saturated	4 g
Sodium	425 mg
Cholesterol	41 mg

AMERICA'S EXCHANGES PER SERVING

2½	Starch
1	Vegetable
1½	Lean Meat

CANADA'S CHOICES PER SERVING

2½	Carbohydrate
2	Meat & Alternatives

3. Reduce heat to medium. Add mushrooms, onion, garlic, thyme and marjoram; cook, stirring often, for 5 minutes or until softened. Sprinkle with flour; stir in broth, tomato paste and Worcestershire sauce. Bring to a boil; reduce heat and simmer, covered, for 8 minutes. Season with pepper to taste.

4. Spread meat mixture in baking dish; layer with corn. Place small spoonfuls of mashed potatoes over corn and spread evenly.

5. *Bread Crumb Topping:* In a small bowl, combine bread crumbs, Parmesan and paprika; sprinkle over top of shepherd's pie.

6. Bake in preheated oven for 25 to 30 minutes or until filling is bubbly.

Tip

This recipe can be prepared through Step 4 up to 1 day ahead. Cover and refrigerate. Increase baking time to 40 minutes.

MAKES 4 BURGERS

If burgers are starting to become mundane, put some excitement in those patties. Instead of cheese on top of the burger, put shredded cheese right in the ground meat mixture for moist burgers with a twist. Mama would be pleased.

Tip

For an easy vegetable topping, cut green or red bell peppers and a large red onion into rounds, brush lightly with olive oil and grill alongside burgers.

Mama's Italian Cheeseburgers

● *Preheat barbecue, sprayed with vegetable cooking spray*

1/4 cup	tomato pasta sauce	50 mL
1/4 cup	grated or minced onion	50 mL
1	clove garlic, minced	1
1/4 tsp	dried basil or oregano leaves	1 mL
1/4 tsp	salt	1 mL
1/4 tsp	freshly ground black pepper	1 mL
1/2 cup	shredded part-skim mozzarella cheese	125 mL
1/3 cup	dry seasoned bread crumbs	75 mL
1 lb	lean ground beef	500 g
4	hamburger buns, split and lightly toasted	4

1. In a bowl, combine tomato pasta sauce, onion, garlic, basil, salt and pepper. Stir in cheese and bread crumbs; mix in beef. Shape into four 3/4-inch (2 cm) thick patties.

2. Place on grill over medium-high heat; cook, turning once, for 6 to 7 minutes on each side or until no longer pink in center. Serve in buns.

NUTRITIONAL ANALYSIS PER SERVING

Calories	307
Carbohydrate	15 g
Fiber	1 g
Protein	27 g
Fat, total	15 g
Fat, saturated	6 g
Sodium	505 mg
Cholesterol	69 mg

AMERICA'S EXCHANGES PER SERVING

1	Starch
3 1/2	Lean Meat
1/2	Fat

CANADA'S CHOICES PER SERVING

1	Carbohydrate
3 1/2	Meat & Alternatives

*We often think of meatballs
with spaghetti, but they
are equally delicious in a
variety of sauces such as
Sweet-and-Sour (see recipe,
page 138).*

Tips

To freeze meatballs, place
in a single layer on a baking
sheet until frozen then
transfer to a covered
container or freezer bag.
To quickly reheat, place
the frozen meatballs in a
casserole dish, cover and
microwave at Medium
(50%) until defrosted.

For Spaghetti with
Meatballs, see recipe,
page 159.

Basic Meatballs

● *Preheat oven to 400°F (200°C)* ● *Baking sheets*

1	large egg	1
2 tbsp	water	25 mL
1/3 cup	fine dry bread crumbs	75 mL
1/3 cup	minced green onions	75 mL
1	clove garlic, minced	1
3/4 tsp	salt	4 mL
1/2 tsp	freshly ground black pepper	2 mL
1 1/2 lbs	lean ground beef	750 g

1. In a large bowl, beat egg with water; stir in bread crumbs, green onions, garlic, salt and pepper. Mix in beef.

2. Form by tablespoonfuls (15 mL) into balls; arrange on baking sheets. Bake for 15 minutes or until browned and no longer pink inside. Drain on paper towels.

**NUTRITIONAL ANALYSIS
PER SERVING**

Calories	168
Carbohydrate	4 g
Fiber	0 g
Protein	17 g
Fat, total	9 g
Fat, saturated	3 g
Sodium	305 mg
Cholesterol	68 mg

**AMERICA'S EXCHANGES
PER SERVING**

2 1/2	Lean Meat
1/2	Fat

**CANADA'S CHOICES
PER SERVING**

2 1/2	Meat & Alternatives

SERVES 8

*Take advantage
of supermarket specials
for lean ground beef and
cook batches of meatballs
ahead. Freeze them (see
tip, page 137) for
this quick dish.*

Tip

Be sure to use unseasoned
rice vinegar, that is, without
added sugar and salt.
Seasoned rice vinegar,
sometimes called sushi
seasoning, contains about
300 mg of sodium per
tablespoon (15 mL).

Everyone's Favorite Sweet-and-Sour Meatballs

1	can (14 oz/398 mL) pineapple chunks	1
1/4 cup	packed brown sugar	50 mL
1/4 cup	rice vinegar (not seasoned)	50 mL
1/4 cup	reduced-sodium soy sauce	50 mL
4 tsp	cornstarch	20 mL
48	Basic Meatballs (see recipe, page 137)	48

1. Drain pineapple chucks and reserve. Measure pineapple juice; add enough water to make 1 cup (250 mL).

2. In a large saucepan, combine pineapple juice, brown sugar, vinegar, soy sauce and cornstarch. Place over medium heat, stirring, until sauce comes to a boil and thickens.

3. Stir in meatballs and pineapple chunks; cook for 3 to 5 minutes or until piping hot.

NUTRITIONAL ANALYSIS PER SERVING

Calories	236
Carbohydrate	21 g
Fiber	1 g
Protein	18 g
Fat, total	9 g
Fat, saturated	3 g
Sodium	550 mg
Cholesterol	68 mg

AMERICA'S EXCHANGES PER SERVING

1/2	Starch
1/2	Fruit
1/2	Other Carbohydrate
2	Medium-fat Meat

CANADA'S CHOICES PER SERVING

1 1/2	Carbohydrate
2 1/2	Meat & Alternatives

Salisbury Steak

Here's a satisfying meat loaf–like dish with a tasty gravy that's wonderful accompanied by creamy mashed potatoes. Peel the potatoes and start them cooking on the stovetop before you begin preparing the patties so both will be ready at about the same time.

Tip

Unless you're using expensive tomato paste from a tube, you can freeze leftover tomato paste. Put tablespoons (15 mL) of leftover canned tomato paste on a waxed paper–lined plate or in ice-cube trays; freeze until firm. Transfer to a small freezer bag and have handy in the freezer to add to recipes.

1	egg	1
2 tbsp	fine dry bread crumbs	25 mL
1	small onion, minced, divided	1
1 tbsp	Worcestershire sauce, divided	15 mL
1/2 tsp	salt	2 mL
1/4 tsp	freshly ground black pepper	1 mL
1 lb	lean ground beef	500 g
2 tsp	vegetable oil	10 mL
1 1/2 cups	chopped mushrooms	375 mL
1	clove garlic, minced	1
1/4 tsp	dried thyme or marjoram leaves	1 mL
1 tbsp	all-purpose flour	15 mL
1 cup	reduced-sodium beef broth	250 mL
1 tbsp	tomato paste	15 mL

1. In a bowl, beat egg; stir in bread crumbs, half the onion, half the Worcestershire sauce, salt and pepper; mix in ground beef. Form into four patties, each 4 inches (10 cm) in diameter.

2. In a large nonstick skillet, heat oil over medium-high heat; brown patties, about 2 minutes on each side. Transfer to a plate and drain fat from pan. Add remaining onion, mushrooms, garlic and thyme to skillet; cook, stirring, for 2 minutes or until softened.

3. Sprinkle with flour; stir in remaining Worcestershire sauce, beef broth and tomato paste. Cook, stirring, for 1 minute or until thickened. Return patties to skillet; reduce heat, cover and simmer, turning once, for 10 minutes or until patties are no longer pink in center.

NUTRITIONAL ANALYSIS PER SERVING	
Calories	270
Carbohydrate	9 g
Fiber	1 g
Protein	25 g
Fat, total	15 g
Fat, saturated	5 g
Sodium	595 mg
Cholesterol	106 mg

AMERICA'S EXCHANGES PER SERVING	
1/2	Starch
1	Vegetable
3	Lean Meat
1	Fat

CANADA'S CHOICES PER SERVING	
1/2	Carbohydrate
3	Meat & Alternatives
1/2	Fat

SERVES 4

Leftover pasta in the fridge is perfect for this pizza-like supper dish that's especially appealing to the younger set.

Tip

It's easy to turn this recipe into a vegetarian dish — just omit the meat. Broccoli can be replaced by zucchini, bell peppers or whatever vegetables you have on hand.

Kids' Favorite Spaghetti Pie

- Preheat oven to 350°F (180°C)
- 9- or 10-inch (23 or 25 cm) glass pie plate, sprayed with vegetable cooking spray

8 oz	lean ground beef or chicken	250 g
2 cups	sliced mushrooms	500 mL
1	small onion, chopped	1
1	large clove garlic, finely chopped	1
1 1/2 tsp	dried oregano leaves	7 mL
2 cups	Big-Batch Tomato Sauce (see recipe, page 156) or commercial tomato-based pasta sauce	500 mL
2 cups	small broccoli florets	500 mL
3 cups	cooked spaghetti or other string pasta (6 oz/175 g uncooked)	750 mL
1 1/2 cups	shredded part-skim mozzarella cheese	375 mL

1. In a medium saucepan over medium-high heat, cook beef, breaking up with a wooden spoon, for 4 minutes or until no longer pink. Drain in sieve to remove any fat. Return to saucepan. Add mushrooms, onion, garlic, and oregano; cook, stirring, for 3 minutes or until vegetables are softened. Add tomato pasta sauce; cover and simmer for 10 minutes.

2. Rinse broccoli; place in a covered casserole dish. Microwave at High for 2 to 2 1/2 minutes or until bright green and almost tender. Rinse under cold water to chill; drain.

3. Arrange spaghetti in pie plate. Spread with meat sauce; top with broccoli and sprinkle with cheese. Bake for 25 to 30 minutes or until cheese is melted. Cut into wedges and serve.

NUTRITIONAL ANALYSIS PER SERVING

Calories	455
Carbohydrate	47 g
Fiber	6 g
Protein	32 g
Fat, total	16 g
Fat, saturated	8 g
Sodium	760 mg
Cholesterol	59 mg

AMERICA'S EXCHANGES PER SERVING

2	Starch
1	Other Carbohydrate
3 1/2	Lean Meat
1	Fat

CANADA'S CHOICES PER SERVING

2 1/2	Carbohydrate
4	Meat & Alternatives

No need to buy pricey packaged dinner mixes when it's easy to create your own. It's just a matter of using pantry staples already in your cupboard. In about the time it takes to fix an accompanying salad, this dish is ready to set on the table.

Tip

Use your own homemade tomato sauce (see Big-Batch Tomato Sauce, page 156) or, to save time, use one of the many top-notch bottled sauces now available in supermarkets. The amount of sodium in commercial sauces can be as high as 700 mg per 1/2 cup (125 mL), so check labels to find a lower-sodium variety.

Beefy Macaroni with Zucchini

1 lb	lean ground beef or turkey	500 g
1	small onion, chopped	1
2	cloves garlic, finely chopped	2
1 tsp	dried basil or oregano leaves	5 mL
1 1/2 cups	Big-Batch Tomato Sauce (see recipe, page 156) or commercial tomato-based pasta sauce	375 mL
1 1/2 cups	reduced-sodium chicken or beef broth (approx.)	375 mL
1 cup	elbow macaroni	250 mL
2	medium zucchini, cut into 1/2-inch (1 cm) cubes	2

1. In a large nonstick skillet over medium-high heat, cook beef, breaking up with a wooden spoon, for 5 minutes or until no longer pink. Add onion, garlic and basil; cook, stirring, for 2 minutes.
2. Add tomato pasta sauce and broth; bring to a boil. Stir in pasta; reduce heat, cover and cook for 2 minutes.
3. Stir in zucchini; cook, covered, stirring occasionally, adding more broth if needed, for 5 to 7 minutes or until pasta and zucchini are tender.

NUTRITIONAL ANALYSIS PER SERVING	
Calories	404
Carbohydrate	33 g
Fiber	4 g
Protein	29 g
Fat, total	17 g
Fat, saturated	6 g
Sodium	545 mg
Cholesterol	68 mg

AMERICA'S EXCHANGES PER SERVING	
1	Starch
1	Other Carbohydrate
3 1/2	Medium-fat Meat

CANADA'S CHOICES PER SERVING	
2	Carbohydrate
3	Meat & Alternatives
1/2	Fat

Beef and Potato Hash

Looking for a fast-track dinner? Convenient frozen hash browns come to the rescue along with quick-cooking ground beef for a family-pleasing meal.

Tips

Oil is used in the manufacture of most frozen potato products, including hash browns. Avoid those prepared with partially hydrogenated oils; these oils are high in trans fatty acids.

To defrost hash browns, place on a plate lined with paper towels; microwave at High for 3 to 4 minutes, stirring once.

1 lb	lean ground beef	500 g
2 tsp	Worcestershire sauce	10 mL
2 tsp	vegetable oil	10 mL
1	medium onion, chopped	1
1	green bell pepper, chopped	1
4 cups	frozen hash brown potatoes, defrosted	1 L
	Freshly ground black pepper	

1. In a large nonstick skillet over medium-high heat, cook beef, breaking up with a wooden spoon, for 5 minutes or until no longer pink. Place in sieve to drain any fat; transfer to a bowl. Stir in Worcestershire sauce.

2. Add oil to skillet; cook onion, green pepper and potatoes, stirring often, for 8 to 10 minutes or until potatoes are golden. Add ground beef; season with pepper to taste. Cook for 2 minutes or until heated through.

NUTRITIONAL ANALYSIS PER SERVING

Calories	244
Carbohydrate	16 g
Fiber	1 g
Protein	16 g
Fat, total	13 g
Fat, saturated	3 g
Sodium	95 mg
Cholesterol	40 mg

AMERICA'S EXCHANGES PER SERVING

1	Starch
½	Vegetable
2	Lean Meat
1	Fat

CANADA'S CHOICES PER SERVING

1	Carbohydrate
2	Meat & Alternatives
1	Fat

SERVES 4

Some days you just don't have time to think about what's for supper. Rather than getting take-out, here's an easy dish that counts on convenient frozen vegetables to get dinner on the table in 20 minutes.

Tips

By draining the fat from the ground beef, you can reduce the fat in this recipe by 5 to 6 g per serving.

Cook extra rice ahead and keep it handy in the fridge. Or use instant rice prepared according to package directions.

Speedy Beef and Vegetable Fried Rice

I lb	lean ground beef or chicken	500 g
3	green onions, sliced	3
I	large clove garlic, minced	I
2 tsp	minced fresh gingerroot	10 mL
2 cups	cooked rice, preferably basmati	500 mL
4 cups	frozen Oriental mixed vegetables (see tip, page 118)	I L
3 tbsp	reduced-sodium soy sauce	45 mL

1. In a large nonstick skillet over medium-high heat, cook beef, breaking up with a wooden spoon, for 5 minutes or until no longer pink. Add green onions, garlic and ginger; cook, stirring, for 1 minute. Stir in rice; cook, stirring, for 2 minutes.

2. Add vegetables and soy sauce. Reduce heat to medium, cover and cook, stirring occasionally, (adding 2 tbsp/25 mL water if necessary to prevent from sticking), for 5 minutes or until vegetables are tender.

NUTRITIONAL ANALYSIS PER SERVING	
Calories	427
Carbohydrate	40 g
Fiber	4 g
Protein	28 g
Fat, total	16 g
Fat, saturated	6 g
Sodium	455 mg
Cholesterol	68 mg

AMERICA'S EXCHANGES PER SERVING	
2	Starch
2	Vegetable
3	Lean Meat
I	Fat

CANADA'S CHOICES PER SERVING	
2½	Carbohydrate
3	Meat & Alternatives
I	Fat

SERVES 6

Looking for an inviting dinner-in-a-dish everyone in the family will enjoy? This hearty chili-flavored beef casserole topped with a tasty cornbread crust fills the bill. I've kept the seasonings tame so it appeals to the sensitive taste buds of young diners, but boost the seasonings if desired.

Tip

Although canned vegetables contain significant amounts of sodium, many frozen vegetables are quite low in sodium. In this recipe, the corn contributes 2 mg of sodium, compared with about 140 mg for the same amount of canned corn.

Tex-Mex Cobbler

● *Preheat oven to 400°F (200°C)*
● *10-cup (2.5 L) casserole dish*

1 lb	lean ground beef	500 g
1	onion, chopped	1
2	cloves garlic, finely chopped	2
1	large green bell pepper, chopped	1
2 tsp	chili powder	10 mL
1 tsp	dried oregano leaves	5 mL
½ tsp	ground cumin	2 mL
2 tbsp	all-purpose flour	25 mL
1½ cups	reduced-sodium beef broth	375 mL
1	can (7½ oz/213 mL) tomato sauce	1
1½ cups	frozen corn kernels	375 mL
	Cheddar Cornbread Crust (see recipe, opposite)	

1. In a large nonstick skillet over medium-high heat, cook beef, breaking up with a wooden spoon, for 5 minutes or until no longer pink.

2. Stir in onion, garlic, green pepper, chili powder, oregano and cumin; cook, stirring, for 4 minutes or until softened.

3. Blend in flour; stir in broth and tomato sauce. Bring to a boil, stirring, until thickened. Reduce heat, cover and simmer for 5 minutes. Stir in corn; cook for 2 minutes or until piping hot. Spoon into casserole dish.

4. Meanwhile, make Cheddar Cornbread Crust. Spoon over beef mixture in an even layer. Bake for 20 to 25 minutes or until top is light golden and filling is bubbly.

NUTRITIONAL ANALYSIS PER SERVING

Calories	379
Carbohydrate	39 g
Fiber	5 g
Protein	25 g
Fat, total	15 g
Fat, saturated	6 g
Sodium	605 mg
Cholesterol	84 mg

AMERICA'S EXCHANGES PER SERVING

2	Starch
1	Vegetable
2½	Lean Meat
1	Fat

CANADA'S CHOICES PER SERVING

2	Carbohydrate
2½	Meat & Alternatives
2	Fat

Cheddar Cornbread Crust

⅔ cup	whole wheat flour	150 mL
½ cup	cornmeal	125 mL
1½ tsp	granulated sugar	7 mL
1½ tsp	baking powder	7 mL
½ cup	shredded light Cheddar cheese	125 mL
1	egg	1
⅔ cup	low-fat milk	150 mL

1. In a bowl, combine flour, cornmeal, sugar and baking powder; mix in cheese.

2. In another bowl, beat together egg and milk. Stir into dry ingredients to make a smooth batter.

Tip

Add 1 tsp (5 mL) additional chili powder and ¼ tsp (1 mL) hot pepper flakes, or to taste, to the ground beef mixture for a more assertive chili flavor.

SERVES 8

This homey dish is a great way to take advantage of the economical vegetables on display at country farm markets in the fall.

Tip

It is quicker not to drain ground beef when cooking it, but you will get less fat and fewer calories when you do. The amount of fat that can be drained varies with the fat content of the ground beef. You will be able to drain about 23 g of fat from 1 lb (500 g) of lean ground beef (around 85% lean/15% fat), and 60 to 65 g from the same amount of regular ground beef (around 75% lean/25% fat).

Example: A recipe making 4 servings calls for 1 lb (500 g) of regular ground beef. If the meat is drained, it will contribute 13 g of fat per serving; undrained, it will contribute about 28 g.

Rice and Beef–Stuffed Peppers

- Preheat oven to 350°F (180°C)
- 13- by 9-inch (3 L) baking dish

4	large green or red bell peppers	4
8 oz	lean ground beef	250 g
8 oz	lean turkey sausages, casing removed	250 g
2 tsp	olive oil	10 mL
4	green onions, sliced	4
2	cloves garlic, finely chopped	2
1 tsp	dried basil leaves	5 mL
2	large tomatoes, peeled, seeded and diced	2
1 cup	frozen or fresh corn kernels	250 mL
1/2 tsp	freshly ground black pepper	2 mL
1 1/2 cups	cooked rice	375 mL
3/4 cup	shredded part-skim mozzarella cheese	175 mL
1/4 cup	freshly grated Parmesan cheese	50 mL
1/2 cup	chicken broth	125 mL

1. Cut peppers in half lengthwise. Remove seeds and membranes. In a large pot of boiling salted water, blanch peppers for 5 minutes; drain and place cut side down on rack to cool.

2. In a large nonstick skillet, cook beef and sausage over medium-high heat, breaking up with a wooden spoon, for 5 to 7 minutes or until no longer pink. Drain in sieve to remove fat; set aside.

NUTRITIONAL ANALYSIS PER SERVING	
Calories	228
Carbohydrate	21 g
Fiber	2 g
Protein	17 g
Fat, total	9 g
Fat, saturated	4 g
Sodium	450 mg
Cholesterol	54 mg

AMERICA'S EXCHANGES PER SERVING	
1	Starch
1 1/2	Vegetable
1 1/2	Medium-fat Meat

CANADA'S CHOICES PER SERVING	
1	Carbohydrate
2	Meat & Alternatives

3. Add oil to skillet; cook green onions, garlic and basil, stirring, for 2 minutes or until softened. Stir in tomatoes, corn and pepper; cook, stirring, for 3 to 5 minutes or until corn is tender. Stir in rice and ground beef; cook, stirring, for 3 minutes or until heated through.

4. In a bowl, combine mozzarella and Parmesan cheeses. Stir half of the cheese into rice mixture. Arrange peppers, cut side up, in casserole dish. Fill with rice mixture; top with remaining cheese. Pour broth into casserole dish; bake peppers in preheated oven for 30 to 35 minutes or until top is golden and filling is piping hot.

Tip

Cook extra rice ahead and keep it handy in the fridge. Or use instant rice prepared according to package directions.

SERVES 4

Serve this one-pot family favorite with warm pita bread along with a cucumber and tomato salad.

Beef and Potato Curry

1 lb	lean ground beef	500 g
1	onion, chopped	1
2	large cloves garlic, finely chopped	2
2 tbsp	tomato paste	25 mL
1 tbsp	mild curry paste or powder	15 mL
1 tbsp	minced fresh gingerroot	15 mL
1/4 tsp	salt	1 mL
4	potatoes, peeled and diced (about 1 1/2 lbs/750 g)	4
2 cups	reduced-sodium beef broth	500 mL
1 1/2 cups	frozen peas	375 mL
1/4 cup	chopped fresh cilantro or parsley (optional)	50 mL

1. In a large Dutch oven or saucepan over medium-high heat, cook beef, breaking up with a wooden spoon, for 5 minutes or until no longer pink. Drain off fat. Add onion, garlic, tomato paste, curry paste, ginger and salt; cook, stirring, for 5 minutes or until onion is softened.

2. Add potatoes and broth; bring to boil. Reduce heat, cover and simmer for 15 minutes. Stir in peas; cook, covered, for 5 minutes or until potatoes and peas are tender. Stir in cilantro, is using.

NUTRITIONAL ANALYSIS PER SERVING

Calories	378
Carbohydrate	36 g
Fiber	5 g
Protein	28 g
Fat, total	13 g
Fat, saturated	5 g
Sodium	700 mg
Cholesterol	58 mg

AMERICA'S EXCHANGES PER SERVING

2	Starch
1	Vegetable
3	Lean Meat
1/2	Fat

CANADA'S CHOICES PER SERVING

2	Carbohydrate
3	Meat & Alternatives

MAKES 12 ROLLS
(2 rolls per serving)

Satisfying casseroles like this one are always a welcome choice when planning make-ahead meals for the freezer.

Tips

Cooked cabbage rolls can be frozen for up to 2 months.

To easily chop canned tomatoes, run a knife through the tomatoes right in the can.

If inner cabbage leaves are not softened, blanch cabbage again in boiling water to soften leaves.

Stuffed Cabbage Rolls

- Preheat oven to 350°F (180°C)
- 12-cup (3 L) casserole dish

1	medium head green cabbage, cored (about 3 lbs/1.5 kg)	1
4 tsp	vegetable oil	20 mL
1	large onion, finely chopped	1
2	large cloves garlic, finely chopped	2
1 tsp	paprika	5 mL
1½ cups	cooked rice	375 mL
1 lb	lean ground beef	500 g
	Freshly ground black pepper	
1	can (28 oz/796 mL) plum tomatoes, including juice	1
2 tsp	packed brown sugar	10 mL

1. In a large pot of boiling salted water, cook cabbage for 5 to 6 minutes or until leaves are softened. Drain; rinse under cold water, carefully separating 12 leaves. Using a knife, trim coarse veins from cabbage leaves.

2. In a large saucepan, heat oil over medium heat; cook onion, garlic and paprika, stirring, for 5 minutes or until softened. In a bowl, combine half the onion mixture, rice, beef, 1 tsp (5 mL) salt and ½ tsp (2 mL) pepper; mix well.

3. In a food processor, purée tomatoes, including juice. Add with brown sugar to onion mixture in saucepan; bring to a boil. Cover and reduce heat; simmer for 15 minutes, stirring occasionally. Season with pepper to taste.

4. Spoon ¼ cup (50 mL) rice mixture onto each cabbage leaf just above stem. Fold ends and sides over filling; roll up. Spoon 1 cup (250 mL) tomato sauce in bottom of Dutch oven or casserole dish. Layer with half the cabbage rolls; pour 1 cup (250 mL) tomato sauce over. Top with remaining cabbage rolls and pour remaining sauce over. Cover and bake for 1 to 1¼ hours or until rolls are tender.

NUTRITIONAL ANALYSIS PER SERVING	
Calories	284
Carbohydrate	22 g
Fiber	2 g
Protein	18 g
Fat, total	14 g
Fat, saturated	4 g
Sodium	350 mg
Cholesterol	45 mg

AMERICA'S EXCHANGES PER SERVING	
½	Starch
2	Vegetable
2	Medium-fat Meat
1	Fat

CANADA'S CHOICES PER SERVING	
1½	Carbohydrate
2	Meat & Alternatives
1	Fat

Amazing Chili

Every cook has a special version of chili. Here's mine — it's meaty and nicely spiced with just the right amount of beans. Not everyone agrees that beans belong in a chili — witness the Texas version dubbed "bowl of red" — but I love the way the beans absorb the spices and rich tomato flavor.

Tip

The flavor of the chili hinges on the quality of chili powder used. Most powders are a blend of dried, ground mild chilies, as well as cumin, oregano, garlic and salt. Read the list of ingredients to be sure you're not buying one with starch and sugar fillers. Chili powder should not be confused with powdered or ground chilies of the cayenne pepper variety.

1 1/2 lbs	lean ground beef	750 g
2	onions, chopped	2
3	cloves garlic, finely chopped	3
2	stalks celery, chopped	2
1	large green bell pepper, chopped	1
2 tbsp	chili powder	25 mL
1 1/2 tsp	dried oregano leaves	7 mL
1 1/2 tsp	ground cumin	7 mL
1/2 tsp	hot pepper flakes or to taste	2 mL
1	can (28 oz/796 mL) tomatoes, including juice, chopped	1
1 cup	reduced-sodium beef broth	250 mL
1	can (19 oz/540 mL) pinto or red kidney beans, drained and rinsed	1
1/4 cup	chopped fresh parsley or cilantro	50 mL

1. In a large Dutch oven or saucepan, cook beef over medium-high heat, breaking up with a wooden spoon, for about 7 minutes or until no longer pink. Place in strainer and drain fat. Return beef to pan.

2. Reduce heat to medium. Add onions, garlic, celery, green pepper, chili powder, oregano, cumin and hot pepper flakes; cook, stirring often, for 5 minutes or until vegetables are softened.

3. Stir in tomatoes with juice and broth. Bring to a boil; reduce heat, cover and simmer, stirring occasionally, for 1 hour.

4. Add beans and parsley; cover and simmer for 10 minutes more.

NUTRITIONAL ANALYSIS PER SERVING	
Calories	263
Carbohydrate	24 g
Fiber	6 g
Protein	22 g
Fat, total	9 g
Fat, saturated	3 g
Sodium	500 mg
Cholesterol	45 mg

AMERICA'S EXCHANGES PER SERVING	
2	Vegetable
1	Other Carbohydrate
3	Lean Meat
1	Fat

CANADA'S CHOICES PER SERVING	
1	Carbohydrate
3	Meat & Alternatives

This beanless chili has a hot kick to it, so reduce the amount of pepper flakes if you prefer it on the tamer side. Ladle into bowls and have ready shredded light Cheddar cheese, sliced green onions, sour cream and chopped cilantro so everyone can choose their fixings. Terrific served with Cheddar Drop Biscuits (see recipe, page 254).

Tip

If you wish to add beans, omit cornmeal; add 2 cans (each 19 oz/540 mL) red kidney beans, drained and rinsed, to chili instead.

Dynamite Beanless Chili

3 lbs	lean ground beef	1.5 kg
1 tbsp	olive oil	15 mL
2	large onions, chopped	2
6	cloves garlic, finely chopped	6
5 to 6	jalapeño peppers, minced	5 to 6
3 tbsp	chili powder	45 mL
1 tbsp	dried oregano leaves	15 mL
1 tbsp	ground cumin	15 mL
2	bay leaves	2
1 tsp	salt	5 mL
2 tsp	hot pepper flakes or to taste	10 mL
1	can (28 oz/596 mL) tomatoes, including juice, chopped	1
2 cups	reduced-sodium beef broth	500 mL
1	can (5 1/2 oz/156 g) tomato paste	1
3	red or green bell peppers, diced	3
1/4 cup	cornmeal	50 mL

1. In a large Dutch oven or stockpot, cook beef over medium-high heat in two batches, breaking up with a wooden spoon, for about 7 minutes or until no longer pink. Place beef in strainer and drain fat. Transfer to a bowl.

2. Reduce heat to medium; add oil to pan. Cook onions, garlic, jalapeño peppers, chili powder, oregano, cumin, bay leaves, salt and hot pepper flakes, stirring, for 5 minutes or until softened.

3. Return meat to pan; add tomatoes with juice, 1 1/4 cups (300 mL) water, broth and tomato paste. Bring to a boil; simmer, covered, for 30 minutes, stirring occasionally. Add bell peppers; cook for 30 minutes more.

4. In a bowl, stir together 1/4 cup (50 mL) water with cornmeal; stir into meat mixture. Cook for 10 minutes or until sauce is thickened. Remove bay leaves before serving.

NUTRITIONAL ANALYSIS PER SERVING	
Calories	260
Carbohydrate	13 g
Fiber	3 g
Protein	23 g
Fat, total	13 g
Fat, saturated	5 g
Sodium	665 mg
Cholesterol	59 mg

AMERICA'S EXCHANGES PER SERVING	
2	Vegetable
3	Lean Meat
1	Fat

CANADA'S CHOICES PER SERVING	
1/2	Carbohydrate
3	Meat & Alternatives

SERVES 6

Here's a streamlined version of chili that's a snap. Make a double batch and have containers stashed away in the freezer for quick microwave meals. Just ladle into bowls and, if desired, top with shredded Monterey Jack cheese. Set out a basket of crusty bread — supper is that easy.

Tips

Add just a pinch of hot pepper flakes for a mild chili; but if you want to turn up the heat, use amount specified in the recipe.

Bottled pasta sauces are great timesavers, but they can be very high in sodium. Compare labels and choose a lower-sodium variety.

20-Minute Chili

1 lb	lean ground beef or turkey	500 g
1	large onion, chopped	1
2	large cloves garlic, finely chopped	2
1	large green bell pepper, chopped	1
4 tsp	chili powder	20 mL
1 tbsp	all-purpose flour	15 mL
1 tsp	dried basil leaves	5 mL
1 tsp	dried oregano leaves	5 mL
1/2 tsp	hot pepper flakes or to taste	2 mL
2 cups	tomato pasta sauce	500 mL
1 1/3 cups	reduced-sodium beef broth	325 mL
1	can (19 oz/540 mL) kidney or pinto beans, drained and rinsed	1
	Freshly ground black pepper	

1. In a large Dutch oven or saucepan over medium-high heat, cook beef, breaking up with a wooden spoon, for 5 minutes or until no longer pink. Drain off fat.

2. Reduce heat to medium. Add onion, garlic, green pepper, chili powder, flour, basil, oregano and hot pepper flakes; cook, stirring, for 4 minutes or until vegetables are softened.

3. Stir in tomato sauce and broth. Bring to a boil; cook, stirring, until thickened. Add beans; season with pepper to taste. Reduce heat and simmer, covered, for 10 minutes.

NUTRITIONAL ANALYSIS PER SERVING

Calories	278
Carbohydrate	29 g
Fiber	9 g
Protein	22 g
Fat, total	9 g
Fat, saturated	3 g
Sodium	640 mg
Cholesterol	40 mg

AMERICA'S EXCHANGES PER SERVING

2	Vegetable
1	Other Carbohydrate
2 1/2	Lean Meat
1/2	Fat

CANADA'S CHOICES PER SERVING

1 1/2	Carbohydrate
2 1/2	Meat & Alternatives

SERVES 4

Ground meats provide versatile options for the harried cook. Serve this tasty ground chicken dish with a salad or green vegetable such as broccoli. Dinner is ready in about 30 minutes.

Chicken Paprika with Noodles

1 lb	extra-lean ground chicken or turkey	500 g
2 tsp	vegetable oil	10 mL
1	medium onion, chopped	1
8 oz	mushrooms, sliced	250 g
1 tbsp	paprika	15 mL
2 tbsp	all-purpose flour	25 mL
1⅓ cups	reduced-sodium chicken broth	325 mL
½ cup	light sour cream	125 mL
2 tbsp	chopped fresh dill or parsley	25 mL
	Freshly ground black pepper	
8 oz	fettuccine or broad egg noodles	250 g

1. In a large nonstick skillet over medium-high heat, cook chicken, breaking up with a wooden spoon, for 5 minutes or until no longer pink. With a slotted spoon, transfer chicken to a plate lined with a paper towel. Drain fat from skillet.

2. Heat oil in skillet. Add onion, mushrooms and paprika; cook, stirring often, for 3 minutes or until vegetables are softened.

3. Sprinkle with flour; stir in broth and return chicken to skillet. Bring to a boil; cook, stirring, until thickened. Reduce heat, cover and simmer for 5 minutes. Remove from heat and stir in sour cream (it may curdle if added over the heat) and dill; season with pepper to taste.

4. Meanwhile, cook pasta in a large pot of boiling salted water until tender but firm. Drain well. Return to pot and toss with chicken mixture. Serve immediately.

NUTRITIONAL ANALYSIS PER SERVING

Calories	468
Carbohydrate	53 g
Fiber	6 g
Protein	32 g
Fat, total	14 g
Fat, saturated	3 g
Sodium	520 mg
Cholesterol	156 mg

AMERICA'S EXCHANGES PER SERVING

3	Starch
1	Vegetable
3	Lean Meat
½	Fat

CANADA'S CHOICES PER SERVING

3	Carbohydrate
3½	Meat & Alternatives

Terrific Chicken Burgers

Accompany these patties with stir-fried rice and vegetables.

I	egg	I
½ cup	fine dry bread crumbs	125 mL
⅓ cup	finely chopped green onions	75 mL
I tsp	ground coriander	5 mL
I tsp	grated lemon zest	5 mL
½ tsp	salt	2 mL
¼ tsp	freshly ground black pepper	I mL
I lb	ground chicken or turkey	500 g
I tbsp	vegetable oil	15 mL

1. In a bowl, beat egg; stir in bread crumbs, green onions, coriander, lemon zest, salt and pepper; mix in chicken. With wet hands, shape into four patties, each 4 inches (10 cm) in diameter.

2. In a large nonstick skillet, heat oil over medium heat; cook patties for 5 to 6 minutes on each side or until golden brown on outside and no longer pink in center.

NUTRITIONAL ANALYSIS PER SERVING	
Calories	291
Carbohydrate	11 g
Fiber	1 g
Protein	23 g
Fat, total	17 g
Fat, saturated	1 g
Sodium	490 mg
Cholesterol	47 mg

AMERICA'S EXCHANGES PER SERVING	
½	Starch
3	Medium-fat Meat
½	Fat

CANADA'S CHOICES PER SERVING	
½	Carbohydrate
3	Meat & Alternatives
1	Fat

Pasta and Grains

Here's an indispensable sauce I always have handy in the freezer to use as a base for my family's favorite pasta dishes. It's a versatile sauce and I've included several ways to serve it in this book.

Tips

In summer, instead of canned tomatoes, I make this sauce with 5 lbs (2.5 kg) of fresh ripe tomatoes, preferably the plum variety. To prepare, remove tomato cores. Cut an X in the bottom of each. Plunge in boiling water for 30 seconds to loosen skins. Chill in cold water; drain. Slip off skins; cut tomatoes in half crosswise and squeeze out seeds. Chop finely.

Instead of dried basil and oregano, replace dried herbs with $\frac{1}{3}$ cup (75 mL) chopped fresh basil; add towards end of cooking.

To save time, chop vegetables in the food processor.

Big-Batch Tomato Sauce

1 tbsp	olive oil	15 mL
1	medium onion, finely chopped	1
2	medium carrots, peeled and finely chopped	2
1	stalk celery, including leaves, finely chopped	1
4	cloves garlic, finely chopped	4
1 tbsp	dried basil leaves	15 mL
1$\frac{1}{2}$ tsp	dried oregano leaves	7 mL
1 tsp	granulated sugar	5 mL
$\frac{1}{2}$ tsp	freshly ground black pepper	2 mL
1	bay leaf	1
2	cans (28 oz/796 mL) plum tomatoes, including juice, chopped	2
1	can (5$\frac{1}{2}$ oz/156 mL) tomato paste	1
$\frac{1}{4}$ cup	finely chopped fresh parsley	50 mL

1. In a large Dutch oven or saucepan, heat oil over medium-high heat. Add onion, carrots, celery, garlic, basil, oregano, sugar, pepper and bay leaf; cook, stirring often, for 5 minutes or until vegetables are softened.

2. Stir in tomatoes with juice, tomato paste and 1 tomato-paste can of water. Bring to a boil; reduce heat and simmer, partially covered, for 35 to 40 minutes, stirring occasionally, until slightly thickened. Remove bay leaf; stir in parsley. Let cool; pack into containers and refrigerate or freeze.

NUTRITIONAL ANALYSIS PER SERVING	
Calories	57
Carbohydrate	11 g
Fiber	2 g
Protein	2 g
Fat, total	1 g
Fat, saturated	0 g
Sodium	210 mg
Cholesterol	0 mg

AMERICA'S EXCHANGES PER SERVING	
2	Vegetable

CANADA'S CHOICES PER SERVING	
$\frac{1}{2}$	Carbohydrate

SERVES 8
(1 tbsp/15 mL per serving)

Pesto keeps well for up to a week in the refrigerator, or pack into a small airtight container and freeze for up to 1 month.

Tip

Whenever you use a spoonful of the pesto, cover the surface of the pesto with a bit more oil to seal in flavors.

Basil Pesto

1 ½ cups	lightly packed fresh basil leaves	375 mL
2	cloves garlic, coarsely chopped	2
2 tbsp	pine nuts or lightly toasted walnuts	25 mL
¼ cup	olive oil (approx.)	50 mL
¼ cup	freshly grated Parmesan cheese	50 mL
	Freshly ground black pepper	

1. In a food processor, combine basil, garlic and pine nuts. While machine is running, add oil in a stream and process until smooth. Add a bit more oil if pesto appears dry.
2. Stir in Parmesan cheese; season with pepper to taste. Place in a small container; cover with a thin layer of oil and refrigerate.

NUTRITIONAL ANALYSIS PER SERVING	
Calories	89
Carbohydrate	1 g
Fiber	0 g
Protein	2 g
Fat, total	9 g
Fat, saturated	2 g
Sodium	60 mg
Cholesterol	2 mg

AMERICA'S EXCHANGES PER SERVING
2 Fat

CANADA'S CHOICES PER SERVING
2 Fat

SERVES 12
(1 tbsp/15 mL per
serving)

For a fast dinner, toss this pesto with 8 oz (250 g) pasta, cooked according to package directions, or swirl it into soup for a wonderful burst of flavor.

Tips

Make sure to purchase sun-dried tomatoes that are not packed in oil.

If fresh basil is unavailable, increase parsley to 1 cup (250 mL) and add 1 tbsp (15 mL) dried basil leaves.

Sun-Dried Tomato Pesto

1/2 cup	sun-dried tomatoes	125 mL
1/2 cup	lightly packed fresh basil leaves (see tip, at left)	125 mL
1/2 cup	lightly packed fresh parsley	125 mL
1	large clove garlic	1
1/3 cup	vegetable broth	75 mL
2 tbsp	olive oil	25 mL
1/3 cup	freshly grated Parmesan cheese	75 mL
1/2 tsp	freshly ground black pepper	2 mL

1. In a bowl, cover sun-dried tomatoes with boiling water; let stand for 10 minutes or until softened. Drain and pat dry; chop coarsely.

2. In a food processor, combine rehydrated tomatoes, basil, parsley and garlic. With motor running, add broth and oil in a stream. Stir in Parmesan cheese and pepper.

NUTRITIONAL ANALYSIS PER SERVING	
Calories	41
Carbohydrate	2 g
Fiber	0 g
Protein	2 g
Fat, total	3 g
Fat, saturated	1 g
Sodium	115 mg
Cholesterol	2 mg

AMERICA'S EXCHANGES PER SERVING
1/2   Fat

CANADA'S CHOICES PER SERVING
1/2   Fat

Spaghetti with Meatballs

This dish is the essence of Italian cooking — comforting, hearty and sure to please.

3 cups	Big-Batch Tomato Sauce (see recipe, page 156)	750 mL
24	Basic Meatballs (half the recipe, see page 137)	24
12 oz	spaghetti or other string pasta	375 g
1/3 cup	freshly grated Parmesan cheese	75 mL

1. In a large saucepan, combine tomato sauce and meatballs; bring to a boil. Reduce heat, cover and simmer for 15 minutes.

2. Cook pasta in a large pot of boiling water until tender but firm; drain well and toss with sauce. Place in serving bowls and sprinkle with Parmesan cheese.

How to Cook Pasta

You can ruin a good pasta dish if you don't cook the pasta properly. The most common error is not using enough water to boil the pasta — with the result that it cooks unevenly and sticks together.

To cook 8 to 12 oz (250 to 375 g) of pasta: Using a large pot, bring 12 cups (3 L) of water to a full rolling boil. Add up to 1 tsp (5 mL) salt and all the pasta at once. (Do not add oil.) Stir immediately to prevent pasta from sticking. Cover with a lid to return water quickly to full boil. Then uncover and stir occasionally. Taste to see if pasta is al dente, or firm to the bite. Drain immediately. Unless directed otherwise, never rinse pasta — this chills it and removes the coating of starch that helps sauce cling to pasta. Return to pot or place in large warmed serving bowl; add the sauce and toss until well coated. Serve immediately.

NUTRITIONAL ANALYSIS PER SERVING	
Calories	436
Carbohydrate	60 g
Fiber	5 g
Protein	25 g
Fat, total	11 g
Fat, saturated	4 g
Sodium	575 mg
Cholesterol	52 mg

AMERICA'S EXCHANGES PER SERVING	
3	Starch
2	Vegetable
2	Medium-fat Meat

CANADA'S CHOICES PER SERVING	
3 1/2	Carbohydrate
2	Meat & Alternatives
1/2	Fat

Intensely flavored thanks to the addition of red wine — this easy pasta dish suits those nights when you crave something simple but satisfying.

Variation

Instead of ground beef, use half veal and half pork or a combination of all three.

Spaghetti with Meat Sauce

12 oz	lean ground beef	375 g
½ cup	red wine or reduced-sodium beef broth	125 mL
3 cups	Big-Batch Tomato Sauce (see recipe, page 156)	750 mL
	Freshly ground pepper and hot pepper flakes	
12 oz	spaghetti	375 g
½ cup	freshly grated Parmesan cheese	125 mL

1. In a large nonstick skillet over medium-high heat, cook beef, breaking up with a wooden spoon, for 5 minutes, or until no longer pink. Drain off fat. Add wine; cook until partly reduced.

2. Stir in tomato sauce; season with pepper and hot pepper flakes to taste. Reduce heat, cover and simmer for 15 minutes.

3. Cook pasta in a large pot of boiling water until tender but firm; drain well and toss with sauce. Place in serving bowls and sprinkle with Parmesan cheese.

Freezing and Refrigerating Pasta

Here are some general guidelines for making pasta dishes ahead and refrigerating or freezing:

- Make pasta sauces up to 2 days ahead and refrigerate, or freeze for up to 2 months. If assembling pasta dish ahead: Cook pasta and chill under cold water; drain. Toss cold pasta with cold sauce and spoon into casserole dish. It's best to assemble casserole no more than a few hours ahead to prevent pasta from absorbing too much of the sauce.

- *To freeze:* Do not add the cheese topping (it goes rubbery when frozen). Cover with plastic wrap, then with foil. Freeze for up to 2 months. Let defrost in refrigerator overnight. Increase baking time by about 10 minutes.

NUTRITIONAL ANALYSIS PER SERVING

Calories	416
Carbohydrate	58 g
Fiber	5 g
Protein	24 g
Fat, total	9 g
Fat, saturated	3 g
Sodium	400 mg
Cholesterol	32 mg

AMERICA'S EXCHANGES PER SERVING

3	Starch
2	Vegetable
1½	Medium-fat Meat

CANADA'S CHOICES PER SERVING

3½	Carbohydrate
2	Meat & Alternatives

Spaghetti with Garlic Tomato Sauce

SERVES 6

Even when my pantry is almost empty, chances are I'll have a can of tomatoes and dried pasta on hand to whip up this easy supper dish.

Tips

For fresher flavor and less sodium, replace canned tomatoes with 4 large ripe tomatoes, peeled and chopped.

Improvise if you don't have any fresh herbs by using 1 tsp (5 mL) each dried basil and dried oregano for the fresh basil and parsley.

1 tbsp	olive oil	15 mL
3	cloves garlic, thinly sliced, then coarsely chopped	3
¼ tsp	hot pepper flakes	1 mL
1	can (28 oz/796 mL) plum tomatoes, including juice, chopped	1
	Freshly ground black pepper	
Pinch	granulated sugar	Pinch
12 oz	spaghetti	375 g
2 tbsp	chopped fresh parsley	25 mL
2 tbsp	chopped fresh basil leaves or chives	25 mL

1. In a large saucepan, heat oil over medium heat; stir in garlic and hot pepper flakes. Reduce heat to low; cook, stirring, for 1 minute or until garlic is light golden. (Do not let garlic brown or sauce will be bitter.)

2. Add tomatoes with juice; season with pepper and sugar to taste. Bring to a boil, reduce heat and simmer, partially covered, stirring occasionally, for 15 minutes.

3. Cook pasta in a large pot of boiling salted water until tender but firm. Drain well; return to pot. Add tomato sauce, parsley and basil; toss well. Add pepper to taste. Serve immediately.

NUTRITIONAL ANALYSIS PER SERVING	
Calories	279
Carbohydrate	52 g
Fiber	4 g
Protein	9 g
Fat, total	4 g
Fat, saturated	1 g
Sodium	385 mg
Cholesterol	0 mg

AMERICA'S EXCHANGES PER SERVING	
3	Starch
1	Vegetable

CANADA'S CHOICES PER SERVING	
3	Carbohydrate
1	Fat

I like to use fusilli in this recipe because the sauce clings nicely to the corkscrew-shaped pasta, but feel free to use whatever pasta you have in your pantry.

Tip

You can make this 5-minute pasta sauce the day ahead and refrigerate. Reheat on stovetop or microwave before tossing with hot cooked pasta.

Fast Fusilli with Mushrooms and Peas

2 tsp	butter	10 mL
2 cups	sliced mushrooms	500 mL
2	green onions, sliced	2
1	package (4 oz/125 g) light herb and garlic cream cheese	1
1 cup	frozen peas	250 mL
1/2 cup	low-fat milk	125 mL
1/3 cup	freshly grated Parmesan cheese	75 mL
8 oz	fusilli, penne or other tube-shaped pasta	250 g
	Freshly ground black pepper	

1. In a large saucepan, melt butter over medium heat. Add mushrooms and green onions; cook, stirring, for 3 minutes or until softened. Add cream cheese, peas, milk and Parmesan; cook, stirring, for 2 minutes or until piping hot.
2. Cook pasta in a large pot of boiling salted water until tender but firm. Drain well. Stir into mushroom mixture; toss to coat well. Season with pepper to taste. Serve immediately.

NUTRITIONAL ANALYSIS PER SERVING	
Calories	398
Carbohydrate	56 g
Fiber	5 g
Protein	17 g
Fat, total	12 g
Fat, saturated	6 g
Sodium	580 mg
Cholesterol	31 mg

AMERICA'S EXCHANGES PER SERVING	
3 1/2	Starch
1/2	Vegetable
1/2	Medium-fat Meat
1 1/2	Fat

CANADA'S CHOICES PER SERVING	
3 1/2	Carbohydrate
1	Meat & Alternatives
1 1/2	Fat

This streamlined mac and cheese is as easy to assemble as the pre-packaged version.

Tips

For a speedy meal-in-one dinner, add 3 to 4 cups (750 mL to 1 L) small broccoli florets to the pot of boiling pasta for the last 3 minutes of cooking; remove from heat when broccoli is tender-crisp.

To reheat leftovers on the stovetop or in the microwave, stir in additional milk until sauce is creamy.

Easy One-Pot Macaroni and Cheese

2 tbsp	all-purpose flour	25 mL
1 1/2 cups	low-fat milk	375 mL
1 1/2 cups	shredded light Cheddar cheese	375 mL
1/4 cup	freshly grated Parmesan cheese	50 mL
1 tsp	Dijon mustard	5 mL
	Cayenne pepper	
2 cups	elbow macaroni	500 mL

1. In a large saucepan, whisk flour with 1/4 cup (50 mL) milk to make a smooth paste; stir in remaining milk until smooth. Place over medium heat; cook, stirring, until mixture comes to a boil and thickens. Reduce heat to low; stir in cheeses and mustard. Cook, stirring, until melted. Season with a pinch of cayenne pepper; keep warm.

2. Cook pasta in a large pot of boiling salted water until tender but firm. Drain well; stir into cheese mixture. Cook for 1 minute or until sauce coats the pasta. Serve immediately.

NUTRITIONAL ANALYSIS PER SERVING	
Calories	269
Carbohydrate	32 g
Fiber	2 g
Protein	15 g
Fat, total	8 g
Fat, saturated	5 g
Sodium	460 mg
Cholesterol	24 mg

AMERICA'S EXCHANGES PER SERVING	
2	Starch
1 1/2	High-fat Meat

CANADA'S CHOICES PER SERVING	
2	Carbohydrate
1	Meat & Alternatives
1	Fat

Company Chicken Tetrazzini

SERVES 6

With leftover cooked chicken or turkey, you can make a wonderful pasta dish that's great for company. To make the dish in advance, cook the sauce, cover and refrigerate. Boil the pasta, rinse under cold water and chill. Combine the cold sauce and pasta up to 4 hours before the dish goes in the oven. (This prevents the pasta from absorbing too much of the sauce.)

- Preheat oven to 350°F (180°C)
- 13- by 9-inch (3 L) baking dish, sprayed with vegetable cooking spray

1 tbsp	butter	15 mL
8 oz	mushrooms, sliced	250 g
4	green onions, finely chopped	4
1 tsp	dried basil leaves	5 mL
1/4 cup	all-purpose flour	50 mL
2 cups	reduced-sodium chicken broth	500 mL
1/2 cup	half-and-half (10%) cream	125 mL
1/4 cup	medium-dry sherry	50 mL
2 cups	cubed cooked chicken or turkey	500 mL
1/2 cup	freshly grated Parmesan cheese	125 mL
	Freshly ground black pepper	
8 oz	broad egg noodles	250 g

1. In a large saucepan, melt butter over medium-high heat. Add mushrooms, green onions and basil; cook for 4 minutes or until softened. In a bowl, blend flour with 1/3 cup (75 mL) broth to make a smooth paste; stir in remaining broth. Pour into saucepan; bring to a boil, stirring, until thickened. Add cream, sherry and chicken; cook over medium heat for 2 to 3 minutes or until heated through. Remove from heat. Stir in half the Parmesan cheese; season with pepper to taste.

2. Cook noodles in a large pot of boiling salted water until almost tender but firm. Drain well. Return to pot; add chicken mixture and toss to coat well.

3. Spoon into prepared baking dish. Sprinkle with remaining Parmesan cheese. Bake for 30 to 35 minutes or until heated through. (If refrigerated, cook 10 minutes more or until piping hot in center.)

NUTRITIONAL ANALYSIS PER SERVING

Calories	376
Carbohydrate	39 g
Fiber	4 g
Protein	26 g
Fat, total	12 g
Fat, saturated	5 g
Sodium	590 mg
Cholesterol	99 mg

AMERICA'S EXCHANGES PER SERVING

2 1/2	Starch
2 1/2	Lean Meat
1/2	Fat

CANADA'S CHOICES PER SERVING

2	Carbohydrate
3	Meat & Alternatives

Easy Lasagna

Everyone loves lasagna, but who has the time to make it from scratch? Try this uncomplicated version that makes even a non-cook look like a pro in the kitchen. It's also the perfect recipe for young cooks, since there's no chopping involved. Once you assemble the ingredients, it takes a mere 15 minutes to prepare and the lasagna is ready for the oven.

Tip

Lasagna freezes well; cover with plastic wrap, then with foil and freeze for up to 2 months. Let defrost in the refrigerator overnight before baking.

- Preheat oven to 350°F (180°C)
- 13- by 9-inch (3 L) baking dish, sprayed with vegetable cooking spray

2 cups	light ricotta cheese	500 mL
2	eggs, beaten	2
1/3 cup	freshly grated Parmesan cheese	75 mL
1/4 tsp	freshly ground black pepper	1 mL
1/4 tsp	freshly grated nutmeg	1 mL
12	oven-ready lasagna noodles	12
1	jar (26 oz/700 mL) tomato sauce	1
1 1/2 cups	shredded part-skim mozzarella cheese	375 mL

1. In a bowl, combine ricotta, eggs and Parmesan cheese; season with pepper and nutmeg.

2. Depending on thickness of the spaghetti sauce, add about ¾ cup (175 mL) water to thin sauce. (Precooked noodles absorb extra moisture while cooking.)

3. Spoon ½ cup (125 mL) sauce in bottom of prepared baking dish. Layer with 3 lasagna noodles. Spread with ¾ cup (175 mL) of the sauce and then one-third of the ricotta mixture. Repeat with two more layers of noodles, sauce and ricotta cheese. Layer with rest of noodles and top with remaining sauce. Sprinkle with mozzarella cheese.

4. Bake, uncovered, in preheated oven for 45 minutes or until cheese is melted and sauce is bubbly.

NUTRITIONAL ANALYSIS PER SERVING	
Calories	332
Carbohydrate	31 g
Fiber	2 g
Protein	21 g
Fat, total	13 g
Fat, saturated	7 g
Sodium	670 mg
Cholesterol	82 mg

AMERICA'S EXCHANGES PER SERVING	
1 1/2	Starch
1/2	Other Carbohydrate
2 1/2	Medium-fat Meat

CANADA'S CHOICES PER SERVING	
2	Carbohydrate
2	Meat & Alternatives
1	Fat

SERVES 8

Today's store-bought tomato sauces and packaged shredded cheeses ease the making of traditional lasagna. This updated version serves a crowd and replaces ground meat with plenty of healthy vegetables.

Tip

To make ahead, cover and refrigerate for up to 2 days or overwrap with foil and freeze for up to 2 months. Let thaw completely in refrigerator for 24 hours.

Roasted Vegetable Lasagna with Spicy Tomato Sauce

- Preheat oven to 400°F (200°C)
- 2 baking sheets
- 13- by 9-inch (3 L) baking dish, sprayed with vegetable cooking spray

ROASTED VEGETABLES

1	red onion	1
2	small zucchini, diced	2
1	large bulb fennel, diced	1
1	large red bell pepper, diced	1
1 tbsp	dried oregano leaves	15 mL
1/2 tsp	freshly ground black pepper	2 mL
2 tbsp	olive oil	25 mL

CHEESE FILLING

2	eggs	2
1/2 tsp	freshly ground black pepper	2 mL
1 1/2 cups	light ricotta cheese	375 mL
1 cup	crumbled light feta cheese (about 4 oz/125 g)	250 mL
1/4 cup	chopped fresh parsley	50 mL

PASTA SAUCE

12	lasagna noodles	12
1	jar (26 oz/700 mL) spicy tomato sauce with roasted red peppers	1
1	can (7 1/2 oz/213 mL) tomato sauce	1
1/3 cup	chopped Kalamata olives (optional)	75 mL
1 1/2 cups	shredded part-skim mozzarella cheese	375 mL

1. *Roasted Vegetables:* In a bowl, combine onion, zucchini, fennel, pepper, oregano and pepper; drizzle with oil and toss to coat. Spread on baking sheets. Roast in preheated oven, stirring occasionally, for 20 to 25 minutes or until tender. Remove and set aside. Reduce oven temperature to 350°F (180°C).

AMERICA'S EXCHANGES PER SERVING	
2	Starch
2	Vegetable
2	High-fat Meat

CANADA'S CHOICES PER SERVING	
2 1/2	Carbohydrate
2 1/2	Meat & Alternatives
1	Fat

2. *Cheese Filling:* In a bowl, beat eggs and pepper; stir in ricotta, feta and parsley.

3. Meanwhile, in a large pot of boiling salted water, cook noodles for 8 minutes or until almost tender. Drain; chill under cold running water. Arrange in single layer on damp tea towel.

4. In a large bowl, combine bottled and canned tomato sauces; spread ¾ cup (175 mL) sauce in baking dish. Stir roasted vegetables and olives, if using, into remaining tomato sauce.

5. Layer 3 noodles in baking dish. Spread with one-quarter of the vegetable sauce; top with one-third of the ricotta mixture. Repeat layers twice. Arrange remaining noodles over top; spread with remaining sauce.

6. Sprinkle top with mozzarella cheese; cover loosely with foil. Bake in 350°F (180°C) oven for 30 minutes; uncover and bake for 20 to 25 minutes more or until bubbly and top is golden. Let stand for 5 minutes before cutting.

Tip

Bottled pasta sauces can be very high in sodium. Compare labels and choose a lower-sodium variety.

Chicken Penne Bake

SERVES 12

This casual country-style dish — perfect for large potluck dinners — is an easy-make-ahead casserole that's a real crowd pleaser.

Tips

For fresher flavor and less sodium, replace canned tomatoes with 4 large ripe tomatoes, peeled and chopped.

This recipe can be prepared through Step 4 up to 1 day ahead. Cover and refrigerate.

- Preheat oven to 350°F (180°C)
- 16-cup (4 L) baking dish, sprayed with vegetable cooking spray

2 tbsp	olive oil, divided	25 mL
2 lbs	boneless skinless chicken thighs, cut into 1-inch (2.5 cm) pieces	1 kg
2	onions, chopped	2
6	cloves garlic, chopped	6
4 cups	sliced mushrooms	1 L
2 tsp	dried basil leaves	10 mL
2 tsp	dried oregano leaves	10 mL
1 tsp	hot pepper flakes	5 mL
1 tsp	salt	5 mL
1	can (28 oz/796 mL) plum tomatoes, including juice	1
1	can (5½ oz/156 mL) tomato paste	1
1½ cups	reduced-sodium chicken broth	375 mL
1	green bell pepper, chopped	1
1	red bell pepper, chopped	1
½ cup	chopped fresh parsley	125 mL
12 oz	penne or other tube-shaped pasta	375 g
1½ cups	shredded part-skim mozzarella cheese	375 mL
½ cup	freshly grated pecorino, Romano or Parmesan cheese	125 mL

1. In a large Dutch oven or saucepan, heat 1 tbsp (15 mL) olive oil over medium-high heat; brown chicken in batches. Transfer to a plate.

2. Add remaining oil; cook onions, garlic, mushrooms, basil, oregano, hot pepper flakes and salt, stirring, for 5 minutes or until softened. Return chicken to pan along with accumulated juices.

NUTRITIONAL ANALYSIS PER SERVING	
Calories	341
Carbohydrate	35 g
Fiber	4 g
Protein	26 g
Fat, total	11 g
Fat, saturated	4 g
Sodium	590 mg
Cholesterol	63 mg

AMERICA'S EXCHANGES PER SERVING	
1½	Starch
1	Other Carbohydrate
3	Lean Meat

CANADA'S CHOICES PER SERVING	
2	Carbohydrate
3	Meat & Alternatives

3. In a food processor, purée tomatoes with juice. Add to chicken mixture with tomato paste and broth. Bring to a boil; reduce heat, cover and cook for 25 minutes. Add green and red peppers; cook, covered, for 10 minutes or until peppers are tender. Stir in parsley. (If making ahead, let cool and refrigerate.)

4. In a large pot of boiling salted water, cook pasta until tender but firm; drain. Rinse under cold water to chill; drain well. Stir pasta into sauce. Spoon half into prepared baking dish; sprinkle with half the mozzarella and pecorino cheeses. Top with remaining pasta and sprinkle with remaining cheeses.

5. Cover and bake in oven for 45 minutes; uncover and bake for 30 minutes more or until piping hot in center and top is golden.

Variation

Sausage and Chicken Penne Bake

Use ½ lb (500 g) mild or hot lean Italian sausages and 1½ lbs (750 g) chicken in this hearty Italian dish. Lightly brown the sausages in 1 tbsp (15 mL) vegetable oil in a large nonstick skillet; remove and slice. Return to pan and stir frequently until thoroughly cooked. Drain off any fat and add along with browned chicken.

Sodium

Nutrition experts tell us we should keep our sodium intake to no more than 2,400 mg per day, the amount in a teaspoon (5 mL) of salt. Salt is a major source of sodium in our food. Here are some typical values for foods prepared with and without salt.

FOOD	SODIUM	
	WITH SALT	WITHOUT
½ cup (125 mL) cooked pasta	70 mg	1 mg
⅓ cup (75 mL) cooked rice	200 mg	1 mg
½ medium boiled potato	200 mg	3 mg
½ cup (125 mL) cooked green beans	150 mg	2 mg

Source: Canadian Nutrient File, 2005

Remember that sodium in salt added at the table can be significant: each shake adds 15 to 40 mg of sodium.

This hearty pasta dish, brimming with chunks of tasty sausage and colorful peppers, makes a delicious feast for any occasion.

Tips

Not all turkey sausages are the same. Check labels carefully and look for those that contain no more than 10 g of fat per 3½ oz (100 g).

For fresher flavor and less sodium, replace canned tomatoes with 4 large ripe tomatoes, peeled and chopped.

Baked Penne with Italian Sausage and Sweet Peppers

● *Preheat oven to 350°F (180°C)*
● *13- by 9-inch (3 L) baking dish, sprayed with vegetable cooking spray*

I tbsp	olive oil, divided	15 mL
8 oz	hot or mild lean turkey Italian sausages	250 g
3	bell peppers (assorted colors)	3
I	large onion, halved lengthwise and thinly sliced	I
2	cloves garlic, finely chopped	2
I tsp	dried basil leaves	5 mL
I tsp	dried oregano leaves	5 mL
½ tsp	hot pepper flakes or to taste	2 mL
I	can (28 oz/796 mL) plum tomatoes, including juice, chopped	I
¼ cup	chopped fresh parsley	50 mL
12 oz	penne or other small tube-shaped pasta	375 g
I cup	shredded part-skim mozzarella cheese	250 mL
½ cup	freshly grated Parmesan cheese	50 mL

1. Prick skins of sausages with a fork. In a large Dutch oven or saucepan, heat oil over medium-high heat; cook sausages for 5 minutes or until browned on all sides. (Sausages will not be cooked through.) Remove from pan, cut into slices and reserve.

2. Drain fat from pan. Add peppers, onion, garlic, basil, oregano, salt and hot pepper flakes; cook, stirring often, for 7 minutes or until softened.

NUTRITIONAL ANALYSIS PER SERVING	
Calories	432
Carbohydrate	60 g
Fiber	5 g
Protein	24 g
Fat, total	II g
Fat, saturated	4 g
Sodium	675 mg
Cholesterol	57 mg

AMERICA'S EXCHANGES PER SERVING	
3	Starch
I	Other Carbohydrate
2	Lean Meat
½	Fat

CANADA'S CHOICES PER SERVING	
3½	Carbohydrate
2	Meat & Alternatives
½	Fat

3. Return sausage slices to pan along with canned tomatoes with juice. Bring to a boil; reduce heat to medium-low; cover and simmer, stirring occasionally, for 20 minutes. Stir in parsley.

4. Meanwhile, cook pasta in a large pot of boiling water until tender but firm. Drain well. Place half of the cooked pasta in prepared baking dish. Pour in half of the sauce. Layer again with remaining pasta and top with remaining sauce.

5. In a bowl, combine mozzarella and Parmesan cheeses; sprinkle over top of casserole. Bake, uncovered, in preheated oven for 30 to 35 minutes or until cheese is melted and lightly colored.

Variation

Vegetarian Penne with Sweet Peppers
For a vegetarian version, omit the sausages. Add 1/3 cup (75 mL) small black olives to the sauce along with the parsley for an added dimension of flavor.

Creamy Tuna Pasta Bake

This modern rendition of a tuna casserole includes a nutritional boost of broccoli in a creamy basil sauce. To prepare the casserole ahead, make the sauce the day before and refrigerate. Assemble the dish no more than 4 hours ahead to prevent pasta from soaking up the sauce.

Tip

If fresh basil is unavailable, substitute 2 tsp (10 mL) dried basil leaves and cook with onions.

- Preheat oven to 350°F (180°C)
- 13- by 9-inch (3 L) baking dish, sprayed with vegetable cooking spray

2 tbsp	butter	25 mL
6	green onions, chopped	6
3	cloves garlic, finely chopped	3
4 cups	sliced mushrooms	1 L
1/2 tsp	freshly ground black pepper	2 mL
1/3 cup	all-purpose flour	75 mL
2 cups	low-fat milk	500 mL
1 1/2 cups	reduced-sodium chicken broth	375 mL
3	tomatoes, seeded and diced	3
2/3 cup	freshly grated Parmesan cheese	150 mL
1/2 cup	chopped fresh basil leaves	125 mL
12 oz	penne	375 g
4 cups	broccoli florets and chopped peeled stems	1 L
2	cans (each 6 1/2 oz/170 g) flaked tuna, drained	2
1 1/2 cups	soft fresh bread crumbs	375 mL
1 cup	shredded part-skim mozzarella cheese	250 mL

1. In a large Dutch oven or saucepan, melt butter over medium-high heat. Cook green onions, garlic, mushrooms and pepper, stirring occasionally, for 5 minutes or until softened.

2. In a bowl, whisk flour with 1 cup (250 mL) milk until smooth; add remaining milk. Add to pan along with broth. Bring to a boil, stirring, for 3 minutes or until sauce thickens. Remove from heat. Stir in tomatoes, Parmesan and basil.

NUTRITIONAL ANALYSIS PER SERVING	
Calories	403
Carbohydrate	50 g
Fiber	5 g
Protein	27 g
Fat, total	11 g
Fat, saturated	6 g
Sodium	660 mg
Cholesterol	36 mg

AMERICA'S EXCHANGES PER SERVING	
2 1/2	Starch
1	Vegetable
1/2	Other Carbohydrate
2 1/2	Lean Meat

CANADA'S CHOICES PER SERVING	
3	Carbohydrate
2 1/2	Meat & Alternatives

3. In a large pot of boiling salted water, cook pasta for 7 minutes or until almost tender. Add broccoli; cook for 2 minutes or until broccoli is bright green and crisp, and pasta is just tender. Drain; chill under cold water. Drain well and return to pot. Stir in tuna and sauce. Spread in baking dish.

4. In a bowl, combine bread crumbs and mozzarella; sprinkle over top. Bake in preheated oven for 40 to 45 minutes or until golden and center is piping hot.

Tip

Sauce can be prepared through Step 2 up to 1 day ahead. Cover and refrigerate. Casserole can be prepared through Step 3 up to 4 hours ahead. Cover and refrigerate. Increase baking time by 15 minutes.

SERVES 6

This recipe takes an old standby to new heights. What's great, too, is that it keeps well in the fridge for up to 2 days before baking. For an effortless meal, just pop it in the oven when you get home from work. Serve with a crisp green salad.

Tip

To make ahead, cook noodles, rinse under cold water to chill; drain. Combine cold noodles and cold sauce; spoon into casserole dish, cover and refrigerate. Add crumb topping just before baking to prevent it from getting soggy. Add 10 minutes to the baking time.

Tuna Noodle Bake with Cheddar Crumb Topping

- Preheat oven to 350°F (180°C)
- 13- by 9-inch (3 L) casserole dish, sprayed

I tbsp	butter	15 mL
8 oz	mushrooms, sliced	250 g
¾ cup	chopped green onions	175 mL
2 tbsp	all-purpose flour	25 mL
I	can (10 oz/284 mL) chicken broth, undiluted	I
I cup	low-fat milk	250 mL
4 oz	light cream cheese, softened	125 g
I	can (6½ oz/170 g) solid white tuna, drained and flaked	I
I cup	frozen peas	250 mL
8 oz	broad egg noodles	250 g

CHEDDAR CRUMB TOPPING

½ cup	dry bread crumbs	125 mL
I cup	shredded light Cheddar cheese	250 mL

I. In a saucepan, melt butter over medium heat. Add mushrooms and green onions; cook, stirring, for 3 minutes or until softened. Blend in flour; pour in broth and milk. Bring to a boil, stirring constantly, until slightly thickened. Stir in cream cheese until melted. Add tuna and peas; cook 2 minutes more or until heated through. Remove from heat.

2. Cook noodles in a large pot of boiling water until tender but still firm. Drain well. Stir noodles into sauce. Spoon into prepared casserole dish.

4. *Cheddar Crumb Topping:* In a bowl, toss bread crumbs with cheese. Just before baking, sprinkle topping over noodles.

5. Bake in preheated oven for about 30 minutes or until top is golden.

NUTRITIONAL ANALYSIS PER SERVING	
Calories	407
Carbohydrate	48 g
Fiber	5 g
Protein	23 g
Fat, total	14 g
Fat, saturated	7 g
Sodium	630 mg
Cholesterol	82 mg

AMERICA'S EXCHANGES PER SERVING	
3	Starch
I	Vegetable
I½	Medium-fat Meat
½	Fat

CANADA'S CHOICES PER SERVING	
3	Carbohydrate
2	Meat & Alternatives
½	Fat

SERVES 6

When I crave a rich and creamy pasta dish, this is it. Since this recipe requires very little preparation time, have all of the ingredients assembled before you start.

Tip

When to use curly versus flat-leaf parsley? While they are interchangeable in recipes, I like the more assertive taste of flat-leaf parsley, especially in recipes such as this one, where it is a vital ingredient and balances nicely with the lemon and garlic.

Fettuccine with Seared Scallops, Lemon and Garlic

1 lb	large scallops	500 g
1/4 tsp	salt	1 mL
	Freshly ground black pepper	
2 tbsp	butter	25 mL
3	cloves garlic, minced	3
1/2 cup	dry white wine	125 mL
1/4 cup	fish broth or reduced-sodium chicken broth	50 mL
1 tbsp	grated lemon zest	15 mL
1 tbsp	freshly squeezed lemon juice	15 mL
3/4 cup	whipping (35%) cream	175 mL
1/4 cup	chopped fresh flat-leaf parsley (see tip, at left)	50 mL
12 oz	fettuccine pasta	375 g

1. Pat scallops dry with paper towels. Halve horizontally and season with salt and pepper.
2. Heat a large nonstick skillet over high heat. Add butter; heat until foamy and butter starts to brown. Add scallops and cook for 1 minute or until lightly browned. Turn and cook second side for about 30 seconds. Do not overcook. Transfer to a plate.
3. Reduce heat to medium. Add garlic and cook, stirring, for 30 seconds or until fragrant. Stir in wine, broth and lemon zest and juice; bring to a boil. Add cream and cook, stirring, until sauce boils and is slightly reduced.
4. Add parsley and season with salt and pepper to taste. Add scallops and cook for 1 minute or just until heated in the sauce. Do not overcook.
5. Meanwhile, in a large pot of boiling salted water, cook pasta until tender but firm. Drain and return to pot.
6. Pour sauce over pasta and toss until well coated. Spoon pasta into warm bowls and serve immediately.

NUTRITIONAL ANALYSIS PER SERVING	
Calories	420
Carbohydrate	46 g
Fiber	3 g
Protein	21 g
Fat, total	16 g
Fat, saturated	9 g
Sodium	440 mg
Cholesterol	74 mg

AMERICA'S EXCHANGES PER SERVING	
3	Starch
2	Medium-fat Meat
1/2	Fat

CANADA'S CHOICES PER SERVING	
3	Carbohydrate
2	Meat & Alternatives
1	Fat

Spinach and Ricotta Cannelloni

To streamline this one-dish pasta dish, I like to use convenient bottled pasta sauces, sold in supermarkets. Check labels and choose one with a lower sodium content. If you have the time to make a sauce from scratch, try Big-Batch Tomato Sauce (page 156).

Tip

To defrost spinach, remove packaging and place in a 4-cup (1 L) casserole dish. Cover and microwave at High, stirring once, for 6 to 8 minutes or until defrosted and hot. Place in a sieve and press out excess moisture.

- Preheat oven to 350°F (180°C)
- 13- by 9-inch (3 L) baking dish, sprayed with nonstick vegetable cooking spray

1 tbsp	olive oil	15 mL
1	package (10 oz/300 g) frozen chopped spinach, thawed, squeezed dry	1
4	green onions, sliced	4
2	cloves garlic, finely chopped	2
1	egg	1
2 cups	ricotta cheese	500 mL
1 1/2 cups	shredded light provolone cheese, divided	375 mL
1/2 cup	freshly grated Parmesan cheese, divided	125 mL
1/3 cup	chopped fresh parsley	75 mL
1/4 tsp	salt	1 mL
1/4 tsp	freshly grated black pepper	1 mL
1/4 tsp	freshly ground nutmeg	1 mL
6	sheets (each 9 by 6 inches/ 23 by 15 cm) fresh lasagna noodles	6
3 cups	tomato pasta sauce	750 mL
1/2 cup	chicken stock	125 mL

1. In a large nonstick skillet, heat oil over medium-high heat; cook spinach, green onions and garlic, stirring, for 3 minutes or until softened. Remove from heat.

2. In a bowl, beat egg; stir in ricotta, 1/2 cup (125 mL) of the provolone cheese, 1/4 cup (50 mL) of the Parmesan cheese, parsley, salt, pepper and nutmeg. Stir in spinach mixture until combined.

NUTRITIONAL ANALYSIS PER SERVING	
Calories	254
Carbohydrate	26 g
Fiber	3 g
Protein	7 g
Fat, total	9 g
Fat, saturated	5 g
Sodium	510 mg
Cholesterol	58 mg

AMERICA'S EXCHANGES PER SERVING	
1	Starch
1 1/2	Vegetable
1 1/2	Medium-fat Meat
1/2	Fat

CANADA'S CHOICES PER SERVING	
2	Carbohydrate
2	Meat & Alternatives
1	Fat

3. In a large pot of boiling salted water, cook lasagna noodles until tender but firm, about 3 minutes. Drain and chill under cold water. Cut each sheet in half crosswise. Place on a damp kitchen towel.

4. In a bowl, combine pasta sauce and stock. Spread 1 cup (250 mL) of the tomato sauce in prepared baking dish.

5. Spoon ⅓ cup (75 mL) of the ricotta filling along one short edge of each lasagna sheet. Roll up and place in baking dish, making two rows. Cover with remaining tomato sauce; sprinkle with remaining provolone and Parmesan cheeses. Bake in preheated oven for 40 to 45 minutes or until sauce is bubbly.

Tip

To make ahead and freeze, cover with plastic wrap, then with heavy-duty foil. Freeze for up to 1 month. Thaw in the refrigerator. Add 15 minutes to the baking time.

Vegetarians in your household will request this dish often and come to think of it as a comfort food. Its vibrant combination of Asian flavors tastes terrific and is nourishing, too. Any leftovers make a great next-day lunch.

Tip

Cut vegetables into uniform 2-inch (5 cm) lengths. This colorful pasta dish takes only a few minutes to cook, so have ingredients assembled before you start.

Spicy Noodles with Vegetables and Peanut Sauce

1/4 cup	light peanut butter	50 mL
1/3 cup	water	75 mL
2 tbsp	reduced-sodium soy sauce	25 mL
2 tbsp	freshly squeezed lime juice	25 mL
2 tbsp	packed brown sugar	25 mL
1/4 tsp	hot pepper flakes or to taste	1 mL
1 tbsp	sesame oil	15 mL
1 tbsp	vegetable oil	15 mL
1 tbsp	minced fresh gingerroot	15 mL
2	cloves garlic, minced	2
1	leek, white and light green part only, cleaned and cut into matchstick strips	1
2	small Italian eggplants, cut into thin strips (about 2 cups/500 mL)	2
2	bell peppers (assorted colors), cut into thin strips	2
12 oz	linguine, broken into thirds	375 g
1/2 cup	chopped fresh cilantro or parsley	125 mL

1. In a small saucepan, combine peanut butter, water, soy sauce, lime juice, brown sugar, hot pepper flakes and sesame oil. Stir over medium heat until mixture is warm and smooth. Set aside.

2. In wok or large nonstick skillet, heat vegetable oil over high heat. Add ginger, garlic, leek and eggplant; cook, stirring, for 2 minutes. Add peppers; cook, stirring, for 1 minute more or until vegetables are just tender-crisp. Stir in peanut sauce until heated through.

3. Meanwhile, in a large pot of boiling salted water, cook linguine until tender but firm. Drain and return to pot. Toss with vegetables and peanut sauce until well coated; sprinkle with cilantro. Serve warm or at room temperature.

NUTRITIONAL ANALYSIS PER SERVING	
Calories	378
Carbohydrate	63 g
Fiber	6 g
Protein	12 g
Fat, total	9 g
Fat, saturated	1 g
Sodium	390 mg
Cholesterol	0 mg

AMERICA'S EXCHANGES PER SERVING	
3	Starch
1	Vegetable
1	Other Carbohydrate
1	Fat

CANADA'S CHOICES PER SERVING	
4	Carbohydrate
2	Fat

Singapore Noodles

SERVES 4

Here's a popular noodle dish you'll spot on many restaurant menus that is easy to recreate in your home kitchen.

Tip

Other pasta such as angel hair can be substituted. Cook noodles according to package directions before adding to recipe.

6 oz	rice vermicelli	175 g
2 tbsp	reduced-sodium soy sauce	25 mL
2 tsp	mild curry paste or powder	10 mL
4 tsp	vegetable oil, divided	20 mL
1	red or green bell pepper, cut into thin strips	1
5	green onions, sliced	5
2	large cloves garlic, minced	2
3 cups	bean sprouts, rinsed and dried	750 mL
12 oz	cooked, peeled baby shrimp	375 g

1. In a large pot of lightly salted boiling water, cook noodles for 3 minutes. Drain; chill under cold water and drain well. Cut noodles using scissors into 3-inch (8 cm) lengths; set aside.

2. In a small bowl, combine soy sauce and curry paste; set aside.

3. Heat a wok or large nonstick skillet over high heat until very hot; add 2 tsp (10 mL) oil, tilting wok to coat sides. Stir-fry pepper strips, green onions and garlic for 1 minute. Add bean sprouts and shrimp; stir-fry for 1 to 2 minutes or until vegetables are tender-crisp. Transfer to a bowl.

4. Add remaining oil to wok; when very hot, add noodles and soy sauce mixture. Stir-fry for 1 minute or until heated through. Return vegetable-shrimp mixture to wok and stir-fry for 1 minute more. Serve immediately.

NUTRITIONAL ANALYSIS PER SERVING

Calories	351
Carbohydrate	46 g
Fiber	3 g
Protein	25 g
Fat, total	7 g
Fat, saturated	1 g
Sodium	570 mg
Cholesterol	143 mg

AMERICA'S EXCHANGES PER SERVING

2½	Starch
2	Vegetable
2	Very Lean Meat
½	Fat

CANADA'S CHOICES PER SERVING

3	Carbohydrate
2½	Meat & Alternatives

SERVES 10

This impressive dish, which features plenty of vegetables, appeals to both vegetarians and meat eaters.

Tip

If you've run out of homemade tomato sauce and have to buy a commercial pasta sauce, be aware that these sauces can have as much as 700 mg of sodium per $\frac{1}{2}$ cup (125 mL), so be sure to check sodium on labels.

Baked Polenta with Roasted Vegetables

- Preheat oven to 425°F (220°C) • 2 baking sheets
- 13- by 9-inch (3 L) baking dish, sprayed with vegetable cooking spray

2	zucchini	2
1	small eggplant (about 1 lb/500 g)	1
1	red bell pepper	1
1	yellow bell pepper	1
1	large red onion	1
2 tbsp	olive oil	25 mL
1 $\frac{1}{2}$ tsp	dried rosemary leaves, crumbled	7 mL
$\frac{1}{2}$ tsp	freshly ground black pepper	2 mL
$\frac{1}{4}$ cup	chopped fresh parsley	50 mL
	Garlic Polenta (see recipe, opposite)	
2 cups	Big-Batch Tomato Sauce (see recipe, page 156)	500 mL
1 $\frac{1}{4}$ cups	shredded part-skim mozzarella cheese	300 mL
$\frac{1}{4}$ cup	freshly grated Parmesan cheese	50 mL

1. Halve zucchini lengthwise and thickly slice. Cut eggplant into $\frac{1}{2}$-inch (1 cm) slices, then cut into 1$\frac{1}{2}$-inch (4 cm) pieces. Cut peppers into 1-inch (2.5 cm) pieces. Cut onion into thin lengthwise wedges. Arrange vegetables on baking sheets. Drizzle with oil; sprinkle with rosemary and pepper. Roast in preheated oven, stirring occasionally, for 25 to 30 minutes or until tender. Transfer to a bowl; stir in parsley.

NUTRITIONAL ANALYSIS PER SERVING

Calories	257
Carbohydrate	34 g
Fiber	5 g
Protein	11 g
Fat, total	9 g
Fat, saturated	4 g
Sodium	395 mg
Cholesterol	17 mg

AMERICA'S EXCHANGES PER SERVING

1$\frac{1}{2}$	Starch
2	Vegetable
$\frac{1}{2}$	High-fat Meat
1	Fat

CANADA'S CHOICES PER SERVING

2	Carbohydrate
$\frac{1}{2}$	Meat & Alternatives
1$\frac{1}{2}$	Fat

2. Cut prepared polenta in half crosswise; using two lifters, gently transfer one half to baking dish. Spread with half the tomato sauce, then half the vegetables and half the mozzarella and Parmesan cheeses. Repeat layers. (Can be prepared up to this point, covered and refrigerated for up to 2 days.) Bake in 350°F (180°C) oven for 50 to 60 minutes or until piping hot in center and cheese is melted.

Garlic Polenta

● *Baking sheet, sprayed with vegetable cooking spray*

3	cloves garlic, minced	3
1/2 tsp	salt	2 mL
2 cups	cornmeal	500 mL
1/4 cup	freshly grated Parmesan cheese	50 mL
1 tbsp	butter	15 mL

1. In a large Dutch oven or saucepan, bring 7 cups (1.75 L) water, garlic and salt to a boil; gradually whisk in cornmeal until thickened. Reduce heat to low; cook, stirring often with wooden spoon, for 15 to 20 minutes or until polenta is thick enough to mound on spoon. Stir in Parmesan cheese and butter.

2. Spread onto prepared baking sheet; cover with plastic wrap. Refrigerate for 30 minutes or until firm.

Tip

To make ahead, cover and refrigerate for up to 1 day.

SERVES 6

Traditional paella is made in a wide shallow pan, but today's nonstick skillet makes a very good substitute and reduces the amount of oil needed for this dish.

Tip

Try a variety of different vegetables, including bite-size pieces of broccoli, cauliflower, asparagus, green beans, bell peppers and zucchini.

Spanish Vegetable Paella

● *Preheat oven to 375°F (190°C)*

4 cups	assorted prepared vegetables (see tip, at left)	1 L
3½ cups	reduced-sodium chicken broth or vegetable broth	875 mL
¼ tsp	saffron threads, crushed	1 mL
Pinch	hot pepper flakes	Pinch
2 tbsp	olive oil	25 mL
4	green onions, chopped	4
3	large cloves garlic, finely chopped	3
1½ cups	short-grain white rice, such as Arborio	375 mL

1. Cook vegetables (except peppers and zucchini) in a saucepan of boiling, lightly salted water, for 1 minute. Rinse under cold water to chill; drain well.

2. In the same saucepan, bring broth to a boil. Add saffron and hot pepper flakes. Keep warm.

3. In a large nonstick skillet, heat oil over medium-high heat. Add green onions and garlic; cook, stirring, for 1 minute. Add vegetables to skillet; cook, stirring often, for 4 minutes or until lightly colored. Stir in rice and hot broth mixture. Reduce heat so rice cooks at a gentle boil: cook, uncovered, without stirring, for 10 minutes or until most of the liquid is absorbed.

4. Cover skillet with lid or foil. (If skillet handle is not ovenproof, wrap in double layer of foil.) Bake in preheated oven for 15 minutes or until all liquid is absorbed and rice is tender. Remove; let stand, covered, for 5 minutes before serving.

NUTRITIONAL ANALYSIS PER SERVING	
Calories	255
Carbohydrate	46 g
Fiber	3 g
Protein	6 g
Fat, total	5 g
Fat, saturated	1 g
Sodium	295 mg
Cholesterol	0 mg

AMERICA'S EXCHANGES PER SERVING	
2½	Starch
1	Vegetable
½	Fat

CANADA'S CHOICES PER SERVING	
3	Carbohydrate
1	Fat

Vegetable Fried Rice

Use this recipe as a guide to create your own versions of fried rice, depending on what type of veggies you have in the fridge. With rice cooked ahead, it takes no time to prepare.

Tip

Instead of peas, try blanched diced carrots, snow peas cut into 1-inch (2.5 cm) pieces, 1 zucchini, halved lengthwise and sliced, or small broccoli florets.

Variation

Chicken or Pork Fried Rice

Cut 8 oz (250 g) chicken breasts or lean boneless pork loin into thin strips. In a skillet, heat 1 tbsp (15 mL) oil over medium-high heat; cook meat, stirring, for 5 minutes or until no longer pink. Remove; keep warm. Continue with recipe as directed. Return meat to skillet with bean sprouts.

1 tbsp	vegetable oil	15 mL
3	green onions, chopped	3
1 1/2 tsp	minced fresh gingerroot	7 mL
1	clove garlic, minced	1
3 cups	cold cooked rice	750 mL
1 cup	frozen peas	250 mL
1/2	red bell pepper, cut into thin strips, 1 1/2 inches (4 cm) long	1/2
2 cups	bean sprouts	500 mL
2 tbsp	reduced-sodium soy sauce	25 mL
1 tsp	mild curry paste or powder (optional)	5 mL

1. In a large nonstick skillet, heat oil over high heat. Add green onions, ginger and garlic; cook, stirring, for 15 seconds or until fragrant. Add rice, peas and pepper; cook, stirring often, for 5 to 7 minutes or until rice is heated through and vegetables are tender.

2. In a small bowl, combine soy sauce and curry paste, if using; stir into rice mixture along with bean sprouts. Cook, stirring, for 1 to 2 minutes or until heated through. Serve immediately.

NUTRITIONAL ANALYSIS PER SERVING	
Calories	164
Carbohydrate	30 g
Fiber	2 g
Protein	5 g
Fat, total	3 g
Fat, saturated	0 g
Sodium	515 mg
Cholesterol	0 mg

AMERICA'S EXCHANGES PER SERVING	
1 1/2	Starch
1	Vegetable
1/2	Fat

CANADA'S CHOICES PER SERVING	
2	Carbohydrate
1/2	Fat

Nutritionists recommend adding more whole grains to our diets. Here's a dish that is not only great-tasting but wholesome besides. Your family will love it.

Tip

Other nuts, such as skinned hazelnuts or unblanched almonds, can be substituted for the walnuts.

Mushroom Barley Pilaf

2 tsp	butter	10 mL
2 cups	sliced mushrooms	500 mL
1	small onion, chopped	1
1/2 tsp	dried thyme or marjoram leaves	2 mL
1 cup	pearl barley, rinsed	250 mL
2 1/2 cups	reduced-sodium chicken broth or vegetable broth (approx.)	625 mL
1/4 cup	finely chopped walnuts or pecans	50 mL
1/4 cup	freshly grated Parmesan cheese	50 mL
2 tbsp	chopped fresh parsley	25 mL
	Freshly ground black pepper	

1. In a medium saucepan, melt butter over medium heat. Add mushrooms, onion and thyme; cook, stirring, for 5 minutes or until softened.

2. Stir in barley and broth; bring to a boil. Reduce heat, cover and simmer, stirring occasionally and adding more broth if necessary, for 30 minutes or until barley is tender.

3. Stir in walnuts, Parmesan and parsley; season with pepper to taste.

NUTRITIONAL ANALYSIS PER SERVING

Calories	195
Carbohydrate	30 g
Fiber	4 g
Protein	6 g
Fat, total	6 g
Fat, saturated	2 g
Sodium	300 mg
Cholesterol	7 mg

AMERICA'S EXCHANGES PER SERVING

1 1/2	Starch
1/2	Other Carbohydrate
1/2	Medium-fat Meat
1/2	Fat

CANADA'S CHOICES PER SERVING

2	Carbohydrate
1	Fat

This herb-infused rice makes the perfect accompaniment to a wide range of dishes. Try it with fish, chicken, beef, lamb or pork.

Tip

To save time, make ahead and reheat in the microwave before serving.

Variation

Saffron Rice Pilaf
Substitute ¼ tsp (1 mL) crushed saffron threads for the thyme.

Herbed Rice Pilaf

l tbsp	olive oil	15 mL
l	small onion, finely chopped	l
l	clove garlic, minced	l
½ tsp	dried thyme leaves	2 mL
	Freshly ground black pepper	
l½ cups	long-grain white rice	375 mL
3 cups	reduced-sodium chicken broth or vegetable broth	750 mL
l	small red bell pepper, finely diced	l
¼ cup	chopped fresh parsley	50 mL

1. In a large saucepan, heat oil over medium heat. Add onion, garlic, thyme and pepper; cook, stirring often, for 3 minutes or until softened.
2. Add rice and broth; bring to a boil. Reduce heat to low; cover and simmer for 15 minutes or until most of broth is absorbed.
3. Stir in red pepper; cover and cook for 7 to 9 minutes more or until rice is tender. Stir in parsley; let stand, uncovered, for 5 minutes.

NUTRITIONAL ANALYSIS PER SERVING

Calories	155
Carbohydrate	29 g
Fiber	1 g
Protein	4 g
Fat, total	2 g
Fat, saturated	0 g
Sodium	185 mg
Cholesterol	0 mg

AMERICA'S EXCHANGES PER SERVING
2 Starch

CANADA'S CHOICES PER SERVING
2 Carbohydrate

SERVES 10

Wild Mushroom Risotto

*Risotto's creamy appeal
makes it a modern comfort
food. It may seem
intimidating to make at
home, but it's easy to do
provided you don't wander
away from the stove.
Risotto waits for no one, so
call everyone to the table
as you add the last ladle
of broth to the saucepan.*

Tip

A proper risotto is made
with Italian short-grain rice.
As it cooks, it gives off some
of the starch from its
surface, and the constant
stirring results in a creamy,
moist texture similar to
porridge. Arborio rice is the
most widely available short-
grain variety; look for the
word "superfino" on the
package to ensure you are
buying a superior grade.
Vialone nano and carnaroli
are two other types of short-
grain Italian rice that make
wonderful risotto. They
do not have quite as much
surface starch as Arborio
and require slightly less
broth in cooking.

5 cups	reduced-sodium chicken broth or vegetable broth (approx.)	1.25 L
1 tbsp	butter	15 mL
1 lb	assorted mushrooms, such as cremini, shiitake and oyster, coarsely chopped	500 g
2	cloves garlic, minced	2
1 tbsp	chopped fresh thyme	15 mL
1/4 tsp	freshly ground black pepper	1 mL
1 tbsp	olive oil	15 mL
1	small onion, finely chopped	1
1 1/2 cups	short-grain rice, such as Arborio	375 mL
1/2 cup	white wine or additional broth	125 mL
1/3 cup	freshly grated Parmesan cheese	75 mL
2 tbsp	chopped fresh parsley	25 mL

1. In a large saucepan, bring broth to a boil; reduce heat to low and keep hot.

2. In a heavy-bottomed medium saucepan, melt butter over medium heat. Add mushrooms, garlic, thyme and pepper; cook, stirring often, for 5 to 7 minutes or until tender. Remove and set aside.

3. Add oil to saucepan; cook onion, stirring, for 2 minutes or until softened. Add rice; stir for 1 minute. Add wine; stir until absorbed. Add 1 cup (250 mL) hot broth; adjust heat to a simmer so broth bubbles and is absorbed slowly. When absorbed, continue adding 1 cup (250 mL) broth at a time, stirring almost constantly, for 15 minutes. Add mushroom mixture; cook, stirring often, adding more broth when absorbed, until rice is just tender but slightly firm in the center. Mixture should be creamy; add more broth or water, if necessary. (Total cooking time will be 20 to 25 minutes.)

4. Add Parmesan cheese; adjust seasoning with pepper to taste. Spoon into warm shallow serving bowls. Sprinkle with parsley; serve immediately.

**NUTRITIONAL ANALYSIS
PER SERVING**

Calories	179
Carbohydrate	30 g
Fiber	2 g
Protein	6 g
Fat, total	4 g
Fat, saturated	2 g
Sodium	320 mg
Cholesterol	6 mg

**AMERICA'S EXCHANGES
PER SERVING**

1 1/2	Starch
1	Vegetable
1/2	Fat

**CANADA'S CHOICES
PER SERVING**

2	Carbohydrate
1	Fat

Skillet Shrimp and Rice Creole

Attractive and colorful, this classic Southern specialty relies on the flavors of tomato, celery, thyme and bay leaf. It's a spicy one-dish meal that takes only 30 minutes to cook.

Tip

Today, supermarkets stock frozen shrimp already peeled and deveined — a convenient option for this recipe.

1 tbsp	vegetable oil	15 mL
1	large onion, chopped	1
2	cloves garlic, finely chopped	2
2	stalks celery, chopped	2
1/2 tsp	dried thyme leaves	2 mL
1	bay leaf	1
1 cup	long-grain white rice	250 mL
1	red bell pepper, diced	1
1	can (14 oz/398 mL) tomatoes, including juice, chopped	1
1 cup	fish broth or reduced-sodium chicken broth	250 mL
Pinch	cayenne pepper	Pinch
2	small zucchini, halved lengthwise and thinly sliced	2
1 lb	large shrimp, peeled and deveined, tails left on	500 g

1. In a large nonstick skillet, heat oil over medium heat. Add onion, garlic, celery, thyme and bay leaf; cook, stirring, for 5 minutes or until softened.

2. Stir in rice and red pepper; cook for 2 minutes. Add tomatoes with juice, broth and a generous pinch cayenne pepper. Bring to a boil; reduce heat, cover and simmer for 15 minutes.

3. Stir in zucchini; bury shrimp in rice. Cover and cook for 8 minutes or until zucchini are tender and shrimp are pink and firm.

NUTRITIONAL ANALYSIS PER SERVING	
Calories	229
Carbohydrate	33 g
Fiber	2 g
Protein	16 g
Fat, total	3 g
Fat, saturated	0 g
Sodium	335 mg
Cholesterol	112 mg

AMERICA'S EXCHANGES PER SERVING	
2	Starch
1/2	Vegetable
1	Very Lean Meat

CANADA'S CHOICES PER SERVING	
2	Carbohydrate
1 1/2	Meat & Alternatives

Bistro Lentils

It's Friday night. You've worked hard all week. Don't even bother setting the table. Here's a supper dish that's easy to balance on your lap while you relax in front of the TV.

3½ cups	reduced-sodium chicken broth or vegetable broth (approx.)	875 mL
1½ cups	lentils, rinsed and sorted	375 mL
½ tsp	dried thyme leaves	2 mL
1 tbsp	olive oil	15 mL
1 cup	diced red onions	250 mL
3	cloves garlic, finely chopped	3
2	carrots, peeled and diced	2
1 cup	diced fennel or celery	250 mL
1	red bell pepper, diced	1
2 tbsp	balsamic vinegar	25 mL
1 cup	diced extra-lean kielbasa or lean ham (about 5 oz/150 g)	250 mL
	Freshly ground black pepper	
¼ cup	chopped fresh parsley	50 mL

1. In a large saucepan, bring broth to a boil over high heat. Add lentils and thyme; reduce heat to medium-low, cover and simmer for 25 to 30 minutes or until lentils are just tender but still hold their shape.

2. Meanwhile, heat oil in a large nonstick skillet over medium heat. Add onions, garlic, carrots and fennel; cook, stirring often, for 8 minutes. Add red pepper; cook, stirring, for 2 minutes more or until vegetables are just tender. Stir in vinegar; remove from heat.

3. Add vegetables and kielbasa to lentils in saucepan; season with pepper to taste. Cover and cook for 5 to 8 minutes more or until sausage is heated through. (Add more broth or water, if necessary, to prevent lentils from sticking.) Stir in parsley. Serve warm or at room temperature.

NUTRITIONAL ANALYSIS PER SERVING	
Calories	261
Carbohydrate	37 g
Fiber	8 g
Protein	19 g
Fat, total	5 g
Fat, saturated	0 g
Sodium	530 mg
Cholesterol	0 mg

AMERICA'S EXCHANGES PER SERVING	
1	Starch
1½	Other Carbohydrate
2½	Very Lean Meat

CANADA'S CHOICES PER SERVING	
2	Carbohydrate
2	Meat & Alternatives

SERVES 6

A simple combo of beans and vegetables is a terrific side dish or main course that will delight not only the vegetarians in the crowd but everyone else as well.

Tips

Canned dried legumes such as kidney beans contain significant amounts of fiber. They are also valuable sources of protein and are included in the meat group. Some other varieties in this group are black beans, black-eyed peas, chickpeas, great Northern beans, lentils, navy beans, pinto beans and split peas. Most are canned with salt, so be sure to drain and rinse them well.

To make 1 cup (250 mL) fresh bread crumbs, process 2 slices crusty bread in a food processor until fine.

Recipe can be prepared through Step 3 up to 1 day ahead; cover and refrigerate.

Baked Italian White Beans

- Preheat oven to 350°F (180°C)
- 8-cup (2 L) shallow baking dish, sprayed with vegetable cooking spray

2 tbsp	olive oil, divided	25 mL
2 cups	chopped Spanish onion	500 mL
3	cloves garlic, finely chopped	3
1 tbsp	balsamic vinegar	15 mL
5	tomatoes, seeded and diced	5
1 tbsp	chopped fresh thyme	15 mL
1	bay leaf	1
	Freshly ground black pepper	
2	small zucchini, halved lengthwise, thickly sliced	2
1	red bell pepper, diced	1
1	yellow bell pepper, diced	1
1	can (19 oz/540 mL) white kidney beans, drained and rinsed	1
1 cup	soft fresh bread crumbs	250 mL
2 tbsp	chopped fresh parsley	25 mL
1	large clove garlic, minced	1

1. In a large saucepan, heat 1 tbsp (15 mL) of the oil over medium heat. Cook onions and garlic, stirring often, for 5 minutes or until softened. Add vinegar and cook until evaporated. Add tomatoes, thyme and bay leaf; season with pepper to taste. Bring to a boil. Reduce heat, cover and simmer for 20 minutes.

2. Add zucchini and peppers; cook for 5 to 7 minutes or until vegetables are tender-crisp. Gently stir in beans. Spoon mixture into prepared baking dish.

3. In a bowl, combine bread crumbs, parsley and garlic. Drizzle with remaining olive oil and toss to coat. Sprinkle over beans; bake for 35 to 45 minutes or until bubbly and top is golden.

NUTRITIONAL ANALYSIS PER SERVING	
Calories	198
Carbohydrate	32 g
Fiber	9 g
Protein	8 g
Fat, total	6 g
Fat, saturated	1 g
Sodium	245 mg
Cholesterol	0 mg

AMERICA'S EXCHANGES PER SERVING	
1	Starch
1	Other Carbohydrate
½	Very Lean Meat
1	Fat

CANADA'S CHOICES PER SERVING	
1½	Carbohydrate
½	Meat & Alternatives
½	Fat

SERVES 8

Here's an old-time favorite that stirs memories of the pioneer spirit. This rustic dish is a winter standby and wonderful when served with home-baked bread.

Variation

Vegetarian Baked Beans

For a vegetarian version, omit bacon and cook onions and garlic in 2 tbsp (25 mL) vegetable oil.

Molasses Baked Beans

- Preheat oven to 300°F (150°C)
- 12-cup (3 L) casserole dish or bean pot

1 lb	dried great Northern or white pea beans, rinsed and picked over (about 2¼ cups/550 mL)	500 g
6	slices lean smoky bacon, chopped	6
1	large onion, chopped	1
3	cloves garlic, finely chopped	3
1	can (7½ oz/213 mL) tomato sauce	1
⅓ cup	fancy molasses	75 mL
¼ cup	packed brown sugar	50 mL
2 tbsp	balsamic vinegar	25 mL
2 tsp	dry mustard	10 mL
1 tsp	salt	5 mL
¼ tsp	freshly ground black pepper	1 mL

1. In a large Dutch oven or saucepan, combine beans with 6 cups (1.5 L) cold water. Bring to a boil over high heat; boil for 2 minutes. Remove from heat, cover and let stand for 1 hour.

2. Drain beans and cover with 8 cups (2 L) cold water. Bring to a boil; reduce heat, cover and simmer for 30 to 40 minutes or until beans are just tender but still hold their shape. Drain, reserving 2 cups (500 mL) cooking liquid. Place beans in casserole dish or bean pot.

3. Meanwhile, in a saucepan, cook bacon over medium heat, stirring often, for 5 minutes or until crisp. Drain fat from pan. Add onion and garlic; cook, stirring, for 3 minutes or until softened.

4. Add 2 cups (500 mL) reserved bean-cooking liquid, tomato sauce, molasses, brown sugar, balsamic vinegar, mustard, salt and pepper. Stir into beans.

5. Cover and bake in preheated oven for 2½ to 3 hours or until most of liquid has been absorbed.

NUTRITIONAL ANALYSIS PER SERVING

Calories	287
Carbohydrate	51 g
Fiber	11 g
Protein	15 g
Fat, total	3 g
Fat, saturated	1 g
Sodium	655 mg
Cholesterol	7 mg

AMERICA'S EXCHANGES PER SERVING	
2	Starch
1	Vegetable
1	Other Carbohydrate
1	Very Lean Meat

CANADA'S CHOICES PER SERVING	
2½	Carbohydrate
1	Meat & Alternatives

Vegetables

SERVES 6

Buttermilk adds a tangy flavor and keeps the potatoes moist so they reheat beautifully the next day.

Variation

Roasted Garlic Mashed Potatoes

Beat in a whole bulb of roasted garlic (instead of fresh garlic) in the above recipe. It may seem like a lot, but once roasted, garlic loses its harsh taste and becomes very mild and buttery.

To roast garlic: Trim 1/4 inch (0.5 cm) off the stem end of a whole bulb of garlic. Place, cut side down, on a sheet of foil. Drizzle with 2 tsp (10 mL) olive oil. Wrap and place in small casserole dish. Roast in 350°F (180°C) oven for about 45 minutes or until soft. Squeeze the bulb so pulp slips out of skins.

Fluffy Garlic Mashed Potatoes

6	large Russet or Yukon Gold potatoes (about 3 lbs/1.5 kg)	6
1 tbsp	butter or olive oil	15 mL
2	cloves garlic, finely chopped, or more to taste	2
1/2 cup	low-fat milk	125 mL
3/4 cup	buttermilk or light sour cream (approx.)	175 mL
	Freshly ground black pepper or nutmeg	

1. Peel potatoes and cut into 3-inch (8 cm) chunks. In a large saucepan, cook potatoes in boiling salted water for about 20 minutes or until fork-tender. (Yukon Gold potatoes take a few minutes longer.) Drain well and return to saucepan. Place over low heat and dry for 1 to 2 minutes.

2. Press potatoes through a food mill or ricer or mash with potato masher or use an electric mixer at low speed until very smooth. (Do not use a food processor or the potatoes will turn into glue.)

3. In a small saucepan, heat butter and garlic over medium-low heat for 1 to 2 minutes; do not let garlic brown. Add milk and heat until piping hot. Beat garlic mixture into potatoes along with enough sour cream to make a smooth purée. Adjust seasoning with pepper or nutmeg to taste.

4. Place over medium heat, stirring occasionally, until potatoes are piping hot. Can be made a few hours ahead and reheated. Beat in additional milk to make potatoes creamy, if necessary.

NUTRITIONAL ANALYSIS PER SERVING

Calories	191
Carbohydrate	34 g
Fiber	2 g
Protein	5 g
Fat, total	4 g
Fat, saturated	1 g
Sodium	385 mg
Cholesterol	6 mg

AMERICA'S EXCHANGES PER SERVING	
2	Starch
1/2	Fat

CANADA'S CHOICES PER SERVING	
2	Carbohydrate
1	Fat

One-Pot Italian Sausages Braised with Potatoes (page 120) ➤
Overleaf: Mama's Italian Cheeseburgers (page 136)

Everyone's favorite do-ahead mashed potato casserole — perfect for a roast turkey or roast beef family dinner. For lump-free mashed potatoes, use a food mill or ricer instead of a potato masher.

Tips

Casserole can be prepared ahead, covered and refrigerated for up to 2 days. Increase baking time by 10 minutes.

Starchy Russet or baking potatoes produce fluffy mashed potatoes. Yellow-fleshed potatoes, such as Yukon Gold, have a slightly buttery taste and make delicious mashed potatoes with a creamier texture. Regular white potatoes also make a creamy purée, although not as flavorful. New potatoes are not suitable for mashing because, unlike storage potatoes, much of the carbohydrate has not yet been converted to starch.

Creamy Mashed Potato Casserole

- Preheat oven to 350°F (180°C)
- 8-cup (2 L) casserole dish, sprayed with vegetable cooking spray

6	large Russet potatoes, peeled and quartered (about 3 lbs/1.5 kg)	6
4 oz	light cream cheese, softened, cubed	125 g
¾ cup	hot low-fat milk (approx.)	175 mL
	Freshly grated nutmeg	
½ cup	shredded light Cheddar cheese	125 mL
¼ cup	fine dry bread crumbs	50 mL
½ tsp	paprika	2 mL

1. Peel potatoes and cut into 3-inch (8 cm) chunks. In a large saucepan, cook potatoes in boiling water for about 20 minutes or until fork-tender. (Yukon Gold potatoes take a few minutes longer.) Drain well and return to saucepan. Place over low heat and dry for 1 to 2 minutes.

2. Press potatoes through a food mill or ricer or mash with potato masher or use an electric mixer at low speed until very smooth. (Do not use a food processor or the potatoes will turn to glue.) Beat in cream cheese and milk until smooth; season with nutmeg to taste. Spoon in prepared casserole dish.

3. In a small bowl, combine Cheddar cheese, bread crumbs and paprika. Sprinke evenly over potatoes.

4. Bake, uncovered, in preheated oven for 40 to 50 minutes or until top is golden and a knife inserted in center is hot to the touch.

NUTRITIONAL ANALYSIS PER SERVING	
Calories	239
Carbohydrate	36 g
Fiber	2 g
Protein	9 g
Fat, total	7 g
Fat, saturated	4 g
Sodium	285 mg
Cholesterol	21 mg

AMERICA'S EXCHANGES PER SERVING	
2	Starch
½	Other Carbohydrate
½	Lean Meat
½	Fat

CANADA'S CHOICES PER SERVING	
2	Carbohydrate
½	Meat & Alternatives
1	Fat

◄ Spaghetti with Meatballs (page 159)
Overleaf: Amazing Chili (page 150)

SERVES 6

I wouldn't dream of serving a baked ham without this favorite side dish. Use your food processor to quickly slice the potatoes.

Tip

To make ahead, layer potatoes in cream sauce in dish, cover and refrigerate for up to 1 day.

Variation

Scalloped Potatoes with Ham and Swiss Cheese
Add 4 oz (125 g) smoked ham, cut into 1-inch (2.5 cm) strips, along with potatoes in the sauce. Substitute light Swiss cheese for the Cheddar.

Classic Scalloped Potatoes

- Preheat oven to 350°F (180°C)
- 11- by 9-inch (2.5 L) baking dish, sprayed with vegetable cooking spray

1 tbsp	butter	15 mL
1	large onion, halved lengthwise, thinly sliced	1
2 tbsp	all-purpose flour	25 mL
1 1/2 cups	low-fat milk	375 mL
2 tsp	Dijon mustard	10 mL
1/2 tsp	salt	2 mL
Pinch	freshly grated nutmeg	Pinch
6	medium potatoes (about 2 lbs/1 kg)	6
1 cup	shredded light Cheddar cheese	250 mL

1. In a saucepan, melt butter over medium heat. Cook onion, stirring often, for 3 minutes or until softened.

2. Place flour in bowl and blend in 1/4 cup (50 ml) milk to make a smooth paste. Stir in rest of milk until smooth. Add mustard, salt and nutmeg. Add to saucepan. Bring to boil, stirring, until sauce thickens.

3. Peel and thinly slice potatoes; rinse under cold water. Drain; wrap in dry clean towel to dry. Stir into sauce; bring to a boil over medium heat. Spoon into baking dish; sprinkle with cheese. Bake for 45 to 50 minutes or until potatoes are tender and top is golden.

NUTRITIONAL ANALYSIS PER SERVING	
Calories	211
Carbohydrate	28 g
Fiber	2 g
Protein	9 g
Fat, total	7 g
Fat, saturated	4 g
Sodium	450 mg
Cholesterol	21 mg

AMERICA'S EXCHANGES PER SERVING	
1 1/2	Starch
1/2	Vegetable
1/2	High-fat Meat
1/2	Fat

CANADA'S CHOICES PER SERVING	
2	Carbohydrate
1/2	Meat & Alternatives
1	Fat

With the shortcut microwave method, you'll also find this versatile dish a breeze to make for quick family suppers.

Easy Parmesan Potato Bake

- Preheat oven to 375°F (190°C)
- 11- by 9-inch (2.5 L) baking dish, sprayed with vegetable cooking spray

6	medium potatoes, peeled and thinly sliced (about 2 lbs/1 kg)	6
1 cup	reduced-sodium chicken broth or vegetable broth	250 mL
1 tbsp	melted butter or olive oil	15 mL
1	large clove garlic, minced	1
1/4 tsp	salt	1 mL
1/4 tsp	freshly ground black pepper	1 mL
1/3 cup	freshly grated Parmesan cheese	75 mL
1 tbsp	chopped fresh parsley	15 mL

1. Layer potatoes in prepared baking dish. In a large glass measuring cup, combine broth, butter, garlic, salt and pepper; pour over potatoes. Sprinkle with Parmesan and parsley.

2. Bake in preheated oven for 50 to 60 minutes or until potatoes are tender and top is golden brown.

Quick Microwave-Broiler Method

1. Preheat broiler. Layer potatoes in baking dish; pour broth mixture over. Cover with lid, or use microwave-safe plastic wrap and turn back one corner to vent. Microwave at High for 8 minutes. Rearrange potato slices. Cover and microwave at High for another 6 to 8 minutes or until potatoes are tender when pierced with a fork. Sprinkle with Parmesan and parsley. Place under broiler, about 5 inches (12 cm) from heat; cook for 2 to 3 minutes or until nicely browned.

NUTRITIONAL ANALYSIS PER SERVING	
Calories	134
Carbohydrate	21 g
Fiber	2 g
Protein	5 g
Fat, total	4 g
Fat, saturated	2 g
Sodium	305 mg
Cholesterol	10 mg

AMERICA'S EXCHANGES PER SERVING	
1 1/2	Starch
1/2	Fat

CANADA'S CHOICES PER SERVING	
1	Carbohydrate
1	Fat

Oven French Fries

If you love french fries (and who doesn't?), but you're concerned about calories, here's the next best thing to deep-frying.

Tips

Dark rimmed baking sheets attract the oven heat and will roast the potatoes faster and give them a more intense color than shiny aluminum ones.

One serving of these french fries contains 30 g of carbohydrate and just 5 g of fat. A comparable quantity of fast-food fries contains the same amount of carbohydrate, but about 14 g of fat and 80 additional calories.

- Preheat oven to 450°F (230°C)
- 2 baking sheets, sprayed with vegetable cooking spray

| 4 | large or 6 medium Russet potatoes (about 2 lbs/1kg) | 4 |
| 4 tsp | olive or vegetable oil | 20 mL |

1. Peel potatoes and cut into long strips ½ inch by ½ inch (1 cm) in diameter. Rinse in several changes cold water to remove surface starch. Cover with cold water until ready to cook. Drain well; wrap in clean dry kitchen towel to dry potatoes thoroughly.

2. Place potatoes on baking sheets; drizzle with oil and toss to coat evenly. Arrange in a single layer. Roast in oven for 25 to 30 minutes, stirring occasionally, until tender and golden brown.

NUTRITIONAL ANALYSIS PER SERVING

Calories	171
Carbohydrate	30 g
Fiber	2 g
Protein	3 g
Fat, total	5 g
Fat, saturated	1 g
Sodium	5 mg
Cholesterol	0 mg

AMERICA'S EXCHANGES PER SERVING

2	Starch
½	Fat

CANADA'S CHOICES PER SERVING

2	Carbohydrate
1	Fat

If you're like me, you'll come to rely on this breezy side dish as the perfect complement to a Sunday roast. I also like it with Quick Bistro-Style Steak (see recipe, page 78) and other grilled meats.

Tip

Peel the potatoes if you like, but I find the potatoes are tastier with the skin left on.

Roasted Garlic Potatoes

- Preheat oven to 400°F (200°C)
- 13- by 9-inch (3 L) baking dish, sprayed with vegetable cooking spray

4	large Russet potatoes, scrubbed and cut into 1-inch (2.5 cm) chunks (about 2 lbs/1 kg)	4
4 tsp	olive oil	20 mL
4	cloves garlic, slivered	4
	Freshly ground black pepper	
1 tbsp	chopped fresh parsley	15 mL

1. Cook potato chunks in a large saucepan of boiling salted water for 5 minutes; drain well. Spread in baking dish. Drizzle with oil and garlic; season with pepper to taste.

2. Roast for 40 minutes, stirring occasionally, until potatoes are tender and golden. Sprinkle with parsley.

NUTRITIONAL ANALYSIS PER SERVING

Calories	138
Carbohydrate	26 g
Fiber	2 g
Protein	3 g
Fat, total	3 g
Fat, saturated	0 g
Sodium	300 mg
Cholesterol	0 mg

AMERICA'S EXCHANGES PER SERVING

1	Starch
½	Other Carbohydrate
½	Fat

CANADA'S CHOICES PER SERVING

1½	Carbohydrate
½	Fat

Potato Pudding

This classic comfort food, called kugel, is a staple in Jewish cooking. It's a delicious accompaniment to roasted meats and chicken.

Tip

Make sure to grate potatoes just before using since they discolor quickly.

- Preheat oven to 350°F (180°C)
- 8-inch (2 L) square baking dish, sprayed with vegetable cooking spray

2	eggs	2
2 tbsp	all-purpose flour	25 mL
I tbsp	chopped fresh parsley	15 mL
I	large clove garlic, minced	I
½ tsp	salt	2 mL
¼ tsp	freshly ground black pepper	I mL
I	medium onion	I
6	medium potatoes (about 2 lbs/I kg)	6

1. In a bowl, beat eggs; stir in flour, parsley, garlic, salt and pepper. Using a food processor, grate onion; fold into egg mixture.

2. Peel potatoes; wash and cut into quarters. Grate using a food processor. Wrap in a large clean kitchen towel; squeeze out excess moisture. Stir into onion mixture until combined. (Do this quickly before potatoes discolor.)

3. Spread evenly in baking dish. Bake in oven for about 1 hour or until top is nicely browned. Cut into squares and serve.

NUTRITIONAL ANALYSIS PER SERVING

Calories	194
Carbohydrate	36 g
Fiber	3 g
Protein	7 g
Fat, total	3 g
Fat, saturated	I g
Sodium	330 mg
Cholesterol	93 mg

AMERICA'S EXCHANGES PER SERVING

2	Starch
½	Other Carbohydrate

CANADA'S CHOICES PER SERVING

2	Carbohydrate
½	Fat

These delicious baked potatoes are great to pack along to work if you have the use of a microwave for reheating.

Tip

Cheddar and broccoli are a classic combo, but get adventurous with whatever cheese and vegetables are in the fridge. Another favorite is part-skim mozzarella cheese and lightly sautéed mushrooms and diced red peppers seasoned with basil.

Broccoli and Cheese–Stuffed Potatoes

- Preheat oven to 400°F (200°C)
- 13- by 9-inch (3 L) baking dish

4	large baking potatoes (each 8 oz/250 g)	4
3 cups	small broccoli florets and chopped peeled stems	750 mL
1/2 cup	plain low-fat yogurt or buttermilk (approx.)	125 mL
2	green onions, chopped	2
3/4 cup	shredded light Cheddar or light Swiss cheese, divided	175 mL
	Cayenne pepper	

1. Scrub potatoes well and pierce skins with a fork in several places to allow steam to escape. Bake or microwave potatoes (see tips, page 200).

2. In a saucepan, cook or steam broccoli until just tender-crisp. (Or place in covered casserole and microwave at High for 3 minutes.) Drain well.

3. Cut a thin slice from tops of warm potatoes. Scoop out potato, leaving a 1/4-inch (0.5 cm) shell, being careful not to tear the skins.

4. In a bowl, mash potato with potato masher or fork; beat in enough yogurt until smooth. Add broccoli, green onions and 1/2 cup (125 mL) cheese. Season with cayenne pepper to taste.

5. Spoon filling into potato shells, moulding the tops. Arrange in shallow baking dish; sprinkle with remaining cheese. Bake in preheated oven for 20 minutes or until cheese melts. Or place on a microwave-safe rack and microwave at Medium-High (70%) for 5 to 7 minutes or until heated through and cheese melts.

NUTRITIONAL ANALYSIS PER SERVING	
Calories	295
Carbohydrate	51 g
Fiber	6 g
Protein	13 g
Fat, total	5 g
Fat, saturated	3 g
Sodium	230 mg
Cholesterol	16 mg

AMERICA'S EXCHANGES PER SERVING	
3	Starch
1/2	Other Carbohydrate
1/2	Lean meat

CANADA'S CHOICES PER SERVING	
3	Carbohydrate
1	Meat & Alternatives

SERVES 4

Baked potatoes stuffed with a variety of fillings is a popular meal in my house. I make them ahead for those nights when everyone is on a different schedule. The potatoes need only a quick reheat in the microwave as each person walks through the door for an instant supper.

Tips

To oven-bake potatoes: Place in 400°F (200°C) oven for 1 hour or until potatoes give slightly when squeezed.

To microwave: Arrange potatoes in a circle 1 inch (2.5 cm) apart on a paper towel. Microwave on High, turning halfway through cooking, until potatoes are just tender when pierced. Microwave cooking times: 1 potato, 4 to 5 minutes; 2 potatoes, 6 to 8 minutes; 4 potatoes, 10 to 12 minutes.

For moist potatoes wrap cooked potatoes individually in foil. For drier potatoes, wrap in a dry towel. Let stand 5 minutes.

NUTRITIONAL ANALYSIS PER SERVING	
Calories	411
Carbohydrate	50 g
Fiber	4 g
Protein	22 g
Fat, total	14 g
Fat, saturated	6 g
Sodium	225 mg
Cholesterol	47 mg

Beef-Stuffed Spuds

- Preheat oven to 400°F (200°C)
- 13- by 9-inch (3 L) baking dish

4	large baking potatoes (each 8 oz/250 g)	4
8 oz	lean ground beef or veal	250 g
1/3 cup	finely chopped onions	75 mL
1	clove garlic, minced	1
1 tsp	Worcestershire sauce	5 mL
	Freshly ground black pepper	
1/2 cup	light sour cream, plain low-fat yogurt or buttermilk (approx.)	125 mL
2/3 cup	shredded light Cheddar cheese	150 mL
2 tbsp	chopped fresh parsley	25 mL

1. Scrub potatoes well and pierce skins with a fork in several places to allow steam to escape. Bake or microwave potatoes (see tips, at left).

2. In a large nonstick skillet over medium-high heat, cook beef, breaking up with a wooden spoon, for 4 minutes or until no longer pink. Reduce heat to medium. Add onions, garlic and Worcestershire sauce; season with pepper. Cook, stirring often, for 4 minutes or until onions are softened.

3. Cut warm potatoes in half lengthwise. Carefully scoop out each potato, leaving a 1/4-inch (0.5 cm) shell; set shells aside.

4. In a bowl, mash potatoes with potato masher or fork; beat in enough sour cream until smooth. Stir in beef mixture, half the cheese and all the parsley; season with pepper to taste. Spoon into potato shells; top with remaining cheese.

5. Arrange in baking dish; bake in preheated oven for 15 minutes or until cheese is melted. Or place on microwave-safe rack or large serving plate; microwave at Medium-High (70%) for 5 to 7 minutes or until heated through and cheese melts.

AMERICA'S EXCHANGES PER SERVING	
3	Starch
1/2	Vegetable
2	Medium-fat Meat

CANADA'S CHOICES PER SERVING	
3	Carbohydrate
2	Meat & Alternatives
1	Fat

SERVES 10

I love the combination of sweet potatoes and apples accented with maple syrup. It's great served with pork or chicken.

Tip

You can make this vegetable dish a day ahead; cover and refrigerate. To reheat, cover and microwave at High until piping hot.

Variation

Butternut Squash Purée with Apples
Instead of sweet potatoes, use 2 lbs (1 kg) butternut squash, peeled and seeds removed.

Microwave Sweet Potato Purée with Apples

● *8-cup (2 L) casserole dish, sprayed with vegetable cooking spray*

2 tsp	butter	10 mL
1	small onion, chopped	1
3	sweet potatoes, peeled and cut into 1½-inch (4 cm) chunks (about 2 lbs/1 kg)	3
2	apples, peeled, cored and chopped	2
¼ cup	pure maple syrup	50 mL
	Freshly ground black pepper and freshly grated nutmeg	

1. In casserole dish, combine butter and onion; microwave at High for 2 minutes or until onion is softened. Add sweet potatoes and apples; drizzle with maple syrup. Cover and microwave at High for 20 to 25 minutes, stirring once, until sweet potatoes are very tender.

2. In a food processor, purée in batches until smooth. Place in a serving dish; season with pepper and nutmeg to taste.

NUTRITIONAL ANALYSIS PER SERVING

Calories	113
Carbohydrate	26 g
Fiber	2 g
Protein	1 g
Fat, total	1 g
Fat, saturated	1 g
Sodium	15 mg
Cholesterol	2 mg

AMERICA'S EXCHANGES PER SERVING

1	Starch
½	Other Carbohydrate

CANADA'S CHOICES PER SERVING

1½	Carbohydrate

SERVES 6

If the soft texture of a squash purée doesn't appeal to you, try this easy stir-fry instead.

Tip

To prepare squash, peel using a vegetable peeler or paring knife. Cut into lengthwise quarters and seed. Cut into thin ¼-inch (0.5 cm) by 1½-inch (4 cm) pieces.

Butternut Squash with Snow Peas and Red Pepper

1 tbsp	vegetable oil	15 mL
5 cups	prepared butternut squash (see tip, at left)	1.25 L
4 oz	snow peas, ends trimmed	125 g
1	red bell pepper, cut into thin strips	1
1 tbsp	packed brown sugar	15 mL
1½ tsp	grated fresh gingerroot	7 mL
	Freshly ground black pepper	

1. In a large nonstick skillet, heat oil over medium-high heat. Cook squash, stirring, for 3 to 4 minutes or until almost tender.
2. Add snow peas, red pepper, brown sugar and ginger. Cook, stirring often, for 2 minutes or until vegetables are tender-crisp. Season with pepper to taste.

NUTRITIONAL ANALYSIS PER SERVING

Calories	95
Carbohydrate	19 g
Fiber	3 g
Protein	2 g
Fat, total	2 g
Fat, saturated	0 g
Sodium	5 mg
Cholesterol	0 mg

AMERICA'S EXCHANGES PER SERVING

1	Starch
½	Fat

CANADA'S CHOICES PER SERVING

1	Carbohydrate

Forget the cranberry sauce the next time you serve roast turkey. Serve these tasty onions to complement a holiday bird or roast pork.

Roasted Pearl Onions with Cranberries

- Preheat oven to 375°F (190°C)
- Large shallow baking dish

2	packages or pint baskets (each 10 oz/284 g) pearl onions	2
½ cup	fresh cranberries	125 mL
¼ cup	ruby Port wine	50 mL
1 tbsp	brown sugar	15 mL
1 tsp	finely chopped fresh rosemary leaves	5 mL
1 tbsp	butter, cut into bits	15 mL
	Freshly ground black pepper	

1. In a large saucepan of boiling salted water, blanch onions for 2 minutes. Drain; run under cold water. Remove stem ends and skins. Place in a baking dish large enough to hold onions in a single layer.

2. Add cranberries, port, brown sugar and rosemary. Dot with butter and season with pepper.

3. Roast in preheated oven, stirring occasionally, for about 35 minutes or until onions are tender and sauce is reduced and slightly thickened. Serve warm or at room temperature.

NUTRITIONAL ANALYSIS PER SERVING	
Calories	105
Carbohydrate	18 g
Fiber	2 g
Protein	2 g
Fat, total	3 g
Fat, saturated	2 g
Sodium	35 mg
Cholesterol	8 mg

AMERICA'S EXCHANGES PER SERVING	
2	Vegetable
½	Other Carbohydrate
½	Fat

CANADA'S CHOICES PER SERVING	
1	Carbohydrate
½	Fat

SERVES 6

I love the way oven-roasting sweetens and concentrates the flavors of these sturdy root vegetables. This dish is a natural with stew and mashed potatoes.

Tip

We're used to roasting potatoes, so moving on to other vegetables isn't that much of a shift in our cooking style. Try this treatment with other vegetables such as peppers, winter squash, beets, cauliflower and even asparagus. You'll be amazed with the results. Use oil instead of butter and add a sprinkling of dried herbs, if you like. Reduce cooking time according to the size and type of vegetables.

Oven-Roasted Root Vegetables

- Preheat oven to 400°F (200°C)
- 13- by 9-inch (3 L) baking dish, sprayed with vegetable cooking spray

3	medium carrots	3
2	medium parsnips	2
½	small rutabaga (about 8 oz/250 g)	½
1	medium red onion, cut into wedges	1
2	cloves garlic, cut into slivers	2
¼ cup	dry sherry or reduced-sodium chicken broth	50 mL
1 tbsp	melted butter	15 mL
½ tsp	salt	2 mL
¼ tsp	freshly ground black pepper	1 mL
2 tbsp	finely chopped fresh parsley	25 mL

1. Peel carrots, parsnips and rutabaga; cut into 2- by ½-inch (5 by 1 cm) strips. Place in prepared baking dish along with onion and garlic.

2. In a small bowl, combine sherry and butter; drizzle over vegetables. Sprinkle with salt and pepper.

3. Cover dish with foil; bake for 30 minutes. Remove foil; bake for 25 to 30 minutes more, stirring occasionally, until vegetables are tender and light golden. Sprinkle with parsley before serving.

NUTRITIONAL ANALYSIS PER SERVING

Calories	101
Carbohydrate	19 g
Fiber	4 g
Protein	2 g
Fat, total	2 g
Fat, saturated	1 g
Sodium	245 mg
Cholesterol	5 mg

AMERICA'S EXCHANGES PER SERVING

1	Vegetable
1	Other Carbohydrate
½	Fat

CANADA'S CHOICES PER SERVING

1	Carbohydrate
½	Fat

Snowy cauliflower topped with cheese and nuts makes the perfect side dish for a Sunday roast. For vegetarians, it becomes a main course dish when served along with grains or a bowl of pasta.

Tip

Sprinkle the garlic-crumb mixture over other vegetables such as broccoli, Brussels sprouts or spinach. Unblanched almonds, pecans or walnuts can replace the hazelnuts.

Cauliflower with Hazelnut Crumb Topping

- *Preheat broiler*
- *12- by 8-inch (2.5 L) shallow baking dish, sprayed with vegetable cooking spray*

I tbsp	butter	15 mL
¼ cup	hazelnuts, finely chopped	50 mL
½ cup	soft fresh bread crumbs	125 mL
I	large clove garlic, minced	I
½ cup	finely shredded light Swiss or light Cheddar cheese	125 mL
2 tbsp	chopped fresh parsley	25 mL
I	medium cauliflower, broken into florets	I

1. In a medium nonstick skillet, melt butter over medium heat. Add hazelnuts and cook, stirring, for 1 minute or until lightly toasted. Add bread crumbs and garlic; cook, stirring, for 1 minute more or until crumbs are lightly colored. Remove from heat; let cool.

2. In a bowl, combine crumb mixture, cheese and parsley.

3. In a large saucepan of boiling salted water, cook cauliflower for 3 to 5 minutes or until tender-crisp. Drain well. Place in baking dish; sprinkle with crumb mixture. Place under preheated broiler for 1 to 2 minutes or until topping is lightly browned.

NUTRITIONAL ANALYSIS PER SERVING	
Calories	133
Carbohydrate	7 g
Fiber	2 g
Protein	8 g
Fat, total	9 g
Fat, saturated	4 g
Sodium	155 mg
Cholesterol	18 mg

AMERICA'S EXCHANGES PER SERVING	
I	Vegetable
I	High-fat Meat

CANADA'S CHOICES PER SERVING	
½	Carbohydrate
I	Meat & Alternatives
I	Fat

SERVES 6
(Makes 1¼ cups/
300 mL sauce)

This simple vegetable side dish appears at all our family gatherings including Christmas and Thanksgiving. It's a hit with everybody. Serve the cheese sauce with other vegetables such as cauliflower and Brussels sprouts.

Tip

To prepare broccoli stems, cut off the woody ends and peel stems. Cut into 2- by ½-inch (5 by 1 cm) pieces.

Steamed Broccoli with Cheddar Cheese Sauce

● *8-cup (2 L) casserole dish*

8 cups	broccoli stems and florets (1 large bunch)	2 L
1 tbsp	cornstarch	15 mL
1 cup	low-fat milk	250 mL
1 cup	shredded light Cheddar cheese	250 mL
	Ground nutmeg and cayenne pepper	

1. Steam broccoli for 5 minutes or until just tender. Drain well and place in casserole dish.

2. Meanwhile, in a small saucepan, combine cornstarch with milk; whisk until smooth. Place over medium heat; cook, whisking constantly, for 5 to 7 minutes or until mixture comes to a boil and thickens. Remove from heat. Whisk in cheese until melted. Season with nutmeg and cayenne pepper to taste. Pour over broccoli and serve immediately.

NUTRITIONAL ANALYSIS PER SERVING	
Calories	112
Carbohydrate	9 g
Fiber	3 g
Protein	9 g
Fat, total	5 g
Fat, saturated	3 g
Sodium	210 mg
Cholesterol	15 mg

AMERICA'S EXCHANGES PER SERVING	
1½	Vegetable
1	Medium-fat Meat

CANADA'S CHOICES PER SERVING	
½	Carbohydrate
1	Meat & Alternatives

SERVES 6

When locally grown asparagus appears at the market, it's one of my rites of spring. I prepare them tossed with crunchy almonds and melting Parmesan — and it's every bit as pleasing as a buttery Hollandaise.

Tip

Try making this dish with green beans. Trim and cut into 1½-inch (4 cm) lengths and cook in boiling water for about 5 minutes or until tender-crisp.

Asparagus with Parmesan and Toasted Almonds

1½ lbs	asparagus	750 g
¼ cup	sliced blanched almonds	50 mL
1 tbsp	butter	15 mL
2	cloves garlic, finely chopped	2
¼ cup	freshly grated Parmesan cheese	50 mL
	Freshly ground black pepper	

1. Snap off asparagus ends; cut spears on the diagonal into 2-inch (5 cm) lengths. In a large nonstick skillet, bring ½ cup (125 mL) water to a boil; cook asparagus for 2 minutes (start timing when water returns to a boil) or until just tender-crisp. Run under cold water to chill; drain and reserve.

2. Dry the skillet and place over medium heat. Add almonds and toast, stirring often, for 2 to 3 minutes or until golden. Remove and reserve.

3. Increase heat to medium-high. Add butter to skillet; cook asparagus and garlic, stirring, for 4 minutes or until asparagus is just tender.

4. Sprinkle with Parmesan; season with pepper. Transfer to serving bowl; top with almonds.

NUTRITIONAL ANALYSIS PER SERVING

Calories	75
Carbohydrate	4 g
Fiber	1 g
Protein	4 g
Fat, total	5 g
Fat, saturated	2 g
Sodium	105 mg
Cholesterol	8 mg

AMERICA'S EXCHANGES PER SERVING

½	Vegetable
½	High-fat Meat

CANADA'S CHOICES PER SERVING

½	Meat & Alternatives
½	Fat

SERVES 4

Roasting brings out the best in many vegetables including asparagus. The oven-roasting method is much simpler and more flavorful than the traditional way of cooking asparagus in a steamer.

Oven-Roasted Asparagus

● *Preheat oven to 425°F (220°C)*
● *Baking sheet, sprayed with vegetable cooking spray*

1 lb	asparagus	500 g
1 tbsp	olive oil	15 mL
	Freshly ground black pepper	
1 tbsp	balsamic vinegar	15 mL

1. Snap off tough asparagus ends. If large, peel stalks. Arrange in single layer on prepared baking sheet. Drizzle with oil; season with pepper.

2. Roast in oven, stirring occasionally, for 12 to 15 minutes or until almost tender.

3. Drizzle balsamic vinegar over asparagus and toss to coat. Roast for 3 to 5 minutes more or until tender-crisp. Serve immediately.

NUTRITIONAL ANALYSIS PER SERVING

Calories	46
Carbohydrate	3 g
Fiber	1 g
Protein	1 g
Fat, total	4 g
Fat, saturated	0 g
Sodium	5 mg
Cholesterol	0 mg

AMERICA'S EXCHANGES PER SERVING

½	Vegetable
1	Fat

CANADA'S CHOICES PER SERVING

1	Fat

Green Beans Stewed with Tomatoes

This is a favorite dish to make in late summer when young beans and ripe tomatoes are at their best. But even in winter, with vine-ripened greenhouse tomatoes and imported fresh beans, this recipe is still good. If bits of tomato skin in the sauce bother you, peel the tomatoes before dicing.

Tip

For a quick supper, toss vegetable sauce with 8 oz (250 g) cooked pasta, such as penne, and a sprinkle of Parmesan cheese. Also substitute other vegetables, such as fennel, asparagus or broccoli, for the beans.

1 lb	green beans	500 g
1 tbsp	olive oil	15 mL
1	small red onion, halved lengthwise, thinly sliced	1
2	cloves garlic, thinly sliced	2
1 tsp	dried basil leaves	5 mL
2	ripe tomatoes, diced	2
1 tbsp	balsamic vinegar	15 mL
2 tbsp	water (approx.)	25 mL
1/4 tsp	salt	1 mL
1/4 tsp	freshly ground black pepper	1 mL

1. Trim ends of beans; cut into 1 1/2-inch (4 cm) lengths. In a saucepan, cook beans in lightly salted boiling water for 3 minutes (start timing when water returns to a boil) or until still crisp. Drain well; reserve.

2. Meanwhile, in a large nonstick skillet, heat oil over medium heat. Add onion, garlic and basil; cook, stirring, for 2 minutes or until softened.

3. Stir in tomatoes, vinegar, water, salt and pepper; cook, stirring often, for 3 minutes or until sauce-like.

4. Add beans; cover and simmer for 8 to 10 minutes, stirring occasionally, until tender. Add more water, if necessary, to keep mixture moist. Serve warm or at room temperature.

NUTRITIONAL ANALYSIS PER SERVING	
Calories	90
Carbohydrate	13 g
Fiber	3 g
Protein	3 g
Fat, total	4 g
Fat, saturated	1 g
Sodium	225 mg
Cholesterol	0 mg

AMERICA'S EXCHANGES PER SERVING	
2	Vegetable
1	Fat

CANADA'S CHOICES PER SERVING	
1/2	Carbohydrate
1	Fat

SERVES 6

*Fresh corn is a real
summer treat. Serve this
tasty summer side dish
with grilled meats.*

Tip

Fresh corn works best,
but frozen kernels can be
substituted. To cut corn
kernels from cobs, stand
ears on end and cut
straight down using a small
sharp knife.

Easy Skillet Corn with Tomatoes and Basil

2 tsp	vegetable or olive oil	10 mL
3	green onions, sliced	3
1	small green bell pepper, diced	1
3 cups	fresh or frozen uncooked corn kernels (about 5 ears of corn)	750 mL
2	tomatoes, seeded and diced	2
2 tbsp	chopped fresh basil leaves or 1 tsp (5 mL) dried	25 mL
Pinch	granulated sugar	Pinch
	Freshly ground black pepper	

1. In a large nonstick skillet, heat oil over medium-high heat. Add green onions, green pepper, corn, tomatoes and basil (if using dried); cook, stirring often, for 5 to 7 minutes (8 to 10 minutes, if using frozen corn) or until corn is tender.

2. Add sugar; season with pepper to taste. Sprinkle with chopped basil (if using fresh).

NUTRITIONAL ANALYSIS PER SERVING	
Calories	99
Carbohydrate	20 g
Fiber	3 g
Protein	3 g
Fat, total	3 g
Fat, saturated	0 g
Sodium	15 mg
Cholesterol	0 mg

AMERICA'S EXCHANGES PER SERVING	
1	Starch
1	Vegetable
½	Fat

CANADA'S CHOICES PER SERVING	
1	Carbohydrate
½	Fat

SERVES 4

This is one of my favorite choices to accompany a holiday roast or turkey. Packages of ready-to-cook, peeled whole baby carrots are widely available in supermarkets. They certainly make a cook's life easier — especially when you're preparing a mammoth family dinner and plan to serve several dishes.

Tips

If doubling the recipe, glaze vegetables in a large nonstick skillet to evaporate the broth quickly.

Try this tasty treatment with a combination of blanched carrots, rutabaga and parsnip strips, too.

Lemon-Glazed Baby Carrots

1 lb	peeled baby carrots	500 g
1/4 cup	reduced-sodium chicken broth or vegetable broth	50 mL
2 tsp	butter	10 mL
1 tbsp	packed brown sugar	15 mL
1/2 tsp	grated lemon zest	2 mL
1 tbsp	freshly squeezed lemon juice	15 mL
1/4 tsp	salt	1 mL
	Freshly ground black pepper	
1 tbsp	finely chopped fresh parsley or chives	15 mL

1. In a medium saucepan, cook carrots in boiling salted water for 5 to 7 minutes (start timing when water returns to a boil) or until just tender-crisp; drain and return to saucepan.

2. Add broth, butter, brown sugar, lemon zest and juice, salt and pepper to taste. Cook, stirring often, for 3 to 5 minutes or until liquid has evaporated and carrots are nicely glazed.

3. Sprinkle with parsley or chives and serve.

NUTRITIONAL ANALYSIS PER SERVING

Calories	75
Carbohydrate	13 g
Fiber	2 g
Protein	1 g
Fat, total	3 g
Fat, saturated	1 g
Sodium	265 mg
Cholesterol	5 mg

AMERICA'S EXCHANGES PER SERVING

1	Vegetable
1/2	Other Carbohydrate
1/2	Fat

CANADA'S CHOICES PER SERVING

1/2	Carbohydrate
1/2	Fat

Teriyaki Vegetable Stir-Fry

Use this recipe as a guideline and then get creative with whatever vegetables you have in the fridge. You'll need about 5 cups (1.25 L) in total.

Tips

Vegetables that take longer to cook, such as carrots, broccoli and cauliflower, should be added to the skillet first before adding quick-cooking ones like peppers and zucchini.

You can also toss the cooked vegetables with 4 oz (125 g) cooked spaghettini for an easy pasta supper.

2 tbsp	light teriyaki sauce or reduced-sodium soy sauce	25 mL
2 tbsp	water	25 mL
1 tbsp	unseasoned rice vinegar	15 mL
2 tsp	packed brown sugar	10 mL
1 tsp	cornstarch	5 mL
1	large clove garlic, minced	1
2 tsp	vegetable oil	10 mL
2 cups	small cauliflower or broccoli florets	500 mL
1	red bell pepper, cut into 2-inch (5 cm) strips	1
2	small zucchini, halved lengthwise and thinly sliced	2

1. In a glass measuring cup, combine teriyaki sauce, water, vinegar, brown sugar, cornstarch and garlic; set aside.

2. In a wok or large nonstick skillet, heat oil over high heat. Add cauliflower and cook, stirring, for 1 minute. Add red pepper and zucchini; cook, stirring, for 2 minutes.

3. Reduce heat to medium. Stir teriyaki sauce and add to skillet. Cook, stirring, until sauce is slightly thickened. Cover and cook for 1 minute or until vegetables are tender-crisp.

NUTRITIONAL ANALYSIS PER SERVING	
Calories	66
Carbohydrate	10 g
Fiber	2 g
Protein	2 g
Fat, total	3 g
Fat, saturated	0 g
Sodium	140 mg
Cholesterol	0 mg

AMERICA'S EXCHANGES PER SERVING	
1½	Vegetable
½	Fat

CANADA'S CHOICES PER SERVING	
½	Carbohydrate
½	Fat

SERVES 8

I consider this recipe a convenience food. I keep containers of sweet-and-sour red cabbage in my freezer, ready to microwave at a moment's notice to serve along with pork chops or roasts.

Tips

Most cooked red cabbage recipes, this one included, call for vinegar or wine. This adds not only flavor, but acidity, which preserves the cabbage's bright red color.

To freeze, pack cabbage into containers; it freezes well for up to 3 months.

Sweet-and-Sour Red Cabbage with Apples

1 tbsp	butter	15 mL
1	large onion, finely chopped	1
2	apples, peeled, cored and diced	2
1 cup	reduced-sodium chicken broth or vegetable broth	250 mL
1/2 cup	red wine or additional broth	125 mL
1/3 cup	red wine vinegar	75 mL
1/3 cup	packed brown sugar	75 mL
1	bay leaf	1
1/2 tsp	salt	2 mL
1/4 tsp	ground cinnamon	1 mL
1/4 tsp	freshly ground black pepper	1 mL
Pinch	ground cloves	Pinch
1	medium red cabbage, finely shredded (about 10 cups/2.5 L)	1
1 1/2 tsp	cornstarch	7 mL
1 tbsp	cold water	15 mL

1. In a large Dutch oven or saucepan, heat butter over medium heat. Add onion and apples; cook, stirring often, for 5 minutes or until softened.

2. Add broth, wine, vinegar, brown sugar, bay leaf, salt, cinnamon, pepper and ground cloves. Bring to a boil; stir in cabbage.

3. Cover and simmer over medium-low heat, stirring occasionally, for 45 minutes or until cabbage is tender.

4. Blend cornstarch with water; stir into cabbage. Cook 3 minutes more or until sauce is slightly thickened. Remove bay leaf before serving.

NUTRITIONAL ANALYSIS PER SERVING	
Calories	101
Carbohydrate	20 g
Fiber	2 g
Protein	1 g
Fat, total	2 g
Fat, saturated	1 g
Sodium	235 mg
Cholesterol	4 mg

AMERICA'S EXCHANGES PER SERVING	
1	Vegetable
1	Other Carbohydrate
1/2	Fat

CANADA'S CHOICES PER SERVING	
1	Carbohydrate
1/2	Fat

This colorful vegetable medley is a great summer side dish.

Variation

Stir 2 tbsp (25 mL) pine nuts in dry skillet over medium heat for 3 to 4 minutes. Add with the basil. These will add ½ Fat Exchange or Choice.

Cherry Tomato and Zucchini Sauté with Basil

2 tsp	olive oil	10 mL
3	small zucchini, halved lengthwise and thinly sliced	3
2 cups	cherry tomatoes, halved	500 mL
½ tsp	ground cumin (optional)	2 mL
2	green onions, sliced	2
2 tsp	balsamic vinegar	10 mL
	Freshly ground black pepper	
2 tbsp	chopped fresh basil or mint leaves	25 mL

1. In a large nonstick skillet, heat oil over high heat. Add zucchini and cook, stirring, for 1 minute. Add cherry tomatoes, cumin, if using, green onions and balsamic vinegar. Cook, stirring, for 1 to 2 minutes or until zucchini is tender-crisp and tomatoes are heated through. Season with pepper to taste.

2. Sprinkle with basil and serve immediately.

NUTRITIONAL ANALYSIS PER SERVING	
Calories	52
Carbohydrate	7 g
Fiber	2 g
Protein	1 g
Fat, total	3 g
Fat, saturated	0 g
Sodium	10 mg
Cholesterol	0 mg

AMERICA'S EXCHANGES PER SERVING	
1½	Vegetable
½	Fat

CANADA'S CHOICES PER SERVING	
½	Carbohydrate
½	Fat

Salads

SERVES 8

The king of tossed salads was named after a Tijuana restaurateur by the name of Caesar Cardini. Here, mayonnaise gives this classic salad an even creamier texture than the original.

Tips

The traditional dressing for Caesar salad contains coddled (slightly cooked) eggs. Mayonnaise is used here instead because there is a small chance that raw eggs may contain salmonella bacteria.

Make sure salad greens are washed and dried thoroughly, preferably in a salad spinner, for best results. Homemade croutons make a definite flavor difference but 3 cups (750 mL) store-bought croutons work in a pinch.

Caesar Salad

¼ cup	olive oil	50 mL
2 tbsp	light mayonnaise	25 mL
2 tbsp	freshly squeezed lemon juice	25 mL
2 tbsp	water	25 mL
1 tsp	Dijon mustard	5 mL
2	cloves garlic, minced	2
3	anchovy fillets, chopped, or 1 tbsp (15 mL) anchovy paste	3
¼ tsp	freshly ground black pepper	1 mL
1	large head Romaine lettuce, torn into bite-size pieces (about 12 cups/3 L)	1
	Garlic croutons (see recipe, below)	
⅓ cup	Freshly grated Parmesan cheese	75 mL

1. In a food processor, combine oil, mayonnaise, lemon juice, water, mustard, garlic, anchovy fillets and pepper; process until smooth and creamy.

2. Arrange lettuce in salad bowl; pour dressing over and toss lightly. Add croutons; sprinkle with Parmesan cheese. Toss again. Taste and season with pepper, if needed. Serve immediately.

Garlic Croutons

● *Preheat oven to 375°F (190°C)*   ● *Baking sheet*

4 cups	cubed crusty bread, cut into ½-inch (1 cm) pieces	1 L
1 tbsp	olive oil	15 mL
1	clove garlic, minced	1
2 tbsp	freshly grated Parmesan cheese	25 mL

1. Place bread cubes in a bowl. Combine oil and garlic; drizzle over bread cubes and toss. Sprinkle with Parmesan and toss again. Arrange on baking sheet in single layer. Toast in preheated oven, stirring once, for about 10 minutes or until golden.

NUTRITIONAL ANALYSIS PER SERVING

Calories	177
Carbohydrate	12 g
Fiber	2 g
Protein	6 g
Fat, total	12 g
Fat, saturated	3 g
Sodium	305 mg
Cholesterol	7 mg

AMERICA'S EXCHANGES PER SERVING

½	Starch
½	Vegetable
½	Medium-fat Meat
2	Fat

CANADA'S CHOICES PER SERVING

½	Carbohydrate
½	Meat & Alternatives
2	Fat

Layered Greek Salad

Remember the layered salads of the 1950s — the ones made with shredded iceberg lettuce, sliced cooked eggs and frozen peas crowned with heavy mayonnaise? This updated version layers colorful vegetables that accent the flavors of Greece with a garlic-yogurt dressing and feta cheese topping.

Tip

To serve, spoon down through the vegetable layers so each serving has a little bit of everything.

To ripen tomatoes, see tip, page 37.

4 cups	plain low-fat yogurt	1 L
2	cloves garlic, minced	2
2 tbsp	olive oil	25 mL
2 tbsp	red wine vinegar	25 mL
1 tsp	salt	5 mL
1 tsp	granulated sugar	5 mL
1 tsp	dried oregano leaves	5 mL
1/4 tsp	freshly ground black pepper	1 mL
1	small head Romaine lettuce, shredded (about 8 cups/2 L, packed)	1
1	small Spanish onion, diced	1
1	red bell pepper, diced	1
1	green bell pepper, diced	1
1/2	seedless cucumber, cubed	1/2
1/4 cup	chopped fresh parsley	50 mL
1 1/2 cups	crumbled light feta cheese (about 6 oz/175 g)	375 mL
2	ripe tomatoes, cut into wedges	2
12	Kalamata olives	12

1. Place yogurt in cheesecloth-lined sieve set over a bowl. Cover and refrigerate for 4 hours or until reduced to about 2 1/2 cups (625 mL). Transfer to bowl; discard whey. Stir in garlic, oil, vinegar, salt, sugar, oregano and pepper.

2. Line bottom of 8- or 9-inch (20 or 23 cm) round glass salad bowl with lettuce. Next, layer separately the onion, red pepper, green pepper and cucumber.

3. Spread top with yogurt mixture. Refrigerate, loosely covered, for 8 hours or overnight. Sprinkle with parsley and feta. Garnish with tomato wedges and olives.

NUTRITIONAL ANALYSIS PER SERVING	
Calories	172
Carbohydrate	15 g
Fiber	2 g
Protein	11 g
Fat, total	9 g
Fat, saturated	4 g
Sodium	695 mg
Cholesterol	12 mg

AMERICA'S EXCHANGES PER SERVING	
1/2	Milk, Fat-free/Low-fat
2	Vegetable
1/2	Medium-fat Meat
1	Fat

CANADA'S CHOICES PER SERVING	
1	Carbohydrate
1	Meat & Alternatives
1	Fat

This party salad is not complicated to make, neither is it expensive to prepare. But the flavors make it special enough to serve for company — with tangy lime juice, mustard and cumin balancing the sweetness of raisins and carrots.

Tip

This colorful salad can be made up to 4 hours ahead and refrigerated. Add the dressing and toss just before serving.

Variation

Use ¾ tsp (4 mL) dried fines herbes instead of cumin.

Spinach, Mushroom and Carrot Salad

1	package (10 oz/300 g) fresh baby spinach, stemmed and coarsely chopped (about 8 cups/2 L)	1
1½ cups	sliced mushrooms	375 mL
2 cups	peeled shredded carrots	500 mL
1½ cups	seedless cucumber, halved lengthwise and sliced	375 mL
1	small red onion, thinly sliced	1
⅓ cup	dark raisins	75 mL

DRESSING

¼ cup	olive oil	50 mL
2 tbsp	freshly squeezed lime juice	25 mL
1 tbsp	liquid honey	15 mL
2 tsp	Dijon mustard	10 mL
¾ tsp	ground cumin	4 mL
1	clove garlic, minced	1
½ tsp	salt	2 mL
¼ tsp	freshly ground black pepper	1 mL

1. In a serving bowl, layer one-third of the chopped spinach, all the sliced mushrooms, another one-third of the spinach, all the shredded carrots, then remaining spinach. Layer cucumbers, onion and raisins over top. Cover and refrigerate for up to 4 hours.

2. *Dressing:* In a bowl, whisk together oil, lime juice, honey, mustard, cumin, garlic, salt and pepper. Just before serving, drizzle over salad and toss gently.

NUTRITIONAL ANALYSIS PER SERVING	
Calories	122
Carbohydrate	14 g
Fiber	2 g
Protein	2 g
Fat, total	7 g
Fat, saturated	1 g
Sodium	220 mg
Cholesterol	0 mg

AMERICA'S EXCHANGES PER SERVING	
½	Fruit
1	Vegetable
1½	Fat

CANADA'S CHOICES PER SERVING	
1	Carbohydrate
1½	Fat

SERVES 4

There are so many wonderful mushroom varieties in supermarkets these days. Feel free to use any mushroom combination, depending on what's available, when you make this earthy starter or luncheon salad. Select apple varieties, such as Cortland or Granny Smith, which resist browning when sliced.

Tips

Most produce stores sell mixes of exotic greens, but you can make your own mixture using radicchio, arugula and oak leaf lettuces.

Toast walnuts in a 350°F (180°C) oven for 7 to 9 minutes.

Variation

Instead of goat cheese, use light Brie or light Camembert.

Warm Mushroom and Goat Cheese Salad

6 cups	mesclun or mixed salad greens	1.5 L
1	large apple, quartered and cored	1
1	light goat cheese log (3½ oz/100 g) cut into 8 slices	1
2 tbsp	olive oil	25 mL
8 oz	cremini mushrooms, thickly sliced	250 g
4 oz	assorted mushrooms, such as oyster, shiitake and porcini, thickly sliced	125 g
½ cup	sliced green onions	125 mL
¼ cup	liquid honey	50 mL
¼ cup	cider vinegar	50 mL
¼ tsp	salt	1 mL
¼ tsp	freshly ground black pepper	1 mL
⅓ cup	coarsely chopped toasted walnuts	75 mL

1. Divide salad greens among four plates. Cut apple quarters into 8 thin slices; arrange in a circle in middle of each plate. Place 2 slices goat cheese in center of each circle. (Can be done shortly before serving, covered and refrigerated.)

2. In a large nonstick skillet, heat oil over medium-high heat. Cook mushrooms, stirring, for 3 to 5 minutes or until tender.

3. Add green onions, honey, vinegar, salt and pepper; cook, stirring, for 15 seconds or until hot. Remove from heat. Spoon warm mushroom mixture over salad greens. Sprinkle with walnuts. Serve immediately.

NUTRITIONAL ANALYSIS PER SERVING	
Calories	260
Carbohydrate	35 g
Fiber	5 g
Protein	9 g
Fat, total	12 g
Fat, saturated	4 g
Sodium	280 mg
Cholesterol	12 mg

AMERICA'S EXCHANGES PER SERVING	
1	Vegetable
2	Other Carbohydrate
1	Medium-fat Meat
1	Fat

CANADA'S CHOICES PER SERVING	
2	Carbohydrate
1	Meat & Alternatives
1	Fat

Creamy Coleslaw

A family barbecue and picnic calls for a generous bowl of old-fashioned cabbage slaw with a creamy mayonnaise-mustard dressing.

Variation

Waldorf Coleslaw
Substitute 2 chopped large stalks celery for the carrots, add 2 diced apples and ¾ cup (175 mL) walnuts.

8 cups	finely shredded green cabbage	2 L
5	green onions, sliced	5
2	carrots, peeled and shredded	2
2 tbsp	chopped fresh parsley	25 mL
½ cup	light mayonnaise	125 mL
2 tbsp	liquid honey	25 mL
2 tbsp	cider vinegar	25 mL
1 tbsp	Dijon mustard	15 mL
½ tsp	celery seeds (optional)	2 mL
½ tsp	salt	2 mL
¼ tsp	freshly ground black pepper	1 mL

1. In a serving bowl, combine cabbage, green onions, carrots and parsley.

2. In another bowl, stir together mayonnaise, honey, vinegar, mustard, celery seeds, if using, salt and pepper. Pour over cabbage mixture; toss to coat well. Refrigerate until ready to serve.

NUTRITIONAL ANALYSIS PER SERVING

Calories	123
Carbohydrate	16 g
Fiber	3 g
Protein	2 g
Fat, total	7 g
Fat, saturated	1 g
Sodium	335 mg
Cholesterol	6 mg

AMERICA'S EXCHANGES PER SERVING

1	Vegetable
½	Other Carbohydrate
1½	Fat

CANADA'S CHOICES PER SERVING

1	Carbohydrate
1½	Fat

This delectable grilled salad can be made with whatever vegetables you have on hand. Other vegetable suggestions include sliced baby eggplant, thickly sliced fennel or thick asparagus spears.

Tip

Soak bamboo skewers in cold water for 15 minutes to prevent them from burning when grilling the vegetables.

Grilled Vegetable Salad

- Preheat barbecue, sprayed with vegetable cooking spray
- Bamboo skewers

1	Vidalia onion	1
1	red bell pepper	1
1	yellow bell pepper	1
3	small zucchini	3

DRESSING

2 tbsp	olive oil	25 mL
1 tbsp	balsamic vinegar	15 mL
1 tbsp	red wine vinegar	15 mL
1 tsp	Dijon mustard	5 mL
1	large clove garlic, minced	1
1 tbsp	finely chopped fresh parsley	15 mL
2 tsp	finely chopped fresh rosemary or thyme leaves	10 mL
½ tsp	salt	2 mL
½ tsp	freshly ground black pepper	2 mL

1. Slice onion into four rounds; insert small bamboo skewers through slices to prevent them from falling apart when grilling. Cut peppers into quarters; remove ribs and seeds. Cut zucchini crosswise into halves and then cut each piece in half lengthwise. Arrange vegetables on a baking sheet.

2. *Dressing:* In a bowl, combine oil, vinegars, mustard, garlic, parsley, rosemary, salt and pepper. Brush vegetables with vinaigrette and let marinate at room temperature for 30 minutes or for up to 4 hours.

3. Place on grill over medium-high heat; grill for 12 to 15 minutes, turning occasionally; remove vegetables as they become tender-crisp. Transfer to a serving platter; serve warm or at room temperature.

NUTRITIONAL ANALYSIS PER SERVING	
Calories	72
Carbohydrate	10 g
Fiber	2 g
Protein	1 g
Fat, total	4 g
Fat, saturated	0 g
Sodium	165 mg
Cholesterol	0 mg

AMERICA'S EXCHANGES PER SERVING	
2	Vegetable
½	Fat

CANADA'S CHOICES PER SERVING	
½	Carbohydrate
1	Fat

Bean Salad with Mustard-Dill Dressing

SERVES 6

Bean salad is another staple we've grown up with over the years. Originally this salad used canned string beans, but fresh beans give it a new lease on taste, as does the addition of fiber-packed chickpeas.

Tip

Some bean salad recipes call for canned green beans. Salt is added to canned beans, so it's better to use fresh or frozen. One-half cup (125 mL) fresh green beans cooked without salt contains 2 mg sodium; the same amount of canned contains 180 mg.

Variation

Instead of chickpeas, you can try canned mixed beans. This includes a combination of chickpeas, red and white kidney beans and black-eyed peas. It's available in supermarkets.

1 lb	green beans	500 g
1	can (19 oz/540 mL) chickpeas, drained and rinsed	1
1/3 cup	chopped red onions	75 mL

DRESSING

2 tbsp	olive oil	25 mL
2 tbsp	red wine vinegar	25 mL
1 tbsp	Dijon mustard	15 mL
1 tbsp	granulated sugar	15 mL
1/4 tsp	salt	1 mL
1/4 tsp	freshly ground black pepper	1 mL
2 tbsp	finely chopped fresh dill	25 mL

1. Trim ends of beans; cut into 1-inch (2.5 cm) lengths. In a large pot of boiling salted water, cook beans for 3 to 5 minutes (start timing when water returns to a boil) or until tender-crisp. Drain; rinse under cold water to chill. Drain well.

2. In a serving bowl, combine green beans, chickpeas and onions.

3. *Dressing:* In a small bowl, whisk together oil, vinegar, mustard, sugar, salt and pepper until smooth. Stir in dill. Pour over beans and toss well. Refrigerate until serving time.

NUTRITIONAL ANALYSIS PER SERVING

Calories	161
Carbohydrate	23 g
Fiber	4 g
Protein	6 g
Fat, total	6 g
Fat, saturated	1 g
Sodium	325 mg
Cholesterol	0 mg

AMERICA'S EXCHANGES PER SERVING

1	Vegetable
1	Other Carbohydrate
1/2	Medium-fat Meat
1	Fat

CANADA'S CHOICES PER SERVING

1	Carbohydrate
1/2	Meat & Alternatives
1	Fat

SERVES 6

When preparing this dish ahead, I like to keep the blanched green beans, tomatoes and dressing separate and toss them just before serving to prevent the salad from getting soggy.

Tip

Use the terrific mustardy dressing with other favorite vegetable salad mixtures and crisp greens.

Green Bean and Plum Tomato Salad

1 lb	young green beans, trimmed	500 g
8	small plum tomatoes (about 1 lb/500 g)	8
2	green onions, sliced	2

DRESSING

1/4 cup	olive oil	50 mL
4 tsp	red wine vinegar	20 mL
1 tbsp	grainy mustard	15 mL
1	clove garlic, minced	1
1/2 tsp	granulated sugar	2 mL
1/4 tsp	salt	1 mL
1/4 tsp	freshly ground black pepper	1 mL
1/4 cup	chopped fresh parsley	50 mL

1. In a medium saucepan of boiling salted water, cook beans for 3 to 5 minutes or until just tender-crisp. Drain and rinse under cold water to chill; drain well. Pat dry with paper towels or wrap in a clean dry towel.

2. Cut plum tomatoes in half lengthwise; using a small spoon, scoop out centers. Cut each piece again in half lengthwise; place in a bowl. Just before serving, combine beans, tomatoes and green onions in a serving bowl.

3. *Dressing:* In a small bowl, whisk together oil, vinegar, mustard, garlic, sugar, salt and pepper. Stir in parsley. Pour dressing over salad and toss well.

NUTRITIONAL ANALYSIS PER SERVING	
Calories	128
Carbohydrate	10 g
Fiber	3 g
Protein	2 g
Fat, total	10 g
Fat, saturated	1 g
Sodium	150 mg
Cholesterol	0 mg

AMERICA'S EXCHANGES PER SERVING	
2	Vegetable
2	Fat

CANADA'S CHOICES PER SERVING	
1/2	Carbohydrate
2	Fat

Best-Ever Potato Salad

SERVES 8

If anything signals the arrival of summer days and backyard barbecues, it's a trusty potato salad. My version goes beyond tossing potatoes with mayonnaise. In this recipe, warm potatoes are steeped in a tasty marinade before mayonnaise is introduced. The result? A summertime family favorite.

6	medium-sized new potatoes (about 2 lbs/1kg)	6
3/4 cup	frozen peas	175 mL
2 tbsp	red wine vinegar	25 mL
1 tbsp	Dijon mustard	15 mL
1	clove garlic, minced	1
4	green onions, sliced	4
2	stalks celery, diced	2
1/4 cup	chopped fresh parsley or dill	50 mL
1/2 cup	light mayonnaise	125 mL
1/4 cup	plain low-fat yogurt or light sour cream	50 mL
3	hard-cooked eggs, chopped	3
	Freshly ground black pepper	

1. In a medium saucepan of boiling salted water, cook whole potatoes for 20 to 25 minutes or until just tender. Drain; when cool enough to handle, peel and cut into 1/2-inch (1 cm) cubes. Place in a serving bowl.

2. Rinse peas with boiling water and drain well.

3. In a small bowl, stir together vinegar, mustard and garlic; pour over warm potatoes and toss gently. Let cool to room temperature. Stir in onions, celery and parsley. Add chopped eggs and peas.

4. In a bowl, combine mayonnaise, yogurt, salt and pepper to taste. Fold into potato mixture until evenly coated. Refrigerate until serving time.

NUTRITIONAL ANALYSIS PER SERVING	
Calories	162
Carbohydrate	20 g
Fiber	2 g
Protein	5 g
Fat, total	7 g
Fat, saturated	1 g
Sodium	395 mg
Cholesterol	75 mg

AMERICA'S EXCHANGES PER SERVING	
1	Starch
1/2	Medium-fat Meat
1	Fat

CANADA'S CHOICES PER SERVING	
1	Carbohydrate
1	Fat

Cut preparation time way down by using store-bought tzatziki in this salad. The garlicky Greek sauce made with yogurt and cucumber is not only great for souvlaki, but also makes a delicious salad dressing to use instead of mayonnaise.

Tips

To seed tomatoes, cut in half crosswise and gently squeeze out seeds.

If you like, you can replace the lemon juice in the tzatziki with the same amount of red wine vinegar.

Tzatziki sauce can be stored in a covered container in the refrigerator for up to 5 days. This recipe makes about 2 cups (500 mL).

Great Greek Pasta Salad

8 oz	penne or spiral pasta	250 g
1	small red onion, chopped	1
2	red bell peppers, diced	2
¾ cup	crumbled light feta cheese	175 mL
½ cup	Kalamata olives	125 mL
¼ cup	chopped fresh parsley	50 mL

DRESSING

¾ cup	Tzatziki Sauce (see recipe, below)	175 mL
1 tbsp	olive oil	15 mL
1 tbsp	red wine vinegar	15 mL
1 tsp	dried oregano leaves	5 mL
¼ tsp	freshly ground black pepper	1 mL

1. Cook pasta in a large pot of boiling salted water until tender but firm. Drain; rinse under cold water to chill. Drain well. In a serving bowl, combine pasta, onion, red peppers, feta, olives and parsley.

2. *Dressing:* In a bowl, combine all ingredients; toss with pasta mixture to coat. Cover and refrigerate. Remove from fridge 30 minutes before serving.

Tzatziki Sauce

3 cups	plain low-fat yogurt	750 mL
1 cup	finely chopped cucumber	250 mL
1 tsp	salt	5 mL
2	cloves garlic, minced	2
2 tsp	freshly squeezed lemon juice	10 mL

1. Place yogurt in a coffee filter or double paper towel–lined sieve set over a bowl; cover and let drain in the refrigerator for 4 hours or until reduced to 1½ cups (375 mL).

2. In a bowl, sprinkle cucumber with salt. Let stand 20 minutes. Drain in a sieve; squeeze out excess moisture and pat dry with paper towels. In a bowl, combine yogurt, cucumber, garlic and lemon juice.

NUTRITIONAL ANALYSIS PER SERVING	
Calories	284
Carbohydrate	41 g
Fiber	4 g
Protein	12 g
Fat, total	9 g
Fat, saturated	3 g
Sodium	570 mg
Cholesterol	9 mg

AMERICA'S EXCHANGES PER SERVING	
1½	Starch
1	Other Carbohydrate
1	High-fat Meat

CANADA'S CHOICES PER SERVING	
2½	Carbohydrate
½	Meat & Alternatives
1	Fat

Pasta salads are always a hit. They brighten up a buffet, backyard barbecue or your dinner table.

Tip

Dried basil and oregano can be replaced with 1 tbsp (15 mL) each chopped fresh. (As a general rule, when substituting fresh for dried herbs use three times the amount of fresh for the dried.)

Italian Pasta Salad

8 oz	pasta, such as fusilli or penne	250 g
4 oz	light provolone cheese, cut into small cubes	125 g
1 cup	cherry tomatoes, halved or quartered, if large	250 mL
1/3 cup	diced red onions	75 mL
1/2	large red bell pepper, cut into thin 1 1/2-inch (4 cm) strips	1/2
1/2	large green bell pepper, cut into thin 1 1/2-inch (4 cm) strips	1/2
1/3 cup	Kalamata olives (optional)	75 mL
1/3 cup	finely chopped fresh parsley	75 mL

DRESSING

1/4 cup	olive oil	50 mL
2 tbsp	red wine vinegar	25 mL
1 tbsp	Dijon mustard	15 mL
1	large clove garlic, minced	1
1 tsp	dried basil leaves	5 mL
1 tsp	dried oregano leaves	5 mL
1/2 tsp	salt	2 mL
1/4 tsp	freshly ground black pepper	1 mL

1. Cook pasta in a large pot of boiling salted water until tender but still firm. Drain; rinse under cold water and drain well.

2. In a large serving bowl, combine pasta, cheese cubes, tomatoes, onions, bell peppers, olives and parsley.

3. *Dressing:* In a bowl, combine oil, vinegar, mustard, garlic, basil, oregano, salt and pepper.

4. Pour dressing over pasta mixture; toss until well-coated. Let stand at room temperature for up to 30 minutes, allowing flavors to blend. Refrigerate if making ahead.

NUTRITIONAL ANALYSIS PER SERVING	
Calories	305
Carbohydrate	36 g
Fiber	3 g
Protein	12 g
Fat, total	13 g
Fat, saturated	3 g
Sodium	375 mg
Cholesterol	6 mg

AMERICA'S EXCHANGES PER SERVING	
1	Starch
1	Vegetable
1	Other Carbohydrate
1	High-fat Meat
1	Fat

CANADA'S CHOICES PER SERVING	
2	Carbohydrate
1	Meat & Alternatives
1 1/2	Fat

Tuna Niçoise Salad

This Mediterranean dish is more of a main course than a salad. Tuna, potatoes, green beans, tomatoes, eggs, capers and black olives give this dish a wonderful balance of flavors. It's simple to make and sophisticated to serve.

¼ cup	olive oil	50 mL
2 tbsp	red wine vinegar	25 mL
1 tbsp	balsamic vinegar	15 mL
1 tbsp	Dijon mustard	15 mL
2	cloves garlic, minced	2
¼ tsp	salt	1 mL
¼ tsp	freshly ground black pepper	1 mL
1 lb	small new potatoes, halved	500 g
8 oz	green beans, ends trimmed, cut into 2-inch (5 cm) pieces	250 g
1	small red onion, thinly sliced	1
1	can (6½ oz/170 g) solid white tuna, drained and flaked	1
2	hard-cooked eggs, peeled and quartered	2
2	ripe tomatoes, cut into wedges	2
12	Niçoise or other black olives	12
2 tbsp	capers, rinsed	25 mL
2 tbsp	chopped fresh parsley or chives	25 mL

1. In a bowl, whisk together oil, red wine and balsamic vinegars, mustard, garlic, salt and pepper.

2. In a large saucepan, cook potatoes in lightly salted boiling water for 10 minutes or until tender. Remove with slotted spoon to a bowl. Add 2 tbsp (25 mL) of the dressing and toss to coat.

3. Add green beans to the same saucepan and bring to a boil; cook for 3 to 5 minutes or until tender-crisp. Drain and chill under cold water; pat dry with paper towels. Place in another bowl with onion. Add 2 tbsp (25 mL) of the dressing and toss to coat.

4. On a serving platter, arrange potatoes in center and surround with green bean mixture. Arrange tuna on top of potatoes. Surround with eggs, tomato wedges and olives. Sprinkle with capers and parsley; drizzle with remaining dressing. Serve immediately.

NUTRITIONAL ANALYSIS PER SERVING	
Calories	338
Carbohydrate	30 g
Fiber	4 g
Protein	14 g
Fat, total	19 g
Fat, saturated	3 g
Sodium	640 mg
Cholesterol	106 mg

AMERICA'S EXCHANGES PER SERVING	
1	Starch
2	Vegetable
1½	High-fat Meat
1½	Fat

CANADA'S CHOICES PER SERVING	
1½	Carbohydrate
1½	Meat & Alternatives
2½	Fat

Your turn to bring the salad to the next reunion or neighborhood get-together? Here's a sure-fire winner that can be easily doubled to feed as many folks as the occasion demands. Even better, it can be made a day ahead.

Tip

To cook the rice, rinse ³⁄₄ cup (175 mL) basmati rice under cold water; drain. In a medium saucepan, bring 1¹⁄₂ cups (375 mL) water to a boil. Add rice and ¹⁄₄ tsp (1 mL) salt; cover and simmer for 15 minutes or until tender. Spread hot rice on baking sheet to cool.

Speedy Mexicali Rice and Black Bean Salad

2¹⁄₂ cups	cooked basmati rice (see tip, at left)	625 mL
I	can (19 oz/540 mL) black beans, drained and rinsed	I
I cup	cooked corn kernels	250 mL
I	red bell pepper, diced	I
4	green onions, sliced	4

DRESSING

¹⁄₂ cup	light sour cream	125 mL
2 tbsp	olive oil	25 mL
4 tsp	freshly squeezed lime or lemon juice	20 mL
I tsp	dried oregano leaves	5 mL
I tsp	ground cumin	5 mL
¹⁄₂ tsp	hot pepper sauce	2 mL
¹⁄₂ cup	chopped fresh cilantro or parsley	125 mL

1. In a large serving bowl, combine rice, black beans, corn, red pepper and green onions.

2. *Dressing:* In a bowl, combine sour cream, olive oil, lime juice, oregano, cumin and hot pepper sauce. Pour over rice mixture; toss well. Cover and refrigerate for up to 8 hours. Stir in cilantro just before serving.

NUTRITIONAL ANALYSIS PER SERVING	
Calories	185
Carbohydrate	31 g
Fiber	4 g
Protein	6 g
Fat, total	5 g
Fat, saturated	I g
Sodium	230 mg
Cholesterol	0 mg

AMERICA'S EXCHANGES PER SERVING	
I	Starch
I	Other Carbohydrate
¹⁄₂	Medium-fat Meat

CANADA'S CHOICES PER SERVING	
2	Carbohydrate
I	Fat

SERVES 8

The Lebanese salad, tabbouleh, made with nutty-tasting bulgur, is a good example of the vibrant comfort foods from the Mediterranean that have become so popular in recent years. This refreshing green salad is often displayed next to traditional favorites, such as potato salad and coleslaw, in the deli section of supermarkets. But you'll find it very inexpensive and easy to make in your home kitchen.

Tips

Bulgur is precooked cracked wheat that has been dried; it needs only to be soaked in water before using.

This salad keeps well for several days. It's better to add the tomatoes as a garnish just before serving to prevent the salad from becoming soggy.

Tabbouleh

¾ cup	fine bulgur	175 mL
2 cups	finely chopped fresh parsley, preferably flat-leaf	500 mL
4	green onions, finely chopped	4
¼ cup	finely chopped fresh mint leaves or 2 tbsp (25 mL) dried crumbled (optional)	50 mL
¼ cup	olive oil	50 mL
¼ cup	freshly squeezed lemon juice	50 mL
1 tsp	salt	5 mL
½ tsp	paprika	2 mL
¼ tsp	freshly ground black pepper	1 mL
2	tomatoes, seeded and diced	2

1. Place bulgur in a bowl; add cold water to cover. Let stand for 30 minutes. Drain in a fine sieve. Using the back of a spoon, or with your hands, squeeze out as much water as possible.

2. In a serving bowl, combine softened bulgur, parsley, onions and mint, if using.

3. In a small bowl, stir together oil, lemon juice, salt, paprika and pepper. Pour over bulgur mixture; toss well. Cover and refrigerate until serving time. Just before serving, sprinkle with tomatoes.

NUTRITIONAL ANALYSIS PER SERVING	
Calories	119
Carbohydrate	13 g
Fiber	3 g
Protein	2 g
Fat, total	7 g
Fat, saturated	1 g
Sodium	0 mg
Cholesterol	305 mg

AMERICA'S EXCHANGES PER SERVING	
½	Starch
½	Vegetable
1½	Fat

CANADA'S CHOICES PER SERVING	
½	Carbohydrate
1½	Fat

*A simple way to trim fat in
salad dressings is to replace
part of the oil called for
with low-sodium chicken
broth and fresh herbs to
give the dressing body and
a boost of fresh flavor.*

Tip

Store in an airtight
container in the refrigerator
for up to 1 week.

Variation

Instead of fresh basil,
use ½ cup (125 mL)
packed fresh parsley
leaves and 1 tsp (5 mL)
dried basil.

Basil-Garlic Vinaigrette

½ cup	packed fresh basil leaves	125 mL
⅓ cup	reduced-sodium chicken broth	75 mL
¼ cup	olive oil	50 mL
¼ cup	white wine vinegar	50 mL
I tbsp	balsamic vinegar	15 mL
I tbsp	Dijon mustard	15 mL
I	large clove garlic	I
¼ tsp	freshly ground black pepper	I mL

I. In a food processor or blender, purée basil, broth,
oil, wine vinegar, balsamic vinegar, mustard, garlic
and pepper.

Olive Oil

There are dozens of varieties of olive oil, each with a
characteristic flavor and many with distinctive colors
ranging from buttery yellow to vivid green. In general,
darker-colored oils have a more robust flavor. The best
quality is extra-virgin olive oil. Its fresh natural flavor
makes it a good choice for both cooking and salads. Don't
be misled by "light" olive oil: it is light in color only, and
has just as much fat as other types. Buy olive oil in small
quantities and use soon after purchase. Store it properly
capped in a cool dark place (but not in the refrigerator).

**NUTRITIONAL ANALYSIS
PER SERVING**

Calories	67
Carbohydrate	I g
Fiber	0 g
Protein	0 g
Fat, total	7 g
Fat, saturated	I g
Sodium	70 mg
Cholesterol	0 mg

**AMERICA'S EXCHANGES
PER SERVING**
1½   Fat

**CANADA'S CHOICES
PER SERVING**
1½   Fat

Cookies, Muffins and Breads

**MAKES
40 COOKIES
(1 cookie per
serving)**

*I'm never short of taste
testers when the first warm
batch of these cookies
come out of the oven. My
family loves them flecked
with chocolate chips and
walnuts. Served with a
cold glass of low-fat milk,
they're pure heaven.*

Variation

**Double Chocolate
Chunk Cookies**
Decrease all-purpose
flour to 1 1/2 cups
(375 mL). Sift flour
with 1/2 cup (125 mL)
unsweetened cocoa
powder and baking soda.
Replace chocolate chips
with white chocolate
chunks instead.

Classic Chocolate Chip Cookies

- Preheat oven to 350°F (180°C)
- Baking sheets, lined with parchment paper

3/4 cup	butter, softened	175 mL
3/4 cup	granulated sugar	175 mL
1/2 cup	packed brown sugar	125 mL
2	eggs	2
2 tsp	vanilla	10 mL
1 3/4 cups	all-purpose flour	425 mL
1/2 tsp	baking soda	2 mL
1/2 tsp	salt	2 mL
1 1/2 cups	semi-sweet chocolate chips	375 mL

1. In a large bowl, using an electric mixer, cream butter with granulated and brown sugars until fluffy; beat in eggs and vanilla until smooth.

2. In another bowl, stir together flour, baking soda and salt. Beat into creamed mixture until combined; stir in chocolate chips.

3. Drop by tablespoonfuls (15 mL) about 2 inches (5 cm) apart onto cookie sheets.

4. Bake one sheet at time on middle rack in preheated oven for 10 to 12 minutes or until edges are firm. (Bake for the shorter time if you prefer cookies with a soft chewy center.) Cool for 2 minutes on baking sheets; remove to wire rack and cool completely.

NUTRITIONAL ANALYSIS PER SERVING	
Calories	110
Carbohydrate	15 g
Fiber	1 g
Protein	1 g
Fat, total	6 g
Fat, saturated	3 g
Sodium	85 mg
Cholesterol	19 mg

AMERICA'S EXCHANGES PER SERVING	
1/2	Starch
1/2	Other Carbohydrate
1	Fat

CANADA'S CHOICES PER SERVING	
1	Carbohydrate
1	Fat

*Kids love home-baked
cookies, especially moist
and chewy ones like
these, made with
wholesome oatmeal.*

Tips

Use whatever combination
of dried fruits and nuts
appeals to your family or
whatever you happen
to have on hand. Just add
1½ cups (375 mL) in total
to the batter.

Let baking sheets cool
completely before using
again to prevent dough from
melting and spreading out
too much during baking.

Scrumptious Oatmeal Cookies

● *Preheat oven to 350°F (180°C)*
● *Baking sheets, lined with parchment paper*

¾ cup	butter, softened	175 mL
1¼ cups	packed brown sugar	300 mL
1	egg	1
1 tsp	vanilla	5 mL
1¼ cups	whole wheat flour	300 mL
½ tsp	baking soda	2 mL
¼ tsp	salt	1 mL
1½ cups	old-fashioned rolled oats	375 mL
¾ cup	sliced almonds or chopped pecans	175 mL
¾ cup	dried cranberries, dried cherries or raisins	175 mL

1. In a bowl, cream butter and sugar until fluffy. Beat in egg and vanilla.

2. In another bowl, stir together flour, baking soda and salt. Stir into butter mixture, mixing well. Stir in rolled oats, almonds and dried cranberries.

3. Drop by heaping tablespoonfuls (15 mL) about 2 inches (5 cm) apart onto prepared cookie sheets and flatten with a fork.

4. Bake one sheet at a time on middle rack in preheated oven for 12 to 14 minutes or until edges are golden. Let stand for 5 minutes; remove cookies with a spatula to a rack and let cool.

NUTRITIONAL ANALYSIS PER SERVING

Calories	113
Carbohydrate	16 g
Fiber	1 g
Protein	2 g
Fat, total	5 g
Fat, saturated	3 g
Sodium	80 mg
Cholesterol	16 mg

AMERICA'S EXCHANGES PER SERVING

½	Starch
½	Other Carbohydrate
1	Fat

CANADA'S CHOICES PER SERVING

1	Carbohydrate
1	Fat

...

**MAKES
40 COOKIES
(1 cookie per
serving)**

*These crisp cookies
are sure to satisfy a
craving for something
sweet and indulgent.*

Tip

Double the recipe,
bake half and freeze the
remaining dough to
bake later.

Peanut Butter Cookies

- *Preheat oven to 375°F (190°C)*
- *Baking sheets, lined with parchment paper*

1/2 cup	butter, softened, or shortening	125 mL
2/3 cup	smooth light peanut butter	150 mL
1 cup	packed brown sugar	250 mL
1	egg	1
1 tsp	vanilla	5 mL
1 3/4 cups	all-purpose flour	425 mL
1/2 tsp	baking soda	2 mL
1/4 tsp	salt	1 mL

1. In a bowl, cream butter, peanut butter and brown sugar until fluffy. Beat in egg and vanilla.
2. In another bowl, stir together flour, baking soda and salt. Stir into creamed mixture.
3. Form into 1-inch (2.5 cm) balls and place 2 inches (5 cm) apart on prepared cookie sheets. Using the tines of a fork, flatten by making criss-cross patterns on tops.
4. Bake one sheet at a time on middle rack in preheated oven for 11 to 13 minutes or until light golden. Transfer to a rack to cool.

**NUTRITIONAL ANALYSIS
PER SERVING**

Calories	85
Carbohydrate	11 g
Fiber	0 g
Protein	2 g
Fat, total	4 g
Fat, saturated	2 g
Sodium	80 mg
Cholesterol	11 mg

**AMERICA'S EXCHANGES
PER SERVING**

1/2	Other Carbohydrate
1	Fat

**CANADA'S CHOICES
PER SERVING**

1/2	Carbohydrate
1	Fat

A favorite since my university days, these spice cookies would provide fuel for cram sessions before exams. Now, continuing the tradition, my kids bake a batch when they have to hit the books.

Tip

Be sure to use fresh baking soda as it makes these cookies crisp and light. Like baking powder, an open box of baking soda has a shelf life of only 6 months, so make sure to replenish both regularly. As a reminder, write the date when they need to be replaced on the containers.

Gingersnaps

- Preheat oven to 350°F (180°C)
- Baking sheets, lined with parchment paper

½ cup	soft margarine	125 mL
½ cup	butter, softened	125 mL
¾ cup	packed brown sugar	175 mL
¼ cup	fancy molasses	50 mL
1	egg	1
2¼ cups	all-purpose flour	550 mL
1½ tsp	baking soda	7 mL
1½ tsp	ground ginger	7 mL
1 tsp	ground cinnamon	5 mL
1 tsp	ground cloves	5 mL
¼ tsp	salt	1 mL
¼ cup	granulated sugar	50 mL

1. In a large bowl, cream shortening and butter with sugar until light and fluffy; beat in molasses and egg until creamy.

2. In another bowl, sift together flour, baking soda, ginger, cinnamon, cloves and salt. Stir into creamed mixture to make a soft dough. Refrigerate for 1 hour or until firm.

3. Shape dough into 1-inch (2.5 cm) balls; roll in bowl of granulated sugar. Arrange 2 inches (5 cm) apart on prepared cookie sheets. Flatten to ¼ inch (0.5 cm) thickness using bottom of large glass dipped in sugar.

4. Bake in preheated oven for 12 to 14 minutes or until golden. Cool 2 minutes on baking sheets; transfer to rack and let cool.

NUTRITIONAL ANALYSIS PER SERVING	
Calories	126
Carbohydrate	16 g
Fiber	0 g
Protein	1 g
Fat, total	6 g
Fat, saturated	2 g
Sodium	160 mg
Cholesterol	14 mg

AMERICA'S EXCHANGES PER SERVING	
½	Starch
½	Other Carbohydrate
1½	Fat

CANADA'S CHOICES PER SERVING	
1	Carbohydrate
1½	Fat

**MAKES
48 COOKIES**
(2 cookies per
serving)

*The secret to this tender,
easy-to-make shortbread
is to have a light touch
and not to over-handle
the dough.*

Tip

Light baking sheets,
particularly the nonstick
variety, are generally better
than dark sheets, which
attract heat and cause
cookies to bake faster
and/or cause the undersides
to darken too quickly.

Scottish Shortbread

- *Preheat oven to 300°F (150°C)*
- *Baking sheets*

1 cup	unsalted butter, softened	250 mL
1/2 cup	superfine sugar	125 mL
2 cups	all-purpose flour	500 mL
1/2 tsp	salt	2 mL

1. In a bowl, cream butter with wooden spoon until fluffy. Beat in sugar, a spoonful at time, until well blended. Stir in flour and salt; gather into a ball.

2. On a lightly floured work surface, gently knead four or five times until smooth. Roll out a portion of the dough on a lightly floured surface to 1/3-inch (8 mm) thickness. Cut out shapes using cooking cutters and place on cookie sheets.

3. Bake one sheet at a time on middle rack in preheated oven for 25 to 30 minutes or until edges are light golden. Transfer cookies to rack to cool.

NUTRITIONAL ANALYSIS PER SERVING	
Calories	122
Carbohydrate	12 g
Fiber	0 g
Protein	1 g
Fat, total	8 g
Fat, saturated	5 g
Sodium	50 mg
Cholesterol	21 mg

AMERICA'S EXCHANGES PER SERVING	
1/2	Starch
1/2	Other Carbohydrate
1 1/2	Fat

CANADA'S CHOICES PER SERVING	
1	Carbohydrate
1 1/2	Fat

**MAKES
48 BISCOTTI
(1 cookie per
serving)**

*These crunchy morsels
make wonderful gifts for
friends and family. Pack
biscotti in fancy containers
or tins, or wrap in clear
cellophane and add a
bright ribbon.*

Tips

To toast and skin hazelnuts,
place on a rimmed baking
sheet in a preheated 350°F
(180°C) oven for 8 to
10 minutes or until lightly
browned. Place in a clean,
dry towel and rub off most
of the skins.

Replenish your spices
regularly; buy the freshest
dried fruits and nuts.

Variation

Dried cranberries add
a sweet-tart flavor;
substitute golden raisins
or chopped dried
apricots, if desired.

Hazelnut and Dried Cranberry Biscotti

- *Preheat oven to 325°F (160°C)*
- *Baking sheets, lined with parchment paper*

1/2 cup	butter, softened	125 mL
1 cup	packed brown sugar	250 mL
2	eggs	2
2 1/3 cups	all-purpose flour	575 mL
1 1/2 tsp	baking powder	7 mL
1 1/2 tsp	ground cinnamon	7 mL
1/4 tsp	ground cloves	1 mL
1/4 tsp	ground allspice	1 mL
1/4 tsp	salt	1 mL
1/2 cup	dried cranberries	125 mL
3/4 cup	hazelnuts, toasted, skinned and coarsely chopped (see tip, at left)	175 mL

1. In a bowl, using an electric mixer, cream butter with brown sugar until light and fluffy; beat in eggs until incorporated.

2. In another bowl, combine flour, baking powder, cinnamon, cloves, allspice and salt. Add to butter mixture to make a soft dough. Fold in dried cranberries and hazelnuts.

3. Turn dough out onto a lightly floured surface. With floured hands, shape into a ball and divide in half. Pat into 2 logs, each about 2 inches (5 cm) wide and 12 inches (30 cm) long. Place on prepared baking sheet, about 2 inches (5 cm) apart.

4. Bake on middle rack of preheated oven for 20 to 25 minutes or until firm to the touch. Let cool for 10 minutes. Using a long spatula, transfer to a cutting board. With a serrated knife, cut diagonally into 1/2-inch (1 cm) slices.

5. Place cookies upright on sheet 1/2-inch (1 cm) apart, using 2 sheets, if necessary. Return to oven and bake for 15 to 20 minutes or until dry and lightly brown. Transfer cookies to a rack to cool.

NUTRITIONAL ANALYSIS PER SERVING	
Calories	76
Carbohydrate	11 g
Fiber	0 g
Protein	1 g
Fat, total	3 g
Fat, saturated	1 g
Sodium	45 mg
Cholesterol	13 mg

AMERICA'S EXCHANGES PER SERVING	
1/2	Other Carbohydrate
1	Fat

CANADA'S CHOICES PER SERVING	
1/2	Carbohydrate
1/2	Fat

**MAKES
32 BROWNIES
(1 brownie per
serving)**

*So moist and chewy, these
brownies will disappear
in no time. Luckily, this
recipe makes a big batch,
so you can stash half in
the freezer.*

Tip

Here's the easiest way to
cut bars or squares. Line
the bottom and sides of
baking pan with foil. Bake
as directed and let bars cool
completely in pan. Place in
freezer for up to 30 minutes
or until partially frozen. Lift
out entire batch and cut
into bars or squares with
a sharp knife. Arrange in a
cookie tin with waxed paper
separating the layers and
freeze. Most bars, like
cookies, freeze well.

Fudgy Chocolate Brownies

- *Preheat oven to 350°F (180°C)*
- *13- by 9-inch (3.5 L) baking pan, lined with foil and sprayed
  with vegetable cooking spray*

1 cup	butter, softened	250 mL
1½ cups	granulated sugar	375 mL
4	eggs	4
2 tsp	vanilla	10 mL
1 cup	all-purpose flour	250 mL
1 cup	unsweetened cocoa powder	250 mL
¾ tsp	baking powder	4 mL
½ tsp	salt	2 mL
1 cup	walnuts, chopped	250 mL

FROSTING

1 cup	confectioner's (icing) sugar	250 mL
⅓ cup	unsweetened cocoa powder	75 mL
2 tbsp	butter, softened	25 mL
2 tbsp	low-fat milk	25 mL

1. In a bowl, using an electric mixer, cream butter with
   sugar until light and fluffy. Beat in eggs, one at a
   time, until incorporated; add vanilla.

2. In a separate bowl, sift together flour, cocoa powder,
   baking powder and salt. Beat into butter mixture to
   make a smooth batter. Fold in walnuts.

3. Spread in prepared baking pan. Bake on middle rack
   in preheated oven for 25 to 30 minutes or until cake
   tester inserted in center comes out clean. Place pan
   on rack to cool completely.

4. *Frosting:* In a bowl, using an electric mixer, beat
   confectioner's sugar, cocoa powder, butter and milk
   until smooth. Spread over slightly warm brownies.
   When set, cut into bars.

**NUTRITIONAL ANALYSIS
PER SERVING**

Calories	164
Carbohydrate	19 g
Fiber	1 g
Protein	2 g
Fat, total	10 g
Fat, saturated	5 g
Sodium	120 mg
Cholesterol	41 mg

**AMERICA'S EXCHANGES
PER SERVING**

½	Starch
½	Other Carbohydrate
2	Fat

**CANADA'S CHOICES
PER SERVING**

1	Carbohydrate
2	Fat

*These classy lemon treats
with a shortbread crust are
always appreciated when
friends are invited for a
fresh-brewed cup of tea
or coffee.*

Luscious Lemon Squares

- *Preheat oven to 350°F (180°C)*
- *8-inch (2 L) square baking pan*

1 cup	all-purpose flour	250 mL
1/4 cup	granulated sugar	50 mL
1/2 cup	butter, cut into pieces	125 mL

FILLING

2	eggs	2
1 cup	granulated sugar	250 mL
2 tbsp	all-purpose flour	25 mL
1/2 tsp	baking powder	2 mL
Pinch	salt	Pinch
1 tbsp	grated lemon zest	15 mL
1/4 cup	freshly squeezed lemon juice	50 mL
2 tbsp	confectioner's (icing) sugar	15 mL

1. In a bowl, combine flour and sugar; cut in butter with a pastry blender to make coarse crumbs. Press into bottom of baking pan. Bake in preheated oven for 18 to 20 minutes or until light golden. Let cool on rack.

2. *Filling:* In a bowl, beat eggs with sugar, flour, baking powder, salt, lemon zest and juice. Pour over base.

3. Bake for 25 to 30 minutes or until filling is set and light golden. Place pan on rack to cool. Dust with confectioner's sugar; cut into small squares.

NUTRITIONAL ANALYSIS PER SERVING

Calories	70
Carbohydrate	11 g
Fiber	0 g
Protein	1 g
Fat, total	3 g
Fat, saturated	2 g
Sodium	35 mg
Cholesterol	17 mg

AMERICA'S EXCHANGES PER SERVING
1/2 Other Carbohydrate
1/2 Fat

CANADA'S CHOICES PER SERVING
1/2 Carbohydrate
1/2 Fat

MAKES 32 BARS
(1 bar per serving)

Ideal for school lunches, these chewy bars travel well. I like to package bars individually in plastic wrap, place in a covered container and freeze. It's so easy to pop a bar from the freezer into lunch bags or take them along for snacks.

Lunch Box Oatmeal-Raisin Bars

- Preheat oven to 350°F (180°C)
- 13- by 9-inch (3.5 L) baking pan, lined with foil and sprayed with vegetable cooking spray

⅔ cup	packed brown sugar	150 mL
⅓ cup	butter	75 mL
⅓ cup	golden corn syrup	75 mL
2½ cups	quick-cooking rolled oats	625 mL
¼ cup	all-purpose flour	50 mL
½ cup	raisins or chopped dried apricots	125 mL
1	egg	1
1 tsp	vanilla	5 mL

1. In a glass bowl, combine brown sugar, butter and corn syrup. Microwave at High for 2 minutes; stir until smooth. Microwave 1 minute more or until sugar dissolves and mixture comes to a full boil.

2. Stir in rolled oats, flour and raisins. In a small bowl, beat egg with vanilla. Stir into rolled-oats mixture.

3. Spread evenly in prepared pan. Bake in preheated oven for 20 to 25 minutes or until golden around edges. Let cool 10 minutes in pan. Lift out foil; cut into 32 bars. Transfer to a rack to complete cooling.

NUTRITIONAL ANALYSIS PER SERVING	
Calories	87
Carbohydrate	15 g
Fiber	1 g
Protein	2 g
Fat, total	3 g
Fat, saturated	1 g
Sodium	30 mg
Cholesterol	11 mg

AMERICA'S EXCHANGES PER SERVING	
½	Starch
½	Other Carbohydrate
½	Fat

CANADA'S CHOICES PER SERVING	
1	Carbohydrate
½	Fat

Caesar Salad (page 216) ➤
Overleaf: Classic Chocolate Chip Cookies (page 232)

*Peanut butter fans
will love these no-bake
bars. They're a breeze
to make and taste so much
better than the expensive
packaged snack bars sold
in supermarkets.*

Tip

Wrap bars individually in
plastic wrap and freeze.
Then, when making
school lunches, just pop a
pre-wrapped bar into each
lunch bag.

Peanutty Cereal Snacking Bars

- *13- by 9-inch (3.5 L) baking pan, lined with foil and sprayed with vegetable cooking spray*

1 cup	smooth or chunky light peanut butter	250 mL
2/3 cup	liquid honey or golden corn syrup	150 mL
4 cups	toasted rice cereal	1 L
2 cups	muesli-type cereal with fruit and nuts	500 mL

1. In a large saucepan, combine peanut butter and honey; cook over medium heat, stirring constantly, until smooth. (Or place in large glass bowl and microwave at High for 2 minutes, or until smooth, stirring once.)

2. Fold in cereals until evenly coated. Press firmly into prepared baking pan. Let cool; cut into 3- by 1½-inch (8 by 4 cm) bars.

NUTRITIONAL ANALYSIS PER SERVING	
Calories	121
Carbohydrate	19 g
Fiber	1 g
Protein	4 g
Fat, total	4 g
Fat, saturated	1 g
Sodium	110 mg
Cholesterol	0 mg

AMERICA'S EXCHANGES PER SERVING	
½	Starch
½	Other Carbohydrate
½	High-fat Meat

CANADA'S CHOICES PER SERVING	
1	Carbohydrate
½	Fat

◄ Lemon Fool with Fresh Berries (page 271)
Overleaf: Bread Pudding with Caramelized Pears (page 267)

*I discovered that these
wholesome muffins have
great appeal. As a food
columnist for The Gazette
newspaper in Montreal,
this recipe was featured in
one of my weekly columns.
The maple syrup amount
was omitted due to a
technical problem when
going to press and the
paper received more than
500 telephone calls from
readers requesting how
much maple syrup to add
to the recipe. Here it is —
with the right amount of
maple syrup!*

Tips

For walnuts, the light-
colored Californian walnuts
are preferred.

Always store nuts in
a container in the
refrigerator or freezer
to keep them fresh.

Maple Walnut Apple Muffins

- Preheat oven to 400°F (200°C)
- Muffin pan, with paper liners

1 1/4 cups	all-purpose flour	300 mL
2 1/2 tsp	baking powder	12 mL
1/2 tsp	baking soda	2 mL
1/4 tsp	salt	1 mL
1/3 cup	finely chopped walnuts	75 mL
1	egg	1
1 cup	quick-cooking rolled oats	250 mL
1 cup	coarsely grated apple	250 mL
2/3 cup	pure maple syrup	150 mL
1/2 cup	plain low-fat yogurt	125 mL
1/4 cup	vegetable oil	50 mL

1. In a bowl, combine flour, baking powder, baking soda, salt and walnuts.

2. In another bowl, beat egg. Stir in oats, grated apple, maple syrup, yogurt and oil. Stir into flour mixture just until combined; do not over-mix.

3. Spoon batter into prepared muffin cups.

4. Bake in preheated oven for 20 minutes or until tops are springy to the touch. Let muffins cool slightly; transfer to rack to cool.

NUTRITIONAL ANALYSIS PER SERVING	
Calories	206
Carbohydrate	30 g
Fiber	2 g
Protein	4 g
Fat, total	8 g
Fat, saturated	1 g
Sodium	170 mg
Cholesterol	16 mg

AMERICA'S EXCHANGES PER SERVING	
1	Starch
1	Other Carbohydrate
1 1/2	Fat

CANADA'S CHOICES PER SERVING	
2	Carbohydrate
1 1/2	Fat

*Packed with fruits and
carrots, these scrumptious
muffins are perfect for
breakfast. But they are
just as tasty for afternoon
snacks or stowed away in
a lunch box.*

Tip

Have only one muffin
pan? Place muffin paper
liners in 6-oz (175 mL)
glass custard cups or small
ramekins and fill with extra
batter. Place in oven and
bake alongside muffin pan.

Carrot-Raisin Muffins

- *Preheat oven to 375°F (190°C)*
- *2 muffin pans, with paper liners*

2 cups	all-purpose flour	500 mL
¾ cup	granulated sugar	175 mL
1½ tsp	ground cinnamon	7 mL
1 tsp	baking powder	5 mL
1 tsp	baking soda	5 mL
½ tsp	freshly grated nutmeg	2 mL
½ tsp	salt	2 mL
1½ cups	grated carrots (about 3 medium)	375 mL
1 cup	grated peeled apples	250 mL
½ cup	raisins	125 mL
½ cup	sweetened shredded coconut	125 mL
2	eggs	2
⅔ cup	plain low-fat yogurt	150 mL
⅓ cup	vegetable oil	75 mL

1. In a large bowl, stir together flour, sugar, cinnamon, baking powder, baking soda, nutmeg and salt. Stir in carrots, apples, raisins and coconut

2. In another bowl, beat eggs; add yogurt and oil. Stir into flour mixture just until combined. (Batter will be very thick.)

3. Spoon batter into prepared muffins cups, filling almost to the top.

4. Bake in preheated oven for 25 to 30 minutes or until tops spring back when lightly touched. Let cool in pans for 5 minutes; transfer muffins to a rack and cool.

**NUTRITIONAL ANALYSIS
PER SERVING**

Calories	189
Carbohydrate	30 g
Fiber	1 g
Protein	3 g
Fat, total	7 g
Fat, saturated	2 g
Sodium	200 mg
Cholesterol	24 mg

**AMERICA'S EXCHANGES
PER SERVING**

1	Starch
½	Fruit
½	Other Carbohydrate
1	Fat

**CANADA'S CHOICES
PER SERVING**

2	Carbohydrate
1½	Fat

When it comes to
celebrating the pleasures
of summer fruits, nothing
beats juicy blueberries.
They are especially
welcome when teamed
with lemon in these
deliciously moist muffins.

Tip

To minimize the problem of
frozen blueberries tinting
the batter blue, place
berries in a sieve and
quickly rinse under cold
water to get rid of any ice
crystals. Blot dry with paper
towels. Place berries in a
bowl and toss with 2 tbsp
(25 mL) of the muffin flour
mixture. Use immediately;
fold into batter with a few
quick strokes.

Blueberry Cornmeal Muffins

- Preheat oven to 400°F (200°C)
- Muffin pan, with paper liners

1 1/2 cups	all-purpose flour	375 mL
1/3 cup	cornmeal	75 mL
1/2 cup	granulated sugar	125 mL
2 1/2 tsp	baking powder	12 mL
1/4 tsp	salt	1 mL
1	egg	1
3/4 cup	low-fat milk	175 mL
1/4 cup	butter, melted	50 mL
1 tsp	grated lemon zest	5 mL
1 cup	fresh or frozen blueberries	250 mL

1. In a bowl, stir together flour, cornmeal, sugar, baking powder and salt.

2. In another bowl, beat egg. Stir in milk, melted butter and lemon zest. Combine with dry ingredients until just mixed. Gently fold in blueberries.

3. Spoon into prepared muffin cups so they are three-quarters full.

4. Bake in preheated oven for 20 to 24 minutes or until top is firm to the touch and lightly browned. Remove from pans and let muffins cool on rack.

MAKES 12 MUFFINS (1 muffin per serving)

Bran muffins are never out of style. Nicely moistened with molasses, these muffins will become a morning favorite.

Tip

Always measure the oil before measuring sticky sweeteners such as molasses or honey. (For recipes that don't call for oil, spray measure with nonstick vegetable spray or lightly coat with oil. You'll find every last drop of sweetener will easily pour out.)

Bran Muffins

- Preheat oven to 400°F (200°C)
- Muffin pan, with paper liners

2	eggs	2
1 cup	buttermilk	250 mL
1/3 cup	packed brown sugar	75 mL
1/4 cup	vegetable oil	50 mL
1/4 cup	fancy molasses	50 mL
1 1/4 cups	whole wheat flour	300 mL
1 cup	natural bran	250 mL
1 tsp	baking soda	5 mL
1/2 tsp	baking powder	2 mL
1/4 tsp	salt	1 mL
1/2 cup	raisins or chopped apricots	125 mL

1. In a bowl, beat eggs. Add buttermilk, brown sugar, oil and molasses.

2. In another bowl, combine flour, bran, baking soda, baking powder and salt. Stir into liquid ingredients to make a smooth batter; fold in raisins.

3. Spoon into prepared muffin cups so they are three-quarters full.

4. Bake in preheated oven for 20 to 24 minutes or until tops spring back when lightly touched. Let cool 10 minutes; remove from pan and cool on racks.

NUTRITIONAL ANALYSIS PER SERVING

Calories	175
Carbohydrate	29 g
Fiber	4 g
Protein	4 g
Fat, total	6 g
Fat, saturated	1 g
Sodium	205 mg
Cholesterol	32 mg

AMERICA'S EXCHANGES PER SERVING

1	Starch
1	Other Carbohydrate
1	Fat

CANADA'S CHOICES PER SERVING

1 1/2	Carbohydrate
1	Fat

Here's a lemony-flavored loaf that stays moist for days — if it lasts that long.

Tip

I like to double this recipe so that I have an extra loaf handy in the freezer. Wrap in plastic wrap, then in foil and freeze for up to 1 month.

Variation

Lemon Poppy Seed Loaf
Stir 2 tbsp (25 mL) poppy seeds into flour mixture before combining with yogurt mixture.

Lemon Yogurt Loaf

- Preheat oven to 350°F (180°C)
- 9- by 5-inch (2 L) loaf pan, sprayed with vegetable cooking spray

1¾ cups	all-purpose flour	425 mL
I tsp	baking powder	5 mL
½ tsp	baking soda	2 mL
¼ tsp	salt	I mL
2	eggs	2
¾ cup	granulated sugar	175 mL
¾ cup	plain low-fat yogurt	175 mL
⅓ cup	vegetable oil	75 mL
I tbsp	grated lemon zest	15 mL

TOPPING

2 tbsp	freshly squeezed lemon juice	25 mL
2 tbsp	granulated sugar	25 mL

1. In a bowl, combine flour, baking powder, baking soda and salt.

2. In another large bowl, beat eggs. Stir in sugar, yogurt, oil and lemon zest. Fold in flour mixture to make a smooth batter.

3. Spoon into prepared pan; bake in preheated oven for 50 to 60 minutes or until cake tester inserted in center comes out clean. Place pan on rack.

4. *Topping:* In a small saucepan, heat lemon juice and sugar; bring to a boil. Cook, stirring, until sugar is dissolved. (Or place in a glass bowl and microwave at High for 1 minute, stirring once.) Pour over hot loaf in pan; let cool completely before turning out of pan.

NUTRITIONAL ANALYSIS PER SERVING	
Calories	170
Carbohydrate	26 g
Fiber	I g
Protein	3 g
Fat, total	6 g
Fat, saturated	I g
Sodium	125 mg
Cholesterol	27 mg

AMERICA'S EXCHANGES PER SERVING	
I	Starch
½	Other Carbohydrate
1½	Fat

CANADA'S CHOICES PER SERVING	
1½	Carbohydrate
I	Fat

This bread is so much easier to bake than pumpkin pie, but still loaded with all the spice-scented flavors we love.

Tip

To measure flour correctly, give it a quick stir, spoon into a dry measure and use a knife to level the top.

Orange-Pumpkin Loaf

- Preheat oven to 350°F (180°C)
- 9- by 5-inch (2 L) loaf pan, sprayed with vegetable cooking spray

I cup	all-purpose flour	250 mL
¾ cup	whole wheat or all-purpose flour	175 mL
2 tsp	baking powder	10 mL
½ tsp	baking soda	2 mL
½ tsp	salt	2 mL
1 ½ tsp	ground cinnamon	7 mL
½ tsp	freshly grated nutmeg	2 mL
¼ tsp	ground cloves or allspice	1 mL
1 ¼ cups	packed brown sugar	300 mL
2	eggs	2
I cup	canned pumpkin purée (not pie filling)	250 mL
⅓ cup	vegetable oil	75 mL
2 tsp	grated orange zest	10 mL
¼ cup	orange juice	50 mL

1. In a bowl, combine flours, baking powder, baking soda and salt; stir well.

2. In a small bowl, combine cinnamon, nutmeg and cloves. Transfer 1 tsp (5 mL) of the spice mixture to another bowl; add 2 tbsp (25 mL) brown sugar. Set aside for topping.

3. Place remaining spices and brown sugar in a bowl; add eggs and beat well. Stir in pumpkin, oil, orange zest and juice. Stir dry ingredients into pumpkin mixture until combined.

4. Spoon batter into prepared loaf pan. Sprinkle top with reserved spiced-sugar mixture. Bake on middle rack in preheated oven for 50 to 55 minutes or until toothpick inserted in center comes out clean. Let pan cool on rack for 15 minutes; turn loaf out and let cool completely.

NUTRITIONAL ANALYSIS PER SERVING

Calories	195
Carbohydrate	33 g
Fiber	2 g
Protein	3 g
Fat, total	6 g
Fat, saturated	1 g
Sodium	185 mg
Cholesterol	27 mg

AMERICA'S EXCHANGES PER SERVING

1	Starch
1	Other Carbohydrate
1	Fat

CANADA'S CHOICES PER SERVING

2	Carbohydrate
1	Fat

**MAKES 2 LOAVES
(1 of 14 slices
per serving)**

*There's nothing more
welcoming than the aroma
of home-baked bread when
you walk in the door. Who
can wait to cut into a
warm loaf so tasty, you
don't need butter?*

Tip

For yeast to work properly,
liquids must be at the
correct temperature to
activate it. Liquids that are
too hot will kill the action
of yeast and dough will not
rise. Cold temperatures
will shock the yeast and
it will not have its full
leavening strength. Use a
thermometer for accuracy.

Honey Oatmeal Bread

● *Two 9- by 5-inch (2 L) loaf pans, sprayed with vegetable
cooking spray*

1	package (2¼ tsp/11 mL) active dry yeast	1
1 tsp	granulated sugar	5 mL
1 cup	low-fat milk	250 mL
¼ cup	dark honey, such as buckwheat, or fancy molasses	50 mL
2 tbsp	butter	25 mL
2½ tsp	salt	12 mL
1 cup	old-fashioned rolled oats	250 mL
2 cups	whole wheat flour	500 mL
3 cups	all-purpose flour (approx.)	750 mL
2 tsp	melted butter	10 mL
1	egg white	1
2 tbsp	additional rolled oats	25 mL

1. Place ½ cup (125 mL) lukewarm water in a glass
   measuring cup; sprinkle with yeast and sugar. Let
   stand until foamy.

2. In a saucepan, combine 1 cup (250 mL) lukewarm
   water, milk, honey, 2 tbsp (25 mL) butter and salt.
   Heat over medium heat, stirring, until bubbles
   appear around edge.

3. Place rolled oats in a large mixing bowl; pour in
   hot mixture. Let cool until lukewarm; if using a
   thermometer, temperature should read 105° to
   115°F (40° to 45°C).

4. Stir in whole wheat flour and dissolved yeast;
   beat vigorously with a wooden spoon for 1 minute
   or until smooth. Stir in enough all-purpose flour
   to make a stiff dough that leaves sides of bowl.

5. Turn out onto a floured board and knead, adding
   just enough flour to prevent dough from sticking,
   for 7 to 9 minutes or until smooth and elastic.

NUTRITIONAL ANALYSIS PER SERVING	
Calories	112
Carbohydrate	21 g
Fiber	2 g
Protein	3 g
Fat, total	2 g
Fat, saturated	1 g
Sodium	225 mg
Cholesterol	3 mg

AMERICA'S EXCHANGES PER SERVING	
1	Starch
½	Other Carbohydrate

CANADA'S CHOICES PER SERVING	
1	Carbohydrate
½	Fat

6. Shape into a ball; place in well-buttered bowl. Turn dough to coat in butter. Cover with plastic wrap, then with clean dry towel; let rise in warm place until doubled in bulk, about $1\frac{1}{2}$ to 2 hours.

7. Punch down dough; knead for 1 minute to get rid of air bubbles. Divide in two. Shape into loaves and place in prepared loaf pans. Brush tops with 2 tsp (10 mL) melted butter. Cover with clean towel; let rise in a warm place for $1\frac{1}{4}$ hours or until almost doubled in bulk. Preheat oven to 375°F (190°C).

8. Lightly beat egg white with 1 tsp (5 mL) water; brush tops of loaves. Sprinkle each loaf with 1 tbsp (15 mL) rolled oats.

9. Bake in preheated oven for 45 minutes or until bottom of loaves when removed from pans sound hollow when tapped. Remove loaves from oven, turn out of pans and let cool on racks.

Tip

Do not work in too much flour when mixing and kneading or dough will be heavy. Depending on the humidity of the flour used, you may need less or more than the amount called for.

**MAKES I LOAF
(1 of 14 slices
per serving)**

*Everyone has a recipe
for banana bread in their
files. I've included my best.
It's a simple bread that just
relies on the flavor of
banana and walnuts.
Honey gives extra moistness
that keeps it fresh for days
— if it lasts that long.*

Tips

Lining the bottom of
baking pan with waxed or
parchment paper ensures
you'll never have trouble
removing the bread from
the pan.

Left with ripe bananas on
your counter but have no
time to bake a bread?
Simply freeze whole
bananas with the peel, then
leave at room temperature
to defrost. Or peel and
mash bananas; pack into
containers and freeze for
up to 2 months. Defrost
at room temperature.
Frozen banana purée may
darken slightly, but this
will not affect the delicious
baked results.

Banana Nut Bread

- Preheat oven to 325°F (160°C)
- 9- by 5-inch (2 L) loaf pan, sprayed with vegetable cooking spray

1¾ cups	all-purpose flour	425 mL
1 tsp	baking soda	5 mL
½ tsp	salt	2 mL
2	eggs	2
1 cup	mashed ripe bananas (about 3)	250 mL
⅓ cup	vegetable oil	75 mL
½ cup	liquid honey	125 mL
⅓ cup	packed brown sugar	75 mL
½ cup	chopped walnuts	125 mL

1. In a bowl, sift together flour, baking soda and salt.

2. In another bowl, beat eggs. Stir in bananas, oil, honey and brown sugar. Stir dry ingredients into banana mixture until combined. Fold in walnuts.

3. Pour batter into prepared loaf pan. Bake in preheated oven for 1¼ hours or until cake tester inserted in center comes out clean. Let pan cool on rack for 15 minutes. Run knife around edge; turn out loaf and let cool on rack.

NUTRITIONAL ANALYSIS PER SERVING

Calories	211
Carbohydrate	31 g
Fiber	1 g
Protein	3 g
Fat, total	9 g
Fat, saturated	1 g
Sodium	185 mg
Cholesterol	27 mg

AMERICA'S EXCHANGES PER SERVING

1	Starch
1	Other Carbohydrate
1½	Fat

CANADA'S CHOICES PER SERVING

2	Carbohydrate
2	Fat

Old-fashioned soda bread is a wonderful accompaniment to a hearty soup or stew. Any leftovers are delicious toasted.

Tip

To measure flour correctly, give it a quick stir, spoon into a dry measure and use a knife to level the top.

Whole-Grain Irish Soda Bread

- Preheat oven to 375°F (190°C)
- Baking sheet, sprayed with vegetable cooking spray

2 cups	whole wheat flour	500 mL
1 2/3 cups	all-purpose flour	400 mL
2/3 cup	old-fashioned rolled oats	150 mL
1 tbsp	granulated sugar	15 mL
1 1/2 tsp	baking soda	7 mL
1/2 tsp	salt	2 mL
2 cups	buttermilk	500 mL

TOPPING

1 tbsp	buttermilk	15 mL
1 tbsp	old-fashioned rolled oats	15 mL

1. In a large bowl, combine flours, rolled oats, sugar, baking soda and salt. Stir well. Make a well in center; add buttermilk. Stir until a soft dough forms.

2. Turn out onto lightly floured board; knead five or six times until smooth. Shape dough into a ball; pat into an 8-inch (20 cm) round. Place on prepared cookie sheet. With a sharp knife dipped in flour, cut a large 1/2-inch (1 cm) deep cross on top of loaf.

3. *Topping:* Brush loaf with buttermilk and sprinkle with oats. Bake in preheated oven for 50 to 60 minutes or until well risen and golden; loaf sounds hollow when tapped on base. Immediately wrap in clean dry tea towel; set aside to cool. This prevents crust from becoming too hard.

NUTRITIONAL ANALYSIS PER SERVING

Calories	166
Carbohydrate	33 g
Fiber	3 g
Protein	6 g
Fat, total	1 g
Fat, saturated	0 g
Sodium	300 mg
Cholesterol	1 mg

AMERICA'S EXCHANGES PER SERVING
2   Starch

CANADA'S CHOICES PER SERVING
2   Carbohydrate

Cut this savory cornbread
into small squares and
serve with a salad. Or cut
into 6 large squares and
slice in half crosswise to
use as sandwich bases.
Spread with herbed cream
cheese or goat cheese, or
layer with your favorite
cold cuts, such as smoked
ham or turkey, topped with
tomato slices and lettuce.

Variation

Jalapeño Cornbread
Add 1 diced small red
bell pepper and 2 tbsp
(25 mL) minced seeded
jalapeño peppers to
flour mixture along
with cheese.

Cheese Cornbread

- Preheat oven to 375°F (190°C)
- 13- by 9-inch (3.5 L) baking pan, sprayed with vegetable cooking spray

1 1/4 cups	all-purpose flour	300 mL
1 cup	cornmeal	250 mL
2 tbsp	granulated sugar	25 mL
1 tbsp	baking powder	15 mL
1/2 tsp	salt	2 mL
3/4 cup	shredded Cheddar cheese	175 mL
2	eggs	2
1 1/4 cups	low-fat milk	300 mL
1/4 cup	vegetable oil	50 mL

1. In a bowl, combine flour, cornmeal, sugar, baking powder and salt. Stir in cheese.

2. In another bowl, beat eggs with milk and oil. Pour over flour mixture and stir until combined.

3. Pour batter into prepared baking pan. Bake in preheated oven for 25 to 30 minutes or until top springs back when lightly touched in center. Let cool on rack. Cut into squares.

NUTRITIONAL ANALYSIS
PER SERVING

Calories	184
Carbohydrate	23 g
Fiber	1 g
Protein	6 g
Fat, total	7 g
Fat, saturated	2 g
Sodium	245 mg
Cholesterol	37 mg

AMERICA'S EXCHANGES
PER SERVING

1 1/2	Starch
1/2	Medium-fat Meat
1/2	Fat

CANADA'S CHOICES
PER SERVING

1 1/2	Carbohydrate
1/2	Meat & Alternatives
1	Fat

MAKES ABOUT 18 SCONES
(1 scone per serving)

Brew a steaming pot of tea, invite some good friends over, then spoil them with these tender, light scones.

Variation

Apricot and Candied Ginger Scones
Substitute ¼ cup (50 mL) slivered dried apricots for the currants and add 2 tbsp (25 mL) finely chopped candied ginger to flour mixture.

Tea Time Scones

- Preheat oven to 400°F (200°C)
- Large baking sheet, sprayed with vegetable cooking spray

2 cups	all-purpose flour	500 mL
¼ cup	granulated sugar	50 mL
1 tbsp	baking powder	15 mL
½ tsp	baking soda	2 mL
½ tsp	salt	2 mL
½ cup	cold butter, cut into pieces	125 mL
½ cup	dried currants or raisins	125 mL
1	egg	1
½ cup	buttermilk	125 mL

TOPPING

1 tbsp	buttermilk	15 mL
2 tsp	granulated sugar	10 mL

1. In a large bowl, stir together flour, sugar, baking powder, baking soda and salt. Cut in butter using a pastry blender or fork to make coarse crumbs. Stir in currants or raisins.

2. In another bowl, beat egg with buttermilk; stir into dry ingredients to make a soft dough.

3. Turn out onto floured board and knead dough gently three to four times; pat or roll out using a floured rolling pin into a circular shape about ¾ inch (2 cm) thick. Cut out rounds using a 2-inch (5 cm) floured cutter; arrange on prepared baking sheet.

4. Brush with buttermilk and sprinkle with sugar. Bake in preheated oven for 16 to 20 minutes or until golden. Transfer to rack.

NUTRITIONAL ANALYSIS PER SERVING

Calories	128
Carbohydrate	17 g
Fiber	1 g
Protein	2 g
Fat, total	6 g
Fat, saturated	3 g
Sodium	210 mg
Cholesterol	24 mg

AMERICA'S EXCHANGES PER SERVING

½	Starch
½	Other Carbohydrate
1	Fat

CANADA'S CHOICES PER SERVING

1	Carbohydrate
1	Fat

*Serve these wonderful
biscuits straight from the
oven. Consider baking a
double batch if expecting
a hungry crowd.*

Tip

To assemble recipe ahead,
place dry ingredients in a
bowl. Cut in butter, add
cheese, cover and
refrigerate. While oven is
preheating, stir in the milk
and continue with recipe.

Cheddar Drop Biscuits

● *Preheat oven to 400°F (200°C)*
● *Baking sheet, sprayed with vegetable cooking spray*

2 cups	all-purpose flour	500 mL
1 tbsp	baking powder	15 mL
1/2 tsp	salt	2 mL
1/3 cup	butter, at room temperature, cut into pieces	75 mL
1 cup	coarsely shredded light Cheddar cheese	250 mL
2 tbsp	chopped fresh chives (optional)	25 mL
1 cup	low-fat milk	250 mL
	Additional chopped chives	

1. In a large bowl, combine flour, baking powder and
salt. Cut in butter using a pastry blender or two
knives to make coarse crumbs. Add cheese and
chives, if using.

2. Stir in milk to make a soft, sticky dough. Use a
1/4-cup (50 mL) measure to drop 15 portions onto
prepared baking sheet. Sprinkle tops with chopped
chives.

3. Bake on middle rack in preheated oven for 18 to
20 minutes or until edges are golden. Transfer
biscuits to a rack to cool.

**NUTRITIONAL ANALYSIS
PER SERVING**

Calories	129
Carbohydrate	14 g
Fiber	1 g
Protein	4 g
Fat, total	6 g
Fat, saturated	4 g
Sodium	245 mg
Cholesterol	17 mg

**AMERICA'S EXCHANGES
PER SERVING**

1	Starch
1	Fat

**CANADA'S CHOICES
PER SERVING**

1	Carbohydrate
1	Fat

Expecting company and want to get a head start on the cooking? Here's a great breakfast dish that can be assembled a day ahead or frozen. When ready to serve, arrange the toasts on greased baking sheets and pop in the oven while you make the coffee.

Tips

Freeze unbaked slices in a single layer on a baking sheet lined with plastic wrap; when frozen, transfer to plastic storage bags and freeze. No need to defrost before baking; just increase baking time by about 5 minutes.

Several no-sugar-added syrups are available. Be sure to check labels, as carbohydrate and calories vary depending on the sweetener(s) used (e.g. Sucralose, sorbitol, aspartame, concentrated fruit juice).

Oven French Toast

- Preheat oven to 425°F (220°C)
- 13- by 9-inch (3 L) baking dish
- Baking sheet, sprayed with vegetable cooking spray

4	eggs	4
1 cup	low-fat milk	250 mL
1 tbsp	granulated sugar	15 mL
1 tsp	vanilla	5 mL
10	slices day-old French bread (about 3½ inches/9 cm in diameter), cut ¾ inch (2 cm) thick	10
¼ cup	melted butter	50 mL
2 tbsp	granulated sugar	25 mL
¾ tsp	ground cinnamon	4 mL

1. In a bowl, whisk together eggs, milk, 1 tbsp (15 mL) granulated sugar and vanilla. Arrange bread slices in a single layer in baking dish. Pour egg mixture over. Turn slices over and let stand until egg mixture is absorbed. Cover and refrigerate until ready to bake. (Recipe can be prepared up to this point the night before.)

2. Arrange toasts in a single layer on prepared sheet and brush tops with half of melted butter.

3. Bake in preheated oven for 10 minutes. Turn slices over; brush tops with remaining melted butter. Bake for 8 minutes longer or until puffed and golden.

4. In a shallow bowl, combine 2 tbsp (25 mL) granulated sugar and cinnamon. Dip baked slices in sugar mixture and lightly coat on both sides. Serve with no-sugar-added syrup and, if desired, accompany with fruit kabobs (see box, page 256).

NUTRITIONAL ANALYSIS PER SERVING	
Calories	168
Carbohydrate	19 g
Fiber	1 g
Protein	6 g
Fat, total	8 g
Fat, saturated	4 g
Sodium	245 mg
Cholesterol	88 mg

AMERICA'S EXCHANGES PER SERVING	
1	Starch
½	Medium-fat Meat
1	Fat

CANADA'S CHOICES PER SERVING	
1	Carbohydrate
½	Meat & Alternatives
1	Fat

**MAKES
18 PANCAKES
(2 pancakes per
serving)**

*If I had to name one dish
that would bring my kids
out from under their down
comforters on a lazy
weekend morning, this
would be it.*

Tips

To keep pancakes warm,
place on rack in warm oven.

Extra pancakes can be
wrapped and frozen, then
popped in the toaster for
a quick breakfast.

To get a head start on
a weekend breakfast,
I measure out the dry
ingredients for several
batches of pancakes in
advance, place in plastic
bags and store in the
cupboard. Beat in the liquid
ingredients and the batter is
ready for the griddle.

Buttermilk Pancakes

1¾ cups	all-purpose flour	425 mL
1 tbsp	granulated sugar	15 mL
2 tsp	baking powder	10 mL
½ tsp	baking soda	2 mL
½ tsp	salt	2 mL
2	eggs	2
2 cups	buttermilk	500 mL
2 tbsp	melted butter	25 mL

1. In a bowl, combine flour, sugar, baking powder,
   baking soda and salt.

2. In another bowl, beat eggs; add buttermilk and
   melted butter. Whisk into flour mixture to make
   a smooth thick batter.

3. On an oiled griddle or in a large nonstick skillet over
   medium heat, drop ¼ cupfuls (50 mL) of batter and
   spread to a 4-inch (10 cm) circle. Cook for about
   1½ minutes or until bubbles appear on top; turn
   over and cook until browned on other side.

Fruit Kabobs

Add colorful fruit kabobs to dress up the breakfast plate.
Thread 5 or 6 chunks of assorted fresh fruit chunks,
such as apple, banana, strawberries, kiwi, pear and
pineapple, onto small 4-inch (10 cm) bamboo skewers.
(Trim or cut skewers in half, if necessary, to get the right
length.) One of these kabobs is an Extras Choice or a
Free Food Exchange.

NUTRITIONAL ANALYSIS PER SERVING	
Calories	156
Carbohydrate	23 g
Fiber	1 g
Protein	6 g
Fat, total	4 g
Fat, saturated	2 g
Sodium	355 mg
Cholesterol	50 mg

AMERICA'S EXCHANGES PER SERVING	
1½	Starch
½	Fat

CANADA'S CHOICES PER SERVING	
1½	Carbohydrate
1	Fat

Special-Occasion Desserts

The desserts that follow are all delicious, but many are higher in calories and fat. Those with diabetes may want to save them for special occasions or choose half-servings. You may also want to discuss with your diabetes educator how you can plan for a rich dessert by choosing your meal carefully.

SERVES 12

I keep individual quick-frozen berries stocked in my freezer to make this delectable cake year-round. It's best served the same day it's baked, warm or at room temperature.

Tips

Individual quick-frozen berries do not need to be defrosted before they are added to batter.

Incorrect measurement is a major cause of baking failures. Use a liquid cup measure for fluids and a dry measure for dry ingredients such as flour. Spoon ingredient into dry measure and level off using a knife. Do not pack the dry measure down by tapping on the counter top; this increases the amount.

Raspberry Coffee Cake

- Preheat oven to 350°F (180°C)
- 9-inch (23 cm) springform pan, sprayed with vegetable cooking spray

1 1/2 cups	all-purpose flour	375 mL
3/4 cup	granulated sugar	175 mL
1/2 cup	sweetened shredded coconut	125 mL
2 tsp	baking powder	10 mL
1/2 tsp	baking soda	2 mL
1/4 tsp	salt	1 mL
1/4 cup	canola oil	50 mL
2	eggs	2
3/4 cup	light sour cream	175 mL
1 tsp	vanilla	5 mL
1 cup	fresh or frozen unsweetened raspberries or blueberries	250 mL

CRUMB TOPPING

3 tbsp	packed brown sugar	45 mL
2 tbsp	quick-cooking rolled oats	25 mL
2 tbsp	all-purpose flour	25 mL
2 tbsp	sweetened shredded coconut	25 mL
1/2 tsp	ground cinnamon	2 mL
2 tbsp	butter, cut into pieces	25 mL

1. In a bowl, combine flour, sugar, coconut, baking powder, baking soda and salt.

2. In another bowl, beat oil with eggs, sour cream and vanilla. Stir in flour mixture; mix well. Gently fold in raspberries; spread batter in prepared pan.

3. *Crumb Topping:* In a bowl, combine brown sugar, oats, flour, coconut and cinnamon. Cut in butter using a pastry blender or two knives to make coarse crumbs. Sprinkle evenly over top.

4. Bake on middle rack in preheated oven for 55 to 60 minutes or until tester inserted in center comes out clean. Set cake on rack to cool.

NUTRITIONAL ANALYSIS PER SERVING	
Calories	241
Carbohydrate	34 g
Fiber	1 g
Protein	4 g
Fat, total	10 g
Fat, saturated	3 g
Sodium	185 mg
Cholesterol	36 mg

AMERICA'S EXCHANGES PER SERVING	
1	Starch
1 1/2	Other Carbohydrate
1 1/2	Fat

CANADA'S CHOICES PER SERVING	
2	Carbohydrate
2	Fat

Mennonite Streusel Cake

SERVES 12

More commonly known as fruit platz, this delectable recipe was given to me by a Mennonite family in Niagara whose ancestors settled the region over two centuries ago. It makes use of seasonal fruits from sweet-and-sour pitted cherries, raspberries, sliced peaches, nectarines, apricots to blue plums.

Tips

For a smaller-size cake to serve 6, halve the ingredients and bake in a buttered 8-inch (2 L) square pan for 35 to 40 minutes.

In baking, always use large eggs, not medium or extra large, either of which can affect the baking result.

To soften butter, microwave on Defrost and check at 15-second intervals.

- Preheat oven to 350°F (180°C)
- 13- by 9-inch (3.5 L) baking pan, sprayed with vegetable cooking spray

2 cups	all-purpose flour	500 mL
1/2 cup	granulated sugar	125 mL
1 tbsp	baking powder	15 mL
1/4 tsp	salt	1 mL
1/3 cup	butter, softened	75 mL
1	egg	1
1 cup	half-and-half (10%) cream	250 mL
1 1/2 tsp	vanilla or grated lemon zest	7 mL
4 cups	fresh or frozen blueberries or other seasonal sliced fruits	1 L

CRUMB TOPPING

1/4 cup	all-purpose flour	50 mL
1/4 cup	packed brown sugar	50 mL
1 tbsp	butter, softened	15 mL

1. In a large bowl, combine flour, sugar, baking powder and salt. Cut in butter using a pastry blender or two knives to make coarse crumbs.

2. In another bowl, beat egg with cream and vanilla. Stir into flour mixture to make a thick batter.

3. Drop tablespoonfuls of batter into prepared baking dish and spread evenly. Top with blueberries in a single layer.

4. *Crumb Topping:* In a bowl, combine flour and brown sugar. Cut in butter using a pastry blender or two knives to make coarse crumbs. Sprinkle evenly over fruit.

5. Bake on middle rack in preheated oven for 45 to 50 minutes or until crumb topping is golden. Place on a rack and let cool. Cut into squares and serve.

NUTRITIONAL ANALYSIS PER SERVING	
Calories	248
Carbohydrate	39 g
Fiber	2 g
Protein	4 g
Fat, total	9 g
Fat, saturated	5 g
Sodium	195 mg
Cholesterol	38 mg

AMERICA'S EXCHANGES PER SERVING	
1	Starch
1/2	Fruit
1	Other Carbohydrate
1 1/2	Fat

CANADA'S CHOICES PER SERVING	
2 1/2	Carbohydrate
2	Fat

This coffee cake is welcome at brunch, afternoon tea or dessert time. Make it year-round with other seasonal fruits such as pears, apples, pitted cherries or plums.

Tips

To peel peaches, plunge in boiling water for 15 to 30 seconds to loosen skins.

Replace your supplies of baking powder and baking soda every 6 months; once opened, they oxidize and lose their leavening power.

For perfect cakes, loaves, bars and squares, it's essential to use the correct size of baking pan specified in each recipe.

Peach Almond Cake

- Preheat oven to 350°F (180°C)
- 9-inch (23 cm) springform pan or cake pan, sprayed with vegetable cooking spray

1 ½ cups	all-purpose flour	375 mL
¾ cup	granulated sugar	175 mL
1 ½ tsp	baking powder	7 mL
½ tsp	baking soda	2 mL
¼ tsp	salt	1 mL
2	eggs	2
⅔ cup	plain low-fat yogurt	150 mL
¼ cup	butter, melted	50 mL
½ tsp	almond extract	2 mL
3	peaches, peeled and sliced	3
3 tbsp	sliced blanched almonds	45 mL
2 tbsp	granulated sugar	25 mL
½ tsp	ground cinnamon	2 mL

1. In a mixing bowl, stir together flour, ¾ cup (175 mL) sugar, baking powder, baking soda and salt.

2. In another bowl, beat eggs, yogurt, melted butter and almond extract until smooth. Stir into dry ingredients to make a smooth thick batter. Spread in prepared pan. Arrange peaches on top in a circular fashion.

3. In a small bowl, combine almonds, 2 tbsp (25 mL) sugar and cinnamon. Sprinkle over peaches. Bake in preheated oven for 50 to 60 minutes or until cake tester inserted in center comes out clean.

NUTRITIONAL ANALYSIS PER SERVING	
Calories	191
Carbohydrate	31 g
Fiber	1 g
Protein	4 g
Fat, total	6 g
Fat, saturated	3 g
Sodium	195 mg
Cholesterol	42 mg

AMERICA'S EXCHANGES PER SERVING	
1	Starch
1	Other Carbohydrate
1	Fat

CANADA'S CHOICES PER SERVING	
2	Carbohydrate
1	Fat

Frozen Strawberry Cake

SERVES 12

Surprisingly easy to prepare, this impressive frozen dessert is sublime when fresh berries are in season.

Tip

Instead of orange-flavored liqueur substitute the same quantity of undiluted frozen orange juice concentrate.

● **9- by 5-inch (2 L) loaf pan, lined with plastic wrap with ends hanging generously over sides of pan**

1	frozen pound cake (10 oz/298 g)	1
6 cups	fresh strawberries, hulled, divided	1.5 L
6 tbsp	orange-flavored liqueur or orange juice, divided	75 mL
4 tbsp	freshly squeezed lime juice, divided	50 mL
1/3 cup	granulated sugar	75 mL
4 cups	low-fat strawberry frozen yogurt, softened slightly	1 L

1. Slightly defrost pound cake. Trim dark crusts from top and sides of cake; cut into 24 slices, each 1/4-inch (0.5 cm) thick.

2. Quarter and slice 2 cups (500 mL) berries. Place in bowl with 3 tbsp (45 mL) orange-flavored liqueur and 2 tbsp (25 mL) lime juice. Set aside.

3. In a food processor, purée remaining berries, orange-flavored liqueur, lime juice and sugar; pour into a bowl.

4. Spread scant 1/4 cup (50 mL) strawberry purée in pan. Layer with 8 slices of cake, arranging them lengthwise with slightly overlapping edges. Spread cake with scant 1/4 cup (50 mL) strawberry purée, then top with 2 cups (500 mL) frozen yogurt and another scant 1/4 cup (50 mL) strawberry puree. Repeat layers of cake, strawberry purée, frozen yogurt and strawberry purée. Arrange remaining cake slices on top and spread with 1/4 cup (50 mL) strawberry purée. Fold plastic wrap over top, pressing gently down on cake. Freeze for 8 hours.

5. Stir reserved purée into sliced strawberry mixture. Cover and refrigerate.

6. To serve, place cake in refrigerator for 30 minutes to soften slightly. Lift out of pan and remove plastic wrap. Cut into slices and arrange on serving plates. Top with a generous spoonful of strawberry mixture.

NUTRITIONAL ANALYSIS PER SERVING	
Calories	269
Carbohydrate	45 g
Fiber	2 g
Protein	4 g
Fat, total	7 g
Fat, saturated	4 g
Sodium	40 mg
Cholesterol	45 mg

AMERICA'S EXCHANGES PER SERVING	
1	Starch
1/2	Fruit
1 1/2	Other Carbohydrate
1 1/2	Fat

CANADA'S CHOICES PER SERVING	
3	Carbohydrate
1 1/2	Fat

SERVES 8

I look forward to indulging in this old-fashioned dessert when local berries and rhubarb are in season. But it's also good in winter, when I turn to my freezer for my stash of summer fruits.

Tips

If using frozen fruit, there's no need to defrost before using.

If you prefer to bake the cobbler earlier in the day, reheat in 350°F (180°C) oven for about 15 minutes.

Strawberry-Rhubarb Cobbler

- Preheat oven to 400°F (200°C)
- 9-inch (2.5 L) round or square baking dish

4 cups	chopped fresh rhubarb	I L
2 cups	sliced strawberries	500 mL
¾ cup	granulated sugar	175 mL
2 tbsp	cornstarch	25 mL
I tsp	grated orange zest	5 mL

BISCUIT TOPPING

I cup	all-purpose flour	250 mL
¼ cup	granulated sugar	50 mL
I ½ tsp	baking powder	7 mL
¼ tsp	salt	I mL
¼ cup	cold butter, cut into pieces	50 mL
½ cup	low-fat milk	125 mL
I tsp	vanilla	5 mL

1. Place rhubarb and strawberries in baking dish. In a small bowl, combine sugar, cornstarch and orange zest; sprinkle over fruit and gently toss.

2. Bake in preheated oven for 20 to 25 minutes (increase to 30 minutes if using frozen fruit), until hot and bubbles appear around edges.

3. *Biscuit Topping:* In a bowl, combine flour, sugar, baking powder and salt. Cut in butter using a pastry blender or fork to make coarse crumbs. In a glass measure, combine milk and vanilla; stir into dry ingredients to make a soft sticky dough.

4. Using a large spoon, drop eight separate spoonfuls of dough onto hot fruit.

5. Bake in preheated oven for 25 to 30 minutes or until top is golden and fruit is bubbly.

NUTRITIONAL ANALYSIS PER SERVING

Calories	245
Carbohydrate	45 g
Fiber	2 g
Protein	3 g
Fat, total	6 g
Fat, saturated	4 g
Sodium	190 mg
Cholesterol	16 mg

AMERICA'S EXCHANGES PER SERVING

I	Starch
½	Fruit
I ½	Other Carbohydrate
I	Fat

CANADA'S CHOICES PER SERVING

3	Carbohydrate
I	Fat

When you pair fresh, ripe peaches with a crumbly nut topping, it's a juicy sweet treat. For a special occasion, served warm with low-fat frozen yogurt, it's the ultimate comfort food dessert.

Tip

Fresh peaches work best, but in a pinch 1 can (28 oz/796 mL) peaches, drained and sliced, can be substituted. Omit the cornstarch.

Irresistible Peach Almond Crumble

- Preheat oven to 375°F (190°C)
- 8-inch (2 L) baking dish, sprayed with vegetable cooking spray

FRUIT

4 cups	sliced peeled peaches or nectarines	1 L
1/4 cup	peach or apricot preserves	50 mL
2 tsp	cornstarch	10 mL

TOPPING

1/2 cup	large-flake rolled oats	125 mL
1/2 cup	all-purpose flour	125 mL
1/4 cup	packed brown sugar	50 mL
1/4 tsp	ground ginger	1 mL
1/4 cup	melted butter	50 mL
2 tbsp	sliced almonds	25 mL

1. *Fruit:* In a large bowl, toss peaches with preserves and cornstarch. Spread in prepared baking dish.

2. *Filling:* In a small bowl, combine oats, flour, brown sugar and ginger. Pour in butter and stir to make coarse crumbs. Sprinkle over fruit and top with almonds.

3. Bake in preheated oven for 30 to 35 minutes or until topping is golden and filling is bubbly. Serve warm or at room temperature.

NUTRITIONAL ANALYSIS PER SERVING

Calories	197
Carbohydrate	34 g
Fiber	2 g
Protein	3 g
Fat, total	6 g
Fat, saturated	3 g
Sodium	60 mg
Cholesterol	14 mg

AMERICA'S EXCHANGES PER SERVING

1/2	Starch
1/2	Fruit
1	Other Carbohydrate
1	Fat

CANADA'S CHOICES PER SERVING

2	Carbohydrate
1	Fat

Saucy fruit topped with a cake batter makes one of the most soothing desserts ever created. This version hails from Quebec, where sweet and snappy Macintosh apples are paired with amber maple syrup.

Tip

Once opened, make sure to store maple syrup in the refrigerator. It can also be frozen.

Warm Maple Apple Pudding

- *Preheat oven to 350°F (180°C)*
- *8-inch (2 L) square baking dish, sprayed with vegetable cooking spray*

4 cups	sliced cored peeled Macintosh apples	1 L
1/2 cup	pure maple syrup	125 mL
1 cup	all-purpose flour	250 mL
1/4 cup	granulated sugar	50 mL
1 1/2 tsp	baking powder	7 mL
1/2 tsp	baking soda	2 mL
1/4 cup	butter, cut into pieces	50 mL
1	egg	1
1/2 cup	buttermilk	125 mL
1 tsp	vanilla	5 mL

1. In a large saucepan, bring apples and maple syrup to a boil; reduce heat and simmer for 3 minutes or until softened. Pour into prepared baking dish.

2. In a large bowl, combine flour, sugar, baking powder and baking soda. Cut in butter, using a pastry blender, to make fine crumbs.

3. In a small bowl, combine egg, buttermilk and vanilla. Pour over flour mixture; stir just until combined. Drop batter by large spoonfuls onto warm apple slices.

4. Bake in preheated oven for 30 minutes or until top is golden and cake tester inserted in center comes out clean. Serve warm.

NUTRITIONAL ANALYSIS PER SERVING

Calories	207
Carbohydrate	36 g
Fiber	1 g
Protein	3 g
Fat, total	6 g
Fat, saturated	3 g
Sodium	190 mg
Cholesterol	35 mg

AMERICA'S EXCHANGES PER SERVING

1/2	Starch
1/2	Fruit
1 1/2	Other Carbohydrate
1	Fat

CANADA'S CHOICES PER SERVING

2 1/2	Carbohydrate
1	Fat

Creamy Rice Pudding

When it comes to comfort food, I put rice pudding at the top of my list. It's creamy, it's luscious and oh-so-satisfying.

Tips

If short-grain rice is unavailable, use long-grain rice (not converted) instead. Long-grain rice is not as starchy, so reduce the amount of milk to 4 cups (1 L) in total. Combine long-grain rice with 3½ cups (875 mL) of the milk and continue with recipe as directed.

Be careful of spillovers and pudding sticking to pan: be sure to turn heat so mixture just simmers gently.

Instead of using vanilla for flavoring, add a 3-inch (8 cm) strip of lemon peel to the milk-rice mixture when cooking. Remove before serving.

½ cup	short-grain rice, such as Arborio	125 mL
5 cups	whole milk, divided	1.25 L
⅓ cup	granulated sugar	75 mL
½ tsp	salt	2 mL
1	egg yolk	1
¼ cup	sultana raisins	50 mL
1 tsp	vanilla	5 mL
	Ground cinnamon (optional)	

1. In a large saucepan, combine rice, 4½ cups (1.125 L) milk, sugar and salt. Bring to a boil; reduce heat to medium-low and simmer, partially covered, stirring occasionally, for about 45 to 50 minutes until rice is tender and mixture has thickened.

2. Beat together remaining ½ cup (125 mL) milk and egg yolk; stir into rice mixture, stirring, for 1 minute or until creamy. Remove from heat. Stir in raisins and vanilla.

3. Serve either warm or at room temperature. (Pudding thickens slightly as it cools.) Sprinkle with cinnamon, if desired.

NUTRITIONAL ANALYSIS PER SERVING	
Calories	194
Carbohydrate	29 g
Fiber	0 g
Protein	6 g
Fat, total	6 g
Fat, saturated	3 g
Sodium	220 mg
Cholesterol	44 mg

AMERICA'S EXCHANGES PER SERVING	
½	Starch
½	Milk, Whole
1	Other Carbohydrate
½	Fat

CANADA'S CHOICES PER SERVING	
2	Carbohydrate
1	Fat

SERVES 9

On a comfort scale, bread puddings, with their old-fashioned appeal, rate as one of the most-loved desserts. This simple bread pudding, featuring cinnamon bread in a custard base, takes no time to put together.

Cinnamon Raisin Bread Pudding

- Preheat oven to 375°F (190°C) ● Baking sheets
- 12- by 8-inch (2.5 L) baking dish, sprayed with nonstick vegetable cooking spray
- Large shallow roasting pan or deep broiler pan

12	slices cinnamon raisin swirl bread (1 lb/500 g loaf)	12
6	eggs	6
2 cups	whole milk	500 mL
1 cup	half-and-half (10%) cream	250 mL
¾ cup	granulated sugar	175 mL
2 tsp	vanilla	10 mL
TOPPING		
2 tbsp	granulated sugar	25 mL
½ tsp	ground cinnamon	2 mL

1. Place bread slices in a single layer on baking sheets and lightly toast in preheated oven for 10 to 12 minutes. Let cool. Leave oven on. Cut bread into cubes and place in prepared baking dish.

2. In a bowl, whisk together eggs, milk, cream, sugar and vanilla. Pour over bread. Let soak for 10 minutes, pressing down gently with a spatula.

3. *Topping:* In a bowl, combine sugar and cinnamon. Sprinkle over top.

4. Place baking dish in roasting or broiler pan; add enough boiling water to come halfway up sides of dish. Bake in preheated oven for 45 to 50 minutes or until top is puffed and custard is set in center. Transfer to a rack to cool. Serve warm or at room temperature.

NUTRITIONAL ANALYSIS PER SERVING

Calories	329
Carbohydrate	50 g
Fiber	2 g
Protein	11 g
Fat, total	10 g
Fat, saturated	4 g
Sodium	275 mg
Cholesterol	140 mg

AMERICA'S EXCHANGES PER SERVING

2	Starch
1½	Milk, Whole
½	Other Carbohydrate
1	Fat

CANADA'S CHOICES PER SERVING

3	Carbohydrate
½	Meat & Alternatives
1½	Fat

Bread Pudding with Caramelized Pears

SERVES 8

In the old days, bread puddings were an economy dish, simply made with stale bread and custard. But there's nothing humble about this recipe. The golden pear topping flecked with raisins transforms it into a special dessert fit for company. Serve either warm or at room temperature.

Tips

Bartlett pears work well in this recipe.

Can't figure out the volume of a baking dish? Look for the measurements on the bottom of dish or measure by pouring in enough water to fill completely.

When a recipe calls for a baking pan, it refers to a metal pan, while a baking dish refers to glass.

- Preheat oven to 350°F (180°C)
- 8-cup (2 L) baking dish, sprayed
- Shallow roasting pan

6	slices whole wheat sandwich bread	6
2 tbsp	butter, softened	25 mL
4	eggs	4
⅔ cup	granulated sugar, divided	150 mL
2 tsp	vanilla	10 mL
2 cups	hot low-fat milk	500 mL
4	pears, peeled, cored and sliced	4
½ tsp	freshly grated nutmeg	2 mL
⅓ cup	raisins	75 mL
¼ cup	sliced blanched almonds	50 mL

1. Trim crusts from bread; butter one side of each bread slice. Cut into 4 triangles each; layer in prepared baking dish, overlapping the triangles.

2. In a large bowl, whisk together eggs, ⅓ cup (75 mL) of the sugar and vanilla. Whisk in hot milk in a stream, stirring constantly. Pour over bread.

3. In a large nonstick skillet over medium heat, cook the remaining sugar and 2 tbsp (25 mL) water, stirring occasionally, until mixture turns a deep caramel color. Immediately add pears and nutmeg (be careful of spatters). Cook, stirring often, for 5 minutes or until pears are tender and sauce is smooth. Stir in raisins; spoon evenly over bread slices. Sprinkle almonds over top.

4. Place baking dish in roasting pan; add enough boiling water to reach halfway up sides of dish. Bake for 40 to 45 minutes or until custard is set in center. Remove from water bath; place on rack to cool.

NUTRITIONAL ANALYSIS PER SERVING	
Calories	247
Carbohydrate	41 g
Fiber	3 g
Protein	7 g
Fat, total	7 g
Fat, saturated	3 g
Sodium	150 mg
Cholesterol	103 mg

AMERICA'S EXCHANGES PER SERVING	
½	Starch
1	Fruit
1	Other Carbohydrate
½	Medium-fat Meat
1	Fat

CANADA'S CHOICES PER SERVING	
2½	Carbohydrate
1	Fat

SERVES 4

Looking for an easy family-pleasing dessert? This one takes only a few minutes to prepare.

Tip

Any kind of fresh, frozen or drained canned fruit can be used. Try sliced strawberries, raspberries, blueberries, peaches or plums, or a combination of several seasonal fresh fruits.

Maple Custard with Fresh Fruit

2	egg yolks	2
1⅓ cups	milk	325 mL
⅓ cup	pure maple syrup	75 mL
2 tbsp	cornstarch	25 mL
2	peaches, pears or bananas, peeled and sliced	2

1. In a small saucepan, whisk together egg yolks, milk, maple syrup and cornstarch until smooth. Cook over medium-low heat, whisking constantly, for 2 to 4 minutes or until boiling and thickened.

2. Arrange fruit in 4 individual serving dishes; pour hot custard over. Cover and refrigerate for 1 hour or until cool.

NUTRITIONAL ANALYSIS PER SERVING

Calories	165
Carbohydrate	30 g
Fiber	1 g
Protein	4 g
Fat, total	3 g
Fat, saturated	1 g
Sodium	45 mg
Cholesterol	98 mg

AMERICA'S EXCHANGES PER SERVING

½	Fruit
1½	Other Carbohydrate
1	Fat

CANADA'S CHOICES PER SERVING

2	Carbohydrate
1	Fat

This self-saucing French custard was the rage in the '70s. Now that French cuisine is back in vogue, so too is this appealing dessert that is surprisingly easy to make and serve.

Tip

Can be made up to 2 days ahead of serving.

Crème Caramel

- Preheat oven to 325°F (160°C)
- 6 individual ramekins or 6-oz (175 mL) custard cups
- 13- by 9-inch (3.5 L) baking pan

CARAMEL

½ cup	granulated sugar	125 mL
¼ cup	water	50 mL

CUSTARD

2	eggs	2
2	egg yolks	2
½ cup	granulated sugar	125 mL
1 tsp	vanilla	5 mL
2½ cups	whole milk	625 mL

1. *Caramel:* In a heavy-bottomed medium saucepan, combine sugar and water. Place over medium heat until sugar melts; increase heat to medium-high and cook until sugar mixture boils (do not stir). When syrup has turned a rich caramel color, remove from heat; pour into ramekins. Quickly rotate dish to spread caramel evenly over bottom.

2. *Custard:* In a bowl, whisk together eggs, egg yolks, sugar and vanilla. In another saucepan, heat milk over medium heat until almost boiling. Pour hot milk mixture in a thin stream into egg mixture, whisking constantly. Strain through a sieve into prepared ramekins.

3. Arrange in baking pan; carefully pour in boiling water to come 1 inch (2.5 cm) up sides of dish. Place pan in oven; bake for 25 minutes or until tester inserted in center comes out clean. Let cool to room temperature; refrigerate. To serve, run a knife around edges to loosen custard. Invert onto serving plate.

NUTRITIONAL ANALYSIS PER SERVING

Calories	196
Carbohydrate	28 g
Fiber	0 g
Protein	6 g
Fat, total	7 g
Fat, saturated	3 g
Sodium	75 mg
Cholesterol	139 mg

AMERICA'S EXCHANGES PER SERVING

½	Milk, Whole
1½	Other Carbohydrate
½	Medium-fat Meat

CANADA'S CHOICES PER SERVING

2	Carbohydrate
1	Fat

Serve this refreshing fresh fruit salad as is, or as a topping for low-fat yogurt.

Tips

Go tropical and use a combination of assorted fruits such as pineapple, mango, kiwi and melon.

Store in an airtight container in the refrigerator for up to 2 days.

Gingery Fresh Fruit Compote

⅔ cup	orange juice	150 mL
2 tbsp	liquid honey	25 mL
1 tbsp	finely chopped candied ginger	15 mL
1 tsp	grated orange zest	5 mL
3 cups	prepared fresh fruit	750 mL

1. In a small saucepan, combine orange juice, honey and candied ginger. Bring to a boil; boil for 2 minutes. (Or place in a 2-cup/500 mL glass measure and microwave at High for 2 to 2½ minutes.) Remove from heat and stir in orange zest. Let cool to room temperature.

2. Place fruit in a serving bowl and pour orange mixture over. Cover and refrigerate for up to 4 hours before serving.

NUTRITIONAL ANALYSIS PER SERVING	
Calories	80
Carbohydrate	20 g
Fiber	1 g
Protein	1 g
Fat, total	0 g
Fat, saturated	0 g
Sodium	0 mg
Cholesterol	0 mg

AMERICA'S EXCHANGES PER SERVING	
1	Fruit
½	Other Carbohydrate

CANADA'S CHOICES PER SERVING	
1	Carbohydrate

Here's an updated version of the traditional "fool" — an old-fashioned dessert with fruit or berries folded into whipped cream or custard. This dessert is ideal for entertaining since it can be assembled earlier in the day.

Tips

Whipped cream is a delicious traditional ingredient in many desserts, but it is high in fat, so combine small amounts with lower-fat ingredients such as the fresh fruit and low-fat yogurt in this recipe.

Instead of individual serving dishes, layer berries and lemon fool in a 6-cup (1.5 L) deep glass serving bowl.

Lemon Fool with Fresh Berries

2 tbsp	cornstarch	25 mL
1/2 cup	cold water	125 mL
2/3 cup	granulated sugar	150 mL
1 tbsp	finely grated lemon zest	15 mL
1/3 cup	freshly squeezed lemon juice	75 mL
2	egg yolks	2
1 cup	plain low-fat yogurt	250 mL
1/2 cup	whipping (35%) cream	125 mL
4 cups	fresh berries, such as sliced strawberries, raspberries or blueberries	1 L
	Additional berries, fresh mint sprigs and grated lemon zest	

1. In a small saucepan, combine cornstarch with water; whisk until smooth. Add sugar, lemon zest, juice and egg yolks; cook over medium heat, whisking constantly, until mixture comes to a full boil; cook for 15 seconds. Remove from heat and pour into a large bowl. Let cool slightly. Cover surface with plastic wrap; refrigerate for 2 hours or until chilled. (Recipe can be prepared to this point up to 1 day ahead.)

2. Whisk lemon mixture until smooth. Whisk in yogurt.

3. In bowl, using electric mixer, beat cream until stiff peaks form. Gently fold into lemon-yogurt mixture.

4. Arrange half the berries in six parfait or large wine glasses. Top with half the lemon fool; layer with remaining berries and lemon fool. (Recipe can be prepared to this point and refrigerated for up to 4 hours.) To serve, garnish with whole berries, mint sprigs and grated lemon zest.

NUTRITIONAL ANALYSIS PER SERVING	
Calories	186
Carbohydrate	29 g
Fiber	2 g
Protein	3 g
Fat, total	7 g
Fat, saturated	4 g
Sodium	30 mg
Cholesterol	68 mg

AMERICA'S EXCHANGES PER SERVING	
1/2	Fruit
1 1/2	Other Carbohydrate
1 1/2	Fat

CANADA'S CHOICES PER SERVING	
1 1/2	Carbohydrate
1 1/2	Fat

SERVES 6

By adding a splash of spirits, you can turn bananas into a special-occasion dessert in a matter of minutes, using your microwave oven.

Bananas in Spiced Rum Sauce

● *8- or 9-inch (20 or 23 cm) round or square shallow baking dish*

1/4 cup	packed brown sugar	50 mL
2 tbsp	orange juice	25 mL
1 tbsp	freshly squeezed lime juice	15 mL
1/4 tsp	ground cinnamon	1 mL
1/4 tsp	freshly grated nutmeg	1 mL
2 tbsp	dark rum	25 mL
4	firm but ripe bananas	4
	Low-fat yogurt (optional)	

1. In a glass measure, combine brown sugar, orange juice, lime juice, cinnamon and nutmeg. Microwave on High for 1 1/2 to 2 minutes or until sauce boils and reduces slightly. Add rum.

2. Peel bananas, halve lengthwise and cut each half into 3 pieces. Arrange banana pieces in a single layer in baking dish and pour sauce over. Cover loosely with waxed paper and microwave on High for 2 1/2 to 4 minutes or until bananas are softened.

3. Serve warm, topped with a dollop of low-fat yogurt, if desired.

NUTRITIONAL ANALYSIS PER SERVING	
Calories	129
Carbohydrate	31 g
Fiber	2 g
Protein	1 g
Fat, total	1 g
Fat, saturated	0 g
Sodium	5 mg
Cholesterol	0 mg

AMERICA'S EXCHANGES PER SERVING	
1	Fruit
1	Other Carbohydrate

CANADA'S CHOICES PER SERVING	
2	Carbohydrate

SERVES 6

This quick dessert sauce is great on its own or over low-fat yogurt. It tastes like old-fashioned apple pie, but without the effort and calories of an actual pie.

Tip

Use apples that hold their shape after cooking, such as Cortland, Granny Smith or Golden Delicious.

Brown Sugar Apple Slices with Dried Cranberries

1/3 cup	orange juice	75 mL
1/4 cup	packed brown sugar	50 mL
1 tsp	cornstarch	5 mL
4	apples, peeled, cored and sliced	4
1/4 cup	dried cranberries	50 mL
1/2 tsp	ground cinnamon	2 mL

1. In a large saucepan, combine orange juice, brown sugar and cornstarch until smooth. Stir in apple slices, cranberries and cinnamon. Cook over medium heat, stirring occasionally, for 7 to 9 minutes or until apples are just tender and sauce is slightly thickened. Serve warm or at room temperature.

NUTRITIONAL ANALYSIS PER SERVING

Calories	111
Carbohydrate	29 g
Fiber	2 g
Protein	0 g
Fat, total	0 g
Fat, saturated	0 g
Sodium	5 mg
Cholesterol	0 mg

AMERICA'S EXCHANGES PER SERVING

1	Fruit
1	Other Carbohydrate

CANADA'S CHOICES PER SERVING

2	Carbohydrate

SERVES 8

When I want elegance and style, I turn to this classic preparation for pears. It's an impressive way to end a special meal.

Tips

Poach the pears the day before. They are best served well-chilled.

Select pears that are not overly ripe so they will hold their shape when sliced.

Wine-Poached Pear Fans

2 cups	red wine (or 1 cup/250 mL pure cranberry juice (not cocktail) plus 1 cup/250 mL water)	500 mL
½ cup	granulated sugar	125 mL
1	cinnamon stick	1
3	whole cloves	3
2	strips (each 3 inches/8 cm) orange peel	2
4	Bartlett pears, peeled, halved and cored	4
	Extra-thick low-fat yogurt	
	Freshly grated nutmeg and fresh mint sprigs	

1. In a medium saucepan, combine wine, sugar, cinnamon stick, cloves and orange peel. Bring to a boil, stirring to dissolve sugar. Add pear halves; reduce heat, cover and simmer for 15 minutes or until just tender when pierced with a knife. Remove with a slotted spoon to a dish; let cool.

2. Bring poaching liquid in saucepan to a boil over high heat; boil until reduced to ¾ cup (175 mL). Strain through a sieve to remove spices; let cool and refrigerate.

3. Place pears cut side down on work surface. Beginning near the stem end, cut each pear half into ¼-inch (5 mm) lengthwise slices. (Do not cut through the stem itself; slices will still be attached at stem end.) Arrange a pear half on each dessert plate, pressing down gently to fan out slices. Spoon syrup over. Garnish with a dollop of yogurt and sprinkle with nutmeg. Garnish with mint sprigs.

NUTRITIONAL ANALYSIS PER SERVING

Calories	127
Carbohydrate	27 g
Fiber	2 g
Protein	2 g
Fat, total	1 g
Fat, saturated	0 g
Sodium	25 mg
Cholesterol	1 mg

AMERICA'S EXCHANGES PER SERVING

1	Fruit
1	Other Carbohydrate

CANADA'S CHOICES PER SERVING

1½	Carbohydrate

Recipe Analysis

Computer-assisted calculation of the recipes was carried out by Food Intelligence (Toronto, Ontario) using Genesis® R&D Nutrition Analysis Program (ESHA Research). The database included current values from the Canadian Nutrient File and USDA Nutrient Database for Standard Reference, supplemented with information from other reliable sources.

Calculations were based on:
* imperial measures unless a metric quantity would typically be purchased and used;
* the first ingredient listed where there is a choice;
* low-fat (1%) milk unless otherwise specified;
* canola vegetable oil and soft non-hydrogenated margarine; and
* trimmed lean meat and skinless poultry portions.

Optional ingredients were excluded from calculations. Recipe variations are similar in nutrient content to the corresponding recipe.

Nutrient values have been rounded to whole numbers. Unrounded values were used in calculating American Exchanges and Canadian Choices, based respectively on American Diabetes Association exchange lists and *Beyond the Basics: Meal Planning, Healthy Eating and Diabetes Prevention and Management* (Canadian Diabetes Association).

Library and Archives Canada Cataloguing in Publication

Burkhard, Johanna
        Diabetes comfort food / Johanna Burkhard; Barbara Selley, nutrition editor. — American ed.

ISBN-13: 978-0-7788-0148-1
ISBN-10: 0-7788-0148-9

1. Diabetes — Diet therapy — Recipes. I. Selley, Barbara. II. Title.

RC662.B876 2006a   641.5'6314   C2006-903901-1

Library and Archives Canada Cataloguing in Publication

Burkhard, Johanna
        Diabetes comfort food / Johanna Burkhard; Barbara Selley, nutrition editor. — Canadian ed.

ISBN-13: 978-0-7788-0151-1
ISBN-10: 0-7788-0151-9

1. Diabetes — Diet therapy — Recipes. I. Selley, Barbara. II. Title.

RC662.B876 2006   641.5'6314   C2006-902544-4

Index

More Great Books from Robert Rose

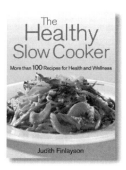

Appliance Cooking

- 125 Best Microwave Oven Recipes
  by Johanna Burkhard
- The Blender Bible
  by Andrew Chase and Nicole Young
- The Mixer Bible
  by Meredith Deeds and Carla Snyder
- The 150 Best Slow Cooker Recipes
  by Judith Finlayson
- Delicious & Dependable Slow Cooker Recipes
  by Judith Finlayson
- 125 Best Vegetarian Slow Cooker Recipes
  by Judith Finlayson
- The Healthy Slow Cooker
  by Judith Finlayson
- 125 Best Rotisserie Oven Recipes
  by Judith Finlayson
- 125 Best Food Processor Recipes
  by George Geary
- The Best Family Slow Cooker Recipes
  by Donna-Marie Pye
- The Best Convection Oven Cookbook
  by Linda Stephen
- 250 Best American Bread Machine Baking Recipes
  by Donna Washburn and Heather Butt
- 250 Best Canadian Bread Machine Baking Recipes
  by Donna Washburn and Heather Butt

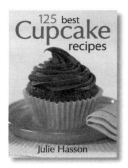

Baking

- 250 Best Cakes & Pies
  by Esther Brody
- 500 Best Cookies, Bars & Squares
  by Esther Brody
- 500 Best Muffin Recipes
  by Esther Brody
- 125 Best Cheesecake Recipes
  by George Geary
- 125 Best Chocolate Recipes
  by Julie Hasson
- 125 Best Chocolate Chip Recipes
  by Julie Hasson
- 125 Best Cupcake Recipes
  by Julie Hasson
- Complete Cake Mix Magic
  by Jill Snider

Healthy Cooking

- 125 Best Vegetarian Recipes
  by Byron Ayanoglu with contributions from Algis Kemezys
- America's Best Cookbook for Kids with Diabetes
  by Colleen Bartley
- Canada's Best Cookbook for Kids with Diabetes
  by Colleen Bartley
- The Juicing Bible
  by Pat Crocker and Susan Eagles
- The Smoothies Bible
  by Pat Crocker

- 125 Best Vegan Recipes
  by Maxine Effenson Chuck and Beth Gurney
- 200 Best Lactose-Free Recipes
  by Jan Main
- 500 Best Healthy Recipes
  Edited by Lynn Roblin, RD
- 125 Best Gluten-Free Recipes
  by Donna Washburn and Heather Butt
- The Best Gluten-Free Family Cookbook
  by Donna Washburn and Heather Butt
- America's Everyday Diabetes Cookbook
  Edited by Katherine E. Younker, MBA, RD
- Canada's Everyday Diabetes Choice Recipes
  Edited by Katherine E. Younker, MBA, RD
- America's Complete Diabetes Cookbook
  Edited by Katherine E. Younker, MBA, RD
- Canada's Complete Diabetes Cookbook
  Edited by Katherine E. Younker, MBA, RD

Recent Bestsellers

- 125 Best Soup Recipes
  by Marylin Crowley and Joan Mackie
- The Convenience Cook
  by Judith Finlayson
- 125 Best Ice Cream Recipes
  by Marilyn Linton and Tanya Linton

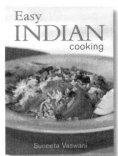

- Easy Indian Cooking
  by Suneeta Vaswani
- Baby Blender Food
  by Nicole Young
- Simply Thai Cooking
  by Wandee Young and Byron Ayanoglu

Health

- The Complete Natural Medicine Guide to the 50 Most Common Medicinal Herbs
  by Dr. Heather Boon, B.Sc.Phm., Ph.D., and Michael Smith, B.Pharm, M.R.Pharm.S., ND
- The Complete Natural Medicine Guide to Breast Cancer
  by Sat Dharam Kaur, ND
- Better Food for Pregnancy
  by Daina Kalnins, MSc, RD, and Joanne Saab, RD
- Help for Eating Disorders
  by Dr. Debra Katzman, MD, FRCP(C), and Dr. Leora Pinhas, MD
- The Complete Doctor's Healthy Back Bible
  by Dr. Stephen Reed, MD, and Penny Kendall-Reed, MSc, ND, with Dr. Michael Ford, MD, FRCSC, and Dr. Charles Gregory, MD, ChB, FRCP(C)
- Crohn's & Colitis
  by Dr. A. Hillary Steinhart, MD, MSc, FRCP(C)
- Chronic Heartburn
  by Barbara E. Wendland, MSc, RD, and Lisa Marie Ruffolo